BAYOU COUNTRY

BAYOU COUNTRY

An Illustrated History of Southeast Arkansas

Rick Joslin

Stephens Press ◉ Las Vegas, Nevada

Credits:
Editor: Kersh E. Hall
Designer: Sue Campbell
Publishing Coordinator: Stacey Fott
Photographer: Ralph Fitzgerald
Proofreader: Judy Normand

ISBN 10: 1932173692
ISBN 13: 9781932173697

Cataloging in Publication.
Joslin, Rick.
Bayou country : an illustrated history of Southeast Arkansas / Rick Joslin.
204 p. : ill., maps, photos ; 30 cm.
Contents: Pioneers and founding fathers – Government – Transportation – Agriculture and industry – Business and tourism – Education – Home and social life – Religious life and eternal rest – War and peace – The good, the bad and the convicted – Disasters – Fun and games – Celebrities and difference makers – Pine Bluff Commercial-125 years – Heritage sponsorships.
Summary: This extensively illustrated work provides a look at the history of Southeast Arkansas based upon newspaper articles, maps, and memorabilia.

ISBN: 1-932173-69-2
ISBN-13: 978-1-932173-69-7
1. Arkansas—History. I. Title.
976.7 dc-22   2007
2006931397
Library of Congress Control Number: 2006931397

STEPHENS PRESS, LLC
A Stephens Media Company

Post Office Box 1600
Las Vegas, NV 89125-1600
www.stephenspress.com

Printed in Hong Kong

Dedicated, with gratitude, to the majestic spirit of our predecessors, especially those among us who have contributed their time and talents in compiling an ongoing chronicle of life here, including such proficient writers as the late William Halliburton, Thomas Nuttall, James W. Leslie, Dave Wallis, and a host of others whose works have aided in recording and maintaining our past so that it can serve as a building block for our lives today and in the future.

George T. Anderson Sr., for making me a better worker by showing me how to be a quality boss;

Jay Bradford, for illustrating the values of compassion and outreach by putting those principles into action each day;

J. Dean Duncan, my college journalism professor, for his patience, perseverance, and (necessary) sense of humor;

Louis L. Ramsay Jr., for being a helpful friend and advisor; and,

Mrs. Cynthia Thornton, possibly the world's "meanest" (and best) high school teacher, for coercing me into learning names, dates, and places in history and, in the process, awakening and nourishing my affection for the subject.

—Rick Joslin

For The People of Southeast Arkansas . . . Past, Present And Future

ADAMSVILLE, ALMYRA, ALTHEIMER, ANDERSON, ANNOVER, ARKANSAS CITY, ARKANSAS POST, AVE
BARKADA, BAYOU METO, BAXTER, BEARDS TOWN, BELFAST, BLANCHTON, BODMAN, BOMBAY, B
CREEK, BUIE, CADES, CADY, CALMER, CANE CREEK, CARMEL, CARTHAGE, CASSCOE, CENTER G
SPUR, COLLINS, COMINTO, COMO, CONSTANCE, COOK, COOPER'S LANDING, CORNERVILLE, CRIGLER,
CORNER, DARYSAW, DEANE, DELUCE, DEWITT, DEXTER, DIALION, DOGWOOD, DOUBLE WELLS, DO
EAGLE CREEK, EBB, EDLIL, ELLISON, ENGLISH, ERIN, ETHEL, FAIRVIEW, FAITH, FANNAGAN, FARELLY
FORDYCE, FRESNO, FURTH, GABE, GARNETT, GARRETT BRIDGE, GARRISON'S LANDING, GETHEM
GOURD, GRADY, GRAPEVINE, GRAVEL RIDGE, GREELEY, GREEN HILL, GREENWALD, GRIFFITH SPR
HAYWOOD, HEBRON, HECKATOO, HERBINE, HERMITAGE, HOOKER, HOLLY SPRINGS, HUMPHREY,
IVY, JACINTO, JEFFERSON, JEROME, JERSEY, JOHNSVILLE, JOSLYN STATION, JUNET, KEARNEY, KEDRON,
LADD, LADELLE, LAKE DICK, LAMONT, LANARK, LEA'S FERRY, LEOLA, LINWOOD, LITTLE GARNE
CORNER, LONO, LUELLA, MACON, MANNING, MARSDEN, MASONVILLE, MCARTHUR, MCGEHEE, M
MILL CREEK, MITCHELLVILLE, MOCCASIN CORNER, MONTICELLO, MONTONGO, MORO BAY, MOSCOW,
MOUNT ZION, NADY, NAPOLEON, NEBO, NELSON, NEW EDINBURG, NEW GASCONY, NEW HOPE, NIX, N
ORION, ORLANDO, OUACHITA, PALACE, PALMYRA, PANSY, PARHAM, PARMA, PASTORIA, PATSVILLE, P
BLUFF, PINE GROVE, PLANTERSVILLE, PLEASANT HILL, PLUM BAYOU, POSSUM FORK, POYEN, PRAGU
RANDALL, RED, REDFIELD, RED FORK, REEDVILLE, RELFS BLUFF, REST, REYDELL, RICHLAND, RI
ROCK SPRINGS, ROHWER, ROSEDALE, ROWELL, RUBY, RYE, SAINT CHARLES, SALINE, SAMPLES, SA
SHERRILL, SIMPSON CREEK, SMEARNEY, SNOW LAKE, SLOVAC, SORRELLS, SOUTHBEND, STAPLE, STAR
SULPHUR SPRINGS, SUMMERVILLE, SUMPTER, SWAN LAKE, SWEDEN, SUX, TAMO, TARRY, TENNESSE
TULIP, TULL, TYRO, VARNER, VICK, WABBASEKA, WALNUT LAKE, WARREN, WASHITA, WATSON,
BLUFF, WHITE OAKS BLUFF, WILDCAT LANDING, WILMAR, WILLOW, WINCHESTER, WOODLAWN

CONTENTS

FOREWORD

Magnolia blooming, Mama smiling,
Mallards sailing on a December wind.
God bless the memories I keep recalling
Like an old familiar friend.

That verse, taken from the state song, "Arkansas (You Run Deep in Me)," personifies life in Arkansas — particularly life in Southeast Arkansas. A portrait representing life in Southeast Arkansas could not be painted without including mallards, magnolias, and especially the smiling faces of the warm and embracing Arkansans — past and present — who have so humbly represented the region.

What I remember most about my years as a pastor in Southeast Arkansas are the people. These are folks who love their families, their church and their heritage. I was there for blessings of birth, heartbreaks of death and every emotion in between. It's the people of this region that you want to share in your joys and turn to in times of need. I have always admired not only the sincerity of the people, but the honored legacies they proudly carry.

The faces that follow in this book represent years of trial and triumph, the hard work of heroes, and a lifestyle cherished and replicated by all of us. We owe it to our ancestors to remember their legacies, and there is no better way to do that than to memorialize them in this way. I am thankful for this historical perspective that will serve as a scrapbook of southern life for decades to come.

There is much to be remembered and rediscovered about the counties portrayed in this book — Jefferson, Grant, Arkansas, Cleveland, Lincoln, Desha, Drew, Dallas, and Bradley counties. Whether you're a history buff and you visit the Civil War sites, an outdoorsman and take in a Nature Center or you prefer to suit up to go hunting or fishing, you can indulge in all of this in this area of the Natural State. Bayou Bartholomew alone is something to be proud of. This bayou is the longest bayou in the United States, beginning in Jefferson County and winding 375 miles where it runs into Morehouse Parish, Louisiana, and eventually empties into the Ouachita River near Sterlington.

I sure hope you enjoy the journey through Southeast Arkansas' history that you are about to encounter. As you read this book, take the time to look into the smiling faces and take in a part of the past. And God bless the memories we keep recalling, like an old familiar friend.

— Governor Mike Huckabee

Introduction

Muddy bayous, their murky waters filled with turtles, fish, snakes, and, in some instances alligators, cut serpentine paths through thousands of acres of Southeast Arkansas.

The most well-known, Bayou Bartholomew, with its head waters north of Pine Bluff, eventually curls its way into northern Louisiana, and is the longest bayou in the world — a fact little known to the thousands of people who cross it daily or live along its banks.

Because bayous are reflective of our landscape, we selected *Bayou Country* as the title of this book to record a diverse written and pictorial history of our ancestry and our future. *Bayou Country* is more a state of mind — recognizing the hard working people who have established a way of life based on survival and perpetual existence.

As *Bayou Country* fell into place, I discovered that Rick Joslin, a member of the editorial staff at *The Pine Bluff Commercial*, possessed a broad, rich knowledge of our history. As you read his words, you will discover and enjoy his unique perspective in telling stories about Southeast Arkansas.

Ralph Fitzgerald added to his daily duties as *The Commercial's* news photographer by capturing the images of the Southeast Arkansas bayous and historical objects. Ralph's visual contribution to *Bayou Country* is outstanding.

I think you will find *Bayou Country* is something you will come back to time and again to reflect on our heritage.

I must say thanks to Governor Mike Huckabee, a former resident of "Bayou Country," for his comments.

And, lastly, a special thank you to the publisher of *The Pine Bluff Commercial*, Charles A. Berry … he made *Bayou Country* possible for you, the readers.

— Kersh E. Hall
Editor, *Bayou Country*

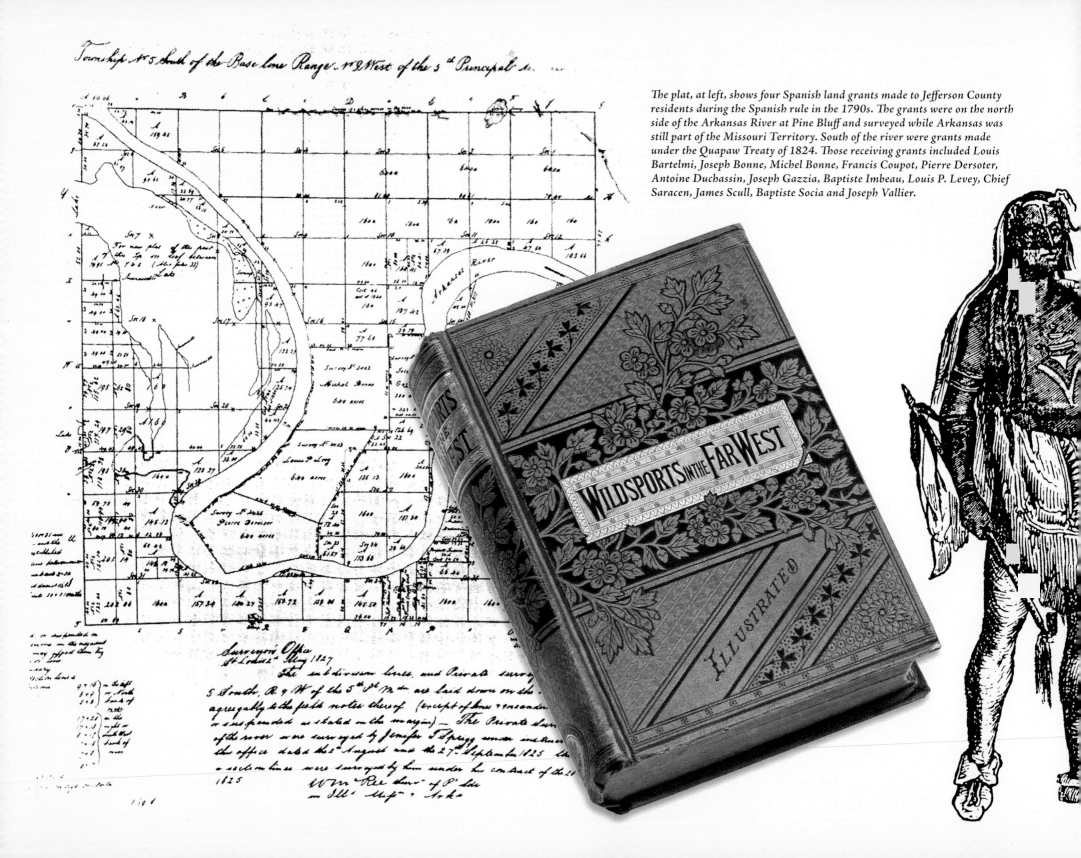

The plat, at left, shows four Spanish land grants made to Jefferson County residents during the Spanish rule in the 1790s. The grants were on the north side of the Arkansas River at Pine Bluff and surveyed while Arkansas was still part of the Missouri Territory. South of the river were grants made under the Quapaw Treaty of 1824. Those receiving grants included Louis Bartelmi, Joseph Bonne, Michel Bonne, Francis Coupot, Pierre Dersoter, Antoine Duchassin, Joseph Gazzia, Baptiste Imbeau, Louis P. Levey, Chief Saracen, James Scull, Baptiste Socia and Joseph Vallier.

CHAPTER ONE

Pioneers and Founding Fathers

No one knows for certain when man first inhabited Arkansas, but until Spanish explorer Hernando DeSoto arrived within the state off the Mississippi River somewhere below the present site of Memphis on June 18, 1541, Indians were the lone occupants and they had never before seen a Caucasian in their homeland.

Other white explorers ventured into the state over the ensuing 145 years, but there was no white settlement until 1686, when Italian explorer Henry de Tonti built one at Arkansas Post along the Arkansas River in what would, in 1813, become Arkansas County, the state's first county.

Thus, the history of the state as a whole is cradled within Southeast Arkansas.

Arkansas — first part of Louisiana and then, following the Louisiana Purchase, part of Missouri until 1819 — was largely an untamed wilderness well into the 1800s. Friedrich Wilhelm Christian Gerstaecker (1816–1872), a German-born author, wrote about his often savage experiences in Arkansas during the late 1830s and early 1840s in the 1845-published *Wild Sports in the Far West*, one of the first documentations of the ruggedness of life within the state.

Civilization did come to Arkansas, but not all at once.

Most Arkansans were directly dependent on land and nature for their daily existence and whatever income they could muster. It was good that game was plentiful, as its meat provided nourishment and its hides brought financial or trade rewards. There was little security beyond one's own means, and individuals had to be alert not only for animal attacks, but also for other persons who might be seeking unlawful gains.

Slavery in America dates back to 1619. The practice in Arkansas dates back to around 1719, when Scottish economist John Law brought in a boatload of slaves from Guinea to work at a Law-created colony near Arkansas Post. The settlement failed after a couple of years.

Only a few early Arkansans owned slaves. Those who did depended upon their slaves' labor for dwellings and other necessities. Many of the first white settlers resided in primitive shelters until other settlers arrived, and they would then help each other in constructing better housing. But, as more affluent newcomers arrived and the number of businesses and large plantations increased, slavery became more and more common.

Most whites became sharecroppers and, depending upon the season or the exaction of overseers or the planters themselves, worked six or seven days a week, alongside the slaves. The sharecroppers were compensated with living quarters and, sometimes, their own livestock and a barn as well as a small section of land on which they could raise fruits and vegetables or cotton.

Life as a sharecropper was certainly better than that of a slave, but it was nevertheless drab, difficult and demanding. The command of the human spirit was evidenced, however, in the ways both slaves and sharecroppers managed to create measures of fun and enjoyment in their lives.

New counties were established as settlements of various sizes were shaped and named and then recognized as communities, towns and cities.

When Congress approved the creation of the Arkansas Territory in early 1819, there were a dozen or so other settlements around Arkansas Post.

Acting Governor Robert Crittenden soon appointed the first officers of Arkansas County, which was enacted in 1813.

Hewes Scull was named sheriff and soon summoned twenty-two men as grand jurors. Surely among the more prominent of the day, those called were Robert Allgore, Daniel H. Baldwin, Jacob Barkman, Peter H. Bennett, Patrick Cassidy, J. H. Cummins, James Curren, Bartley Harrington, John Harrington, Samuel Lemmons, John McCartney, Shiloh Mather, Frederic Notrebe, Richmond Peeler, James S. Polet, Samuel H. Rutherford, James Scull, Harold Stillwell, Joseph Stillwell, John Taylor, John Weane and James Young.

Arkansas County was then much larger, so its inhabitants were scattered across a wide area.

Jefferson County was constituted in 1829. Joseph Bonne, a French hunter and trapper who in 1819 built a wigwam along the Arkansas River, was the first white to permanently settle in the county. For some time, his only companion was his dog.

But others — including Antoine Barraque, Ambrose Bartholomew, John Derresseaux, Israel Dodge, Antoine Duchesson, Euclid Johnson, David Musick, Frances Villier and the Dardenne and Vaugine families — arrived over the next few years and, like Bonne, made their homes near the river.

The 1830 U.S. Census shows respective population counts of 1,426 and 772 for Arkansas and Jefferson counties respectively.

JOSEPH BONNE CABIN

In 1818 a French trapper, Joseph Bonne landed on the south bank of the Arkansas River with his dog and gun near the location of the original Jefferson County Courthouse. Driven to this high bluff after flood waters had threatened his homesite at Arkansas Post, Bonne and his family erected a cabin and became one of the first white settlers in the region which has become Pine Bluff. The Bonne hand-constructed log cabin became the first seat of government, and history reports that Joseph Bonne operated the first tavern in the area.

Blacks may have been freed after the Civil War but, for many, their overall living conditions improved little over the next forty to fifty years. This postcard depicts the home of several black sharecroppers on a Pine Bluff-area farm around 1900, but the photograph could have easily dated back to the late 1860s or 1870s.

Antoine Barraque, born in France in 1773, was one of Jefferson County's earliest settlers. After arriving here around 1816, he acquired land below Pine Bluff. His holdings gave birth to a community he named New Gascony in tribute to Gascony, France. New Gascony served as the Jefferson County seat for a brief time. Barraque died in Pine Bluff in 1858. The city's Barraque Street was named as a tribute to him. It is the only such-named street in the entire United States.

Desha County was instituted in 1838. The Arkansas and Mississippi rivers meet within the county, which borders the Mississippi. Thus, the county encompassed a major port area.

Some of the county's earliest settlers were the Cooper, Jamison, Morris and Watson families.

In the 1840 census, Arkansas County counted 1,346 residents, Jefferson County 2,566 and Desha County 1,598.

Among the first settlers of Bradley County, established in 1840, were Alexander Beard, Frank Berry, Capt. Hugh Bradley (for whom the county is named), Dr. John T. Carleen, Bryant Gardner, Aaron Johnston, Isaac Pennington, Jacob Pennington, Charles H. Seay and Henry Wise.

Dallas County was incorporated in 1845. Noted citizens of the time included P. S. Bethel, Hawes Coleman, Henry Gray, James Kennedy, Moses Overton, William Owen, Albert Phillips, Squire Ramsay and Presley Watts.

Drew County was created in 1846. Believed to be the county's first permanent white residents were Reece Bowden and Stephen Gaster, who settled along Bayou Batholomew in 1832.

Among others who lived in the county before it was incorporated were Hugh Fannin, John S. Handly, Jesse Hunt, Benjamin Martin, Benjamin Nettles, Bynum Nichols, Ezekiel Owens, J. W. Ridgell and Jesse Whitaker.

Respective populations in the 1850 census for Arkansas, Jefferson, Desha, Bradley, Dallas and Drew Counties were 3,245; 5,834; 2,911; 3,829; 6,877; and 3,276. The 1860 counts, in the same order, were 8,844; 14,971; 6,459; 8,388; 8,283; and 9,078.

Grant County, in 1869, became the first county established after the Civil War. Only a few whites resided in the county prior to 1840, but it experienced a boon the following year when Merrill Alley, Seth Atchley, Hugh Berry,

Jonas Black, Edward Calvert, James Hester, John B. Hester, Benjamin Hubbard, Francis Posey and James Rogers settled there, along with the Fenters, Porter, Tull and Williams families.

The 1870 census listed the following county populations: Arkansas 8,268; Jefferson 15,733; Desha 6,125; Bradley 8,646; Dallas 5,707; Drew 9,960; and Grant 3,943.

Lincoln County was formulated in 1871. Earliest residents included William Adkins, J. E. Cox, J. L. Hunter, Calvin Jones, Shelby Richardson, William Sanders, John Sweeney, Dr. C. M. Taylor, F. R. Smith, W. F. Varner and the Atkinson, Bachelor and Pendleton families.

Among the first settlers of Cleveland County, established in 1873, were Thomas Atkinson, W. T. Brewer, Joseph Gray, William Hall, M. J. Harrison, Stephen Johnson, William Moseley, John Powers, John Seymour, H. W. Rogers and the Barnett, Blankenship, Kennedy and Springer families.

MR. BEN. J. ALTHEIMER.
Lawyer.
PINE BLUFF, ARKANSAS.

The 1880 census had the following county populations: Arkansas 8,038; Jefferson 22,386; Desha 8,973; Bradley 6,285; Dallas 6,505; Drew 12,231; Grant 6,185; and Lincoln 9,255. Cleveland County wasn't listed in the 1880 count.

Pine Bluff, the region's primary city, was incorporated in 1839. Its population more than tripled between 1880 and 1890, from 3,203 to 9,952.

In recent times, the City of Altheimer has found itself struggling to simply survive, but the generosity of its founding family continues to grow and serve.

Brothers Joseph and Louis Altheimer founded the city in 1884. A primary reason behind the town's organization was an effort to gain railroad service.

Louis Altheimer proposed the matter to the Cotton Belt Railroad and surveyed a line from

North Little Rock to Altheimer. He convinced Cotton Belt officials that a potential wealth of commerce awaited in the Altheimer area.

The Altheimer brothers donated land for a depot and switching tracks and, with the help of supporting neighbors, donated $1,200 for the depot's construction. Within three years, work on the line was underway and the City of Altheimer would soon experience a boon.

The brothers, who purchased a number of large land tracts in Jefferson County, dissolved their partnership in 1892, but the family's devotion to the city that bears its name has only strengthened over the years.

Ben J. Altheimer, a son of Joseph Altheimer, was born in 1877. He became an attorney and had a successful practice in Chicago. But he always maintained a love of Arkansas, especially its farming and natural areas. He also possessed a deep appreciation for and admiration of farm workers and actively sought to improve their financial and educational opportunities. In the early 1930s, he renovated an old plantation home near Altheimer. When he retired in 1939, he left Chicago and established residency at "The Elms" house. In 1942, he established the Ben J. Altheimer Foundation to benefit Arkansas churches, civic endeavors and education. Ben Altheimer's Jefferson County friends and neighbors would and continue to enjoy the foundation's devoted assistance. School buildings, annual scholarships, medical facilities and equipment, church donations and a $100,000 matching grant program are among the many benefits that have been provided by the trust.

Reflecting Ben Altheimer's passion for farming, the charity also sponsors three chairs in the agriculture department of the University of Arkansas system. And illustrating his devotion to law, the organization established the Ben J. Altheimer Law Library in Pine Bluff, supported construction of the University of Arkansas at Little Rock's School of Law and provided for the university system's Ben J. Altheimer Distinguished Professorship and Ben J. Altheimer Lecture Series.

Ben Altheimer died in 1946, but his and the Altheimer family's productive legacy is alive and thriving.

IMPORTANT DATES IN PINE BLUFF'S HISTORY:

1814 — First settlements recorded in what is now Jefferson County.

1818 — First Quapaw Treaty signed.

1819 — Arkansas admitted to the U.S. as a territory.

1824 — Second Quapaw Treaty signed.

1829 — Jefferson County established.

1836 — Arkansas admitted to the U.S. as a state.

1839 — Pine Bluff first incorporated.

1863 — Battle of Pine Bluff.

1870 — First public school built.

1873 — Railroad service arrived.

1875 — Branch Normal College (University of Arkansas at Pine Bluff) began classes.

1885 — Telephone service began.

1902 — First electric street cars.

1906 — Union Station Depot constructed.

1914 — First concrete road (the Dollarway Road) completed between Pine Bluff and Little Rock.

1927 — The Great Flood impacts the Pine Bluff area, as well as seven states.

1941 — Construction of the Pine Bluff Arsenal began.

1976 — Fire destroyed the Jefferson County Courthouse.

CHAPTER TWO

Government

Issac S. and Belle Suddeth McClellan of near Sheridan were so dedicated to the Democratic Party that when Mrs. McClellan gave birth to a son on February 25, 1896, the couple named him in honor of Democratic Congressman John Little.

Not too many people remember John Little, but John L. McClellan remains a giant in Arkansas politics, serving as a U.S. senator from 1942 until his death in 1977. He was one of the Senate's most powerful — and, to some, most feared — members, having commanded several of the body's more memorable investigations.

McClellan's father was an attorney, and McClellan found the field to be fascinating. At the age of seventeen, McClellan was admitted to the Arkansas Bar Association, becoming the nation's youngest lawyer.

Following military service, McClellan entered into private law practice in Malvern, where he became city attorney. At the age of thirty, he was elected as a prosecuting attorney. He then served in the U.S. House of Representatives from 1935-38, when he unsuccessfully challenged U.S. Senator Hattie Caraway.

McClellan then moved his practice to Camden, where in 1942 he ran for and won the state's other Senate seat.

McClellan was re-elected five times, but not without some difficulties. He narrowly defeated former Governor Sid McMath in 1954 and U.S. Congressman (and future Governor and U.S. Senator) David Pryor in 1974.

As a senator, McClellan became highly influential by gaining chairmanships of several powerful panels, including the Committees on Appropriations and Government Operations and the Senate Permanent Subcommittee on Investigations. In the latter post, he led a Democratic walk-out of the Republican-controlled subcommittee in protest of publicity-seeking Senator Joseph McCarthy's shameless actions on identifying "communists."

McClellan then led investigations on such matters as organized crime and federal contract misappropriations, gaining a reputation for fairness and forcefulness.

Additionally, McClellan was respected for his support of law enforcement and government accountability. He sponsored legislation that created the General Services Administration, which oversees the federal government's business operations.

Unfortunately, McClellan was saddled by several personal setbacks. His mother died three weeks after his birth. His first marriage, to Eula Hicks in 1913, ended in a bitter divorce eight years later. His second wife, the former Lucille Smith, died of spinal meningitis in 1936.

During World War II, McClellan's son Max, an Army colonel serving in North Africa, also died of spinal meningitis. The younger McClellan's body wasn't sent home until six years later, and on the day of the funeral, McClellan's son, John Jr., died of injuries

Senator John L. McClellan

JOHN GRAY LUCAS
1864–1944

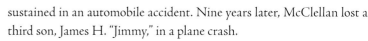

Because of his skin color, John Gray Lucas didn't receive a fair opportunity to display his full leadership ability in Arkansas, but the graduate of what is now the University of Arkansas at Pine Bluff was so highly skilled that, in just a few years, he nevertheless created an impressive political legacy here.

Born in Texas in 1864, he wound up in Pine Bluff as a youngster, receiving a public school education here before earning a degree at Branch Normal College (UAPB). He was engaged in merchandising during and for a couple of years after graduating from college.

Lucas then entered the Boston, Mass., University School of Law, winning academic honors as the lone black among the 52 students of the 1887 graduating class.

During his time at the law school, the Boston Daily Globe newspaper interviewed him for an article focusing on Pine Bluff race relations.

Lucas boasted of Pine Bluff's and Arkansas' positive atmosphere for blacks, pointing out the city's and Jefferson County's highly integrated political system and declaring that Arkansans, in the area of public transportation, were not discriminatory. He told the newspaper that Arkansas would be a great home for "more colored men from the North."

Lucas returned to Pine Bluff, was admitted to the state bar and soon became an assistant prosecuting attorney in Jefferson County. Receiving quick respect in legal circles, he was then appointed as a commissioner of the U.S. Circuit Court's Eastern Arkansas District.

Seen as a rising star in the state's Republican Party, he was elected as a state representative in 1890. As a legislator, both the Arkansas Democrat and Arkansas Gazette statewide newspapers editorially saluted him for his debating and speaking talents. Journalists described him as able and brilliant.

As one of the legislature's 12 black members in 1891, he won acclaim for his stirring speech against a bill designed to allow racial segregation within state railroads.

Nevertheless, the measure passed. Also approved was legislation that weakened the influence of black voters and greatly reduced prospects for blacks to continue to be able to compete for — let alone win — elective posts.

Realizing his future in Arkansas had been made limited, Lucas moved to Chicago, where he developed a reputation as a gifted attorney, eventually arguing before the U.S. Supreme Court on four occasions. He became a leading Republican in local affairs and received several political appointments, but changed to the Democratic Party after the start of the Great Depression.

He as named an assistant U.S. attorney for Cook County in 1934, remaining in that post until his death in 1944.

sustained in an automobile accident. Nine years later, McClellan lost a third son, James H. "Jimmy," in a plane crash.

McClellan sought solace in alcohol, but a close friend challenged him to "lay off the bottle." Before smashing a couple of bottles of bourbon, McClellan said, "I am going to show you that I am the master of my own soul."

McClellan never again consumed liquor.

The cause of his death at the age of 81 was a heart disorder.

The Joslyn Legacy of Public Service

While it's common knowledge that Lincoln County was named in tribute to President Abraham Lincoln, the man perhaps most responsible for the county's birth and whose family greatly contributed to its early prosperity has quietly faded from public recognition over time.

George H. Joslyn, born near Ithaca, New York, on August 19, 1840, had been a resident of the area only a couple of years before he became a state representative. He introduced the legislation establishing the county and was insistent that it be named in honor of President

Lincoln, the man he most admired and who had been assassinated only six years before.

Lincoln County was structured from about 175 square miles of lands previously in Arkansas, Bradley, Desha, Drew and Jefferson Counties.

From farming to military service

George Joslyn's father, J. H. Joslyn, was a hard-working, successful farmer who enjoyed the support of his wife and children. The family moved to Flint, Michigan, and Lyons, Iowa, before George Joslyn migrated to Chicago, where in 1861 he joined a militia group — the Chicago Zouaves — that was mustered into the U.S. Army as the Nineteenth Illinois Volunteer Infantry.

The regiment saw action in several key Civil War battles in Kentucky, Missouri and Tennessee. Joslyn also participated in General Philip Sheridan's siege of Atlanta.

He followed Sheridan to Texas, engaging in battles supporting President Lincoln's stance against Maximilian securing Mexican rule. Joslyn was discharged from service in August 1865.

Remaining in Texas, he married Sophia J. Cook. The couple's only child, son Max A. Joslyn, was born in Galveston in 1867.

The young family moved to Lincoln County the next year when George Joslyn acquired two plantations, one on Cook's Island, and the other in what would become Gould. The estates totaled 5,000 acres.

Triumph, Tragedy and Renewal

Joslyn was appointed Lincoln County's first county and probate judge, serving from 1871–1876. Meanwhile, his brother, John J. Joslyn, a former lieutenant colonel with U.S. Army's First Missouri Cavalry, was Lincoln County clerk from 1874–1880.

At the time of George Joslyn's arrival there, what is now the City of Gould was a settlement known as Palmer's Switch. But Joslyn's standing there was of such strength that the community soon became known as Joslyn's Post Office and finally as simply Joslyn. The family's influence would be evident again after the city

was incorporated as Gould — named after railroad pioneer Jay Gould — in 1907.

George Joslyn and his family enjoyed a good life highlighted by his farming, business and political successes, but that happiness vanished when his wife Sophia died in 1893. Max Joslyn was a young teenager at the time.

After a period of mourning, George Joslyn began putting his life together again. In 1898, at the age of 58, he married Ophelia Morgan. They would have three children — a son, George H. Jr., and daughters Carrie Belle, and Nellie Elizabeth.

In 1904, the family moved to the Pulaski Heights section of Little Rock. He and Ophelia believed their children would have better educational opportunities there.

Two years later, Pulaski Heights became an independent city. Joslyn was elected its first mayor, and re-elected to a second term.

Helping Gould Get Started

Max Joslyn was among thirty-two Gould petitioners and George Joslyn was the group's agent when it appeared before the Lincoln County Quorum Court and gained the court's approval for Gould's incorporation as a city on August 6, 1907. George Joslyn began serving as the city's treasurer.

In 1911, Max Joslyn was elected mayor. After leaving the office for a time, he won a second term in 1917.

Envelopes bearing United States Congressional Postage marks of Senators John L. McClellan, Hattie Caraway, and Congressman Joe T. Robinson.

Max Joslyn took over the family's farming operations and also became a Gould businessman. He is credited with founding the Gould School Board shortly after the city's incorporation and was the city's postmaster from 1910–1920.

George Joslyn Sr. had served as Gould's first postmaster from 1904–1910. George Joslyn Jr. held the job from 1925–1935.

A Continuing Tradition

George Joslyn Sr. died in Little Rock in 1928. He was buried at Roselawn Memorial Park there, where he shares a family plot.

But the Joslyn family's tradition of leadership continued.

Max Joslyn married Belle Paschall in 1901. The couple had two children, a son, James Allen, who died in childhood, and daughter, Frances Maxine.

Frances Maxine Joslyn married William Herschel Carder on August 6, 1933. Their only child, son William Herschel Jr., was the great-grandson of George Joslyn Sr. and grandson of Max Joslyn.

In 1970, William Herschel Carder Jr., just as his grandfather had been fifty-nine years before, was elected as Gould's mayor. Two years later, he would also repeat his grandfather's achievement of winning a second term.

Carder's initial election was a fitting closure to the 100 years that had passed since George Joslyn Sr. had victoriously led the effort to attain Lincoln County's creation. And his re-election gave birth to a second century of the family's on-going legacy of public service.

Violence in Early Arkansas.

To find an example of the lawlessness that abounded in Arkansas politics during much of the 1800s, one needs only to review the state's first-ever legislative session, at Little Rock in 1837, the year after Arkansas was awarded statehood by the U.S. Congress.

Speaker of the House John Wilson of Clark County and State Representative J. J. Anthony of Randolph County had a spat over legislation dealing with, of all things, state bounties for wolf hides.

After Anthony ridiculed Wilson, Wilson left his podium and began walking toward his adversary. Both drew knives — big ones. Anthony's knife reportedly measured twelve inches; Wilson's nine.

Another legislator attempted to cool the confrontation by throwing his chair between the combatants. But both Anthony and Wilson grabbed the chair in mid-air and employed it as a shield as they began slashing at one another. Wilson sustained a severe wound to a wrist. Anthony then threw his knife at Wilson, but missed. Wilson responded by thrusting his knife deep into and ripping it across Anthony's stomach.

Anthony, completely eviscerated, fell to the floor and was dead within seconds.

Wilson was arrested, expelled from the State House and tried for murder. He was eventually freed with a verdict of "excusable homicide."

Political violence unfortunately impacted Jefferson County as well during the century — not once, but twice. Two assassinations, one at a Pine Bluff residence and the other in Plumerville (Conway County), produced vastly different outcomes, and the latter gained national attention and was the subject of a book published by Duke University Press in 1999.

Deadly Resentment: The Slaying of Dr. James T. Pullen

Dr. J. T. Pullen was highly respected throughout Southeast Arkansas. The Pine Bluff resident was elected Jefferson County clerk in 1830 and appointed postmaster in 1834.

The exact circumstances are unknown, but at dusk on Tuesday, June 11, 1839, Pullen was shot while standing within the doorway of his home. Witnesses said the assailant was John N. Outlaw. Other than having long held some sort of grudge against Pullen, little is known of Outlaw.

Pullen was gravely injured and died the following morning.

Press accounts of the time noted that a posse — directed by County Sheriff Stanislaus Dardenne and John W. Pullen, brother of the clerk — began a pursuit of Outlaw, who had scurried toward Memphis.

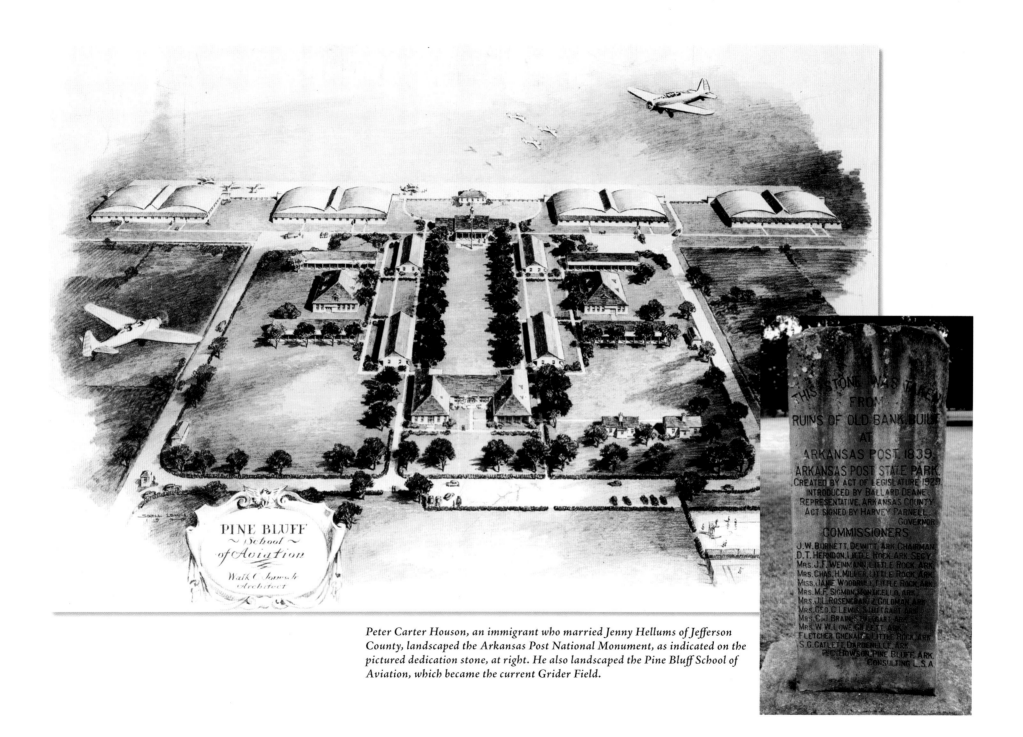

Peter Carter Houson, an immigrant who married Jenny Hellums of Jefferson County, landscaped the Arkansas Post National Monument, as indicated on the pictured dedication stone, at right. He also landscaped the Pine Bluff School of Aviation, which became the current Grider Field.

These two photos show the razing of the old Pine Bluff City Hall at Barraque and State in the 1990s.

Mary Newberry, who in 1976 became Jefferson County's first elected tax collector, is congratulated after winning re-election in 1992. She was re-elected nine times, retiring from the post in 1996. Newberry was a delegate to the 1992 and 1996 National Democratic Party Conventions. She died in Memphis, Tennessee, in 2005 at the age of 54.

The determined posse remained hot on Outlaw's trail until he finally found himself surrounded just shy of Memphis, on the Arkansas bank of the Mississippi River.

Posse member Samuel Butler requested Outlaw's surrender. Meanwhile, Outlaw defiantly loaded his pistol, cocked it and answered Butler by shooting at him. Outlaw missed, and Butler again urged him to give up. Outlaw ignored the invitation and jumped onto his horse, hoping to extend his desperate flight.

But another posse member put a quick end to Outlaw's resumed run, shooting him dead with a musket.

Greed, Terror, and Fraud: Who shot John?

John Middleton Clayton, a Pennsylvania native who came to Jefferson County in 1867, was a younger brother of Colonel Powell Clayton, commander of the Union forces that occupied the county through most of the Civil War.

The elder Clayton was despised by many Confederate sympathizers here, but wasn't totally void of supporters, especially among the wealthy. Like a number of other carpetbaggers, he acquired a hefty amount of acreage after the war. He married a Helena woman and became a planter.

The younger Clayton traveled here specifically to manage his brother's large plantation while the elder, who had become a state Republican leader, ran a successful gubernatorial campaign.

Colonel Clayton was not a popular governor. His term was marred by his declaration of martial law in 14 counties. Division gripped the state, and one of the few things most could agree upon was disgust in the governor's unwillingness, if not inability, to bring about accord.

John Clayton, however, was warmly received in Jefferson County. He was urged to seek a justice of the peace position, and won. In 1870, he was elected to the State House of Representatives. Two years later, he was voted into the State Senate. His state colleagues, even opposing Democrats, were as impressed by his leadership skills as much as was the Jefferson County electorate.

In 1876, John Clayton was elected county sheriff and served five terms before retiring from the post a decade later. He was a revered public servant statewide. Reacting to his supporters' strong promptings, he then became a candidate in the 1878 U.S. Representative race in the Second Congressional District.

A POLITICAL HIT

Pine Bluff's first elected mayor and Jefferson County's first resident to be elected governor were dangerously close to becoming registered fatalities of the political violence that marked their era.

Pine Bluff held its first political elections on January 4, 1847, and James De Baun Jr. was chosen mayor.

Early on the morning of June 24, 1847, the mayor and his father, James De Baun Sr., were walking to the elder's business, a store near the Arkansas River. As they neared White's Tavern, a riverside saloon and eatery, two assailants at the door of the pub's dining room opened fire with shotguns.

The elder De Baun died instantly. The mayor, despite five severe buckshot wounds, would survive.

The gunmen escaped in boats.

The *Arkansas Gazette* reported only that a "Dr. Embree" was the lone identified shooter. The late James W. Leslie of Pine Bluff, who wrote three books on Jefferson County and Southeast Arkansas history, researched the matter and determined that Israel Embree and Jordan N. Embree were major landowners in nearby Rob Roy, but neither was known as a physician.

Leslie also found records showing Israel Embree had been charged with murder in 1830, but was not convicted.

There is no record of a trial in the murder of James De Baun Sr., but an 1848 circuit court docket discloses that felony assault charges against Mayor De Baun were dropped because an unnamed witness failed to appear.

Perhaps the mayor had sought revenge against "Dr. Embree" in the killing of the elder De Baun, but no records have been located to confirm that suspicion.

Just over a month after the De Baun ambush, former State Representative John S. Roane of Pine Bluff and nationally-known Masonic leader and frontiersman Albert Pike engaged in a duel on an Arkansas River sandbar in the Cherokee Nation of the Oklahoma Territory.

Roane asked for the showdown after Pike publicly criticized Roane's performance as a commander in the Mexican War of 1846.

Dueling was illegal in Arkansas and carried a death sentence, so Pike and Roane traveled to Fort Smith and then boated with their seconds to the sandbar, where they aligned back-to-back, took an agreed-upon number of steps and turned to face and fire their pistols at each other.

Though they were both marksmen, neither struck their target.

If one was scared, the other was glad, because they shook hands, hastily settled their differences and returned to Fort Smith to dine together.

Roane, who became governor in 1850, was as inept a governor as he was a dueler. His term was largely highlighted by his ineffectiveness, and he wisely decided not to seek re-election.

Roane returned to Pine Bluff, resumed a legal career and died — of natural causes — in 1867.

A Bill For

an act to be entitled an act for the submission of the question of State-wide prohibition of the liquor traffic to a vote of qualified electors to know whether the people prefer State wide prohibition to local option

Be it enacted by the General Assembly of the State of Arkansas

Section 1 That at the general election to be held throughout the state on the second monday in september in the year nineteen hundred and twelve (1912) there shall be submitted to the qualified electors of the state the question of the sale of intoxicating liquors of any character, whether of alcohol or any alcoholic, spirituous, ardent, vinous, malt or fermented liquors, or any compound or preparation therof, commonly called tonics, bitters, beer, or medicated liquors or intoxicating spirits of any character, which are used and drank, as a beverage in any quantity or for any purpose whatever, except as already provided by law for prohibition or dry counties, townships, wards or special districts for saccramental, and mechanical purposes

Section 2 That the ballots of said general election shall have printed on them, for state wide prohibition, and against state-wide prohibition, and for license and against license as now provided by law

Section 3 That the vote for and against state-wide prohibition shall be certified to the same

He lost to Democrat Major Clifton R. Breckinridge by 746 votes of the over 34,000 cast. Immediately, the outcome fell into question when numerous complaints were aired by Breckinridge foes. John Clayton officially contested the results and contracted the services of the distinguished Pinkerton Detective Agency for an investigation.

At the time, the state Democratic Party had pockets of corruption and successfully controlled many elections by gerrymandering, changing some township or precinct elections into at-large votes, and implementing poll taxes that prevented poorer whites and most blacks from even receiving ballots. And if all that failed, armed violence was an alternative practice. In fact, the Ku Klux Klan openly fronted the party in some locations.

A group of both black and white citizens in Plumerville — a small, predominantly black city near Morrilton — voiced accusations of voter fraud, charging that a ballot box had been stolen from a polling place utilized by a predominantly black and Republican electorate. There were similar reports of ballot box thefts throughout the district, even though a federal supervisor had monitored the election.

As Pinkerton agents pressed in their inquiry, a brother of Conway County Deputy Sheriff Oliver Bentley indicated a desire to speak to the detectives. According to Kenneth C. Barnes, author of the aforementioned book *Who Killed John Clayton? Political Violence and the Emergence of the New South, 1861–1893*, the deputy soon after "accidentally" shot his brother — five times. Bentley was cleared in a local, sham investigation. Two weeks later, an unknown gunman shot the federal election supervisor through a window. He survived, minus part of an ear.

John Clayton, despite recommendations from both Democrats and fellow Republicans not to do so, traveled to Plumerville to gather depositions for his election appeal. He obtained a room in a boarding house owned by a Mrs. Cravens. On Tuesday evening, January 29, 1889, he took a seat at a table within his room and began writing a letter to his

At left, a hand-written proposed bill seeking a vote to prohibit liquor traffic in Arkansas. The proposal was prepared by Representative N. B. Kersh, who represented Lincoln County in the Arkansas House of Representatives in the early 1900s.

children. A shotgun blast from outside a window behind his chair nearly decapitated him. The murder earned front-page coverage in newspapers across the nation.

Barnes theorizes that John Clayton was slain by either Deputy Sheriff Bentley or Plumerville saloon owner Bob Pate. Bentley wound up as the lead investigator in the shooting, while Pate and his bartender were named to a coroner's jury.

Bentley and the jury panel officially determined that John Clayton's killer, or killers, could not be identified.

The pain didn't end there for John Clayton's family, which received a bill from the boarding house manager for damages to his room, including the removal of blood and tissue from walls, a rug and furnishings.

When news of the assassination reached Jefferson County, it was met with much anger, disbelief, and sadness. A group of prominent county leaders — both white and black, Democrat and Republican — journeyed to Little Rock and accompanied John Clayton's body on its return to Pine Bluff.

His funeral, held at First Methodist Church, remains among the most-attended in county history. He was buried in Bellwood Cemetery.

Emotions continued to run high over John Clayton's murder for much of the next two decades, and the event would lead to various changes within state politics, including a reformation of the Democratic Party. Powell and William Henry Clayton devoted much money, time and effort in trying to bring their brother's slaughter to a judicious close, but to no avail.

Conway County lawmen would point fingers of guilt at suspects in California and Montana, but whatever "evidence" might have been possessed was easily disproved. Deputy Sheriff and Justice of the Peace Bentley presided over what rated as nothing more than a mock trial for the Montana man, who was instantly exonerated when he showed that he had been in an Oregon jail at the time of the crime.

Conway County authorities received an out-of-town letter in which someone hailing himself "Jack the Ripper," then the scourge of London, claimed responsibility for John Clayton's demise. The writer said he was seeking revenge for the killing of his father and brother, charging Colonel Clayton was responsible and his true target.

Predictably, no one was ever convicted of John Clayton's murder.

The Desha County Courthouse following its multi-million dollar renovation completed in 2005.

KATE ADAMS

KATE ADAMS

Lake Kate Adams in Arkansas City is named for the old steamer by the same name. The boat frequented the river dock there when the lake was part of the main channel of the Mississippi River. The boat was employed in Universal Studios' 1927 movie Uncle Tom's Cabin. The craft burned shortly after filming was completed.

The Arkansas River has long been a corridor for shipping and transportation. This postcard shows a steamboat loaded with cotton.

CHAPTER THREE

Transportation

Southeast Arkansas was long a transportation pacesetter and may experience a new boon with its future connection to the planned Interstate 69 expressway, which will span from Mexico to Canada.

The state's first road, authorized by Congress on April 30, 1816, started in St. Louis and extended southward into the old city of Davidsonville (Randolph County) in Northeast Arkansas and onward to Arkansas Post in Arkansas County. At the time, Arkansas was still part of the Missouri Territory and three years shy of breaking away as the Arkansas Territory.

A state map from 1836, the year in which Arkansas was granted statehood, shows a road from the south side of the Arkansas River at Little Rock to Pine Bluff and onward to the Bartholomew Post Office (near Warren) and Washita (now Monroe), Louisiana.

In July 1817, Arkansas Post became the second city to establish a post office, and several mail routes were soon charted in the region.

But land travel at the time represented little more than trails. Waterways provided the primary means of getting from one place to another, and there was plenty of migration as people were searching for areas in which to settle as the frontier stretched westward.

A revolutionary new form of travel made its debut in the region in 1868, when the Little Rock, Pine Bluff and New Orleans Railroad was incorporated. By 1874, rail services had extended to Arkansas City, McGehee and between Dermott and Warren.

The St. Louis Southwestern Railroad, more commonly known as the Cotton Belt, came to Arkansas in 1882 as the Texas and St. Louis

Railway and fell into financial straits. Samuel W. Fordyce, vice president and treasurer of the railroad, became receiver. The City of Fordyce would be named in tribute to him.

The company's line soon advanced into Pine Bluff, Altheimer, Rison, Fordyce, Stuttgart and Gillett.

The Mississippi, Ouachita and Red River Railroad incorporated on January 8, 1851, and eventually gave way to the Warren and Ouachita Valley Railroad, which serviced Warren, Banks and a few other stops before going out of business.

Other railway companies that operated within Southeast Arkansas included the Ashley, Drew and Northern; Fordyce and Princeton; Louisiana and Pine Bluff; Pine Bluff and Northern; Pine Bluff, Sheridan and Southern; Warren and Ouachita Valley; and Warren and Saline River.

Union Pacific Railroad took over Missouri Pacific in 1982 and Cotton Belt in 1996.

Almost every city and town and even a few non-populated spots had railroad depots, as trains were responsible for moving much of the freight, including livestock, from here to there for several decades before yielding to trucks and state and national highways.

Trains also carried people from place-to-place within the region and beyond even a few decades after automobiles, planes, buses and electric streetcars became common. Horse- and mule-drawn streetcars were popular in the 1880s and 1890s.

Rail service has long been a mainstay of Southeast Arkansas, especially Pine Bluff.

Loading Cotton, Pine Bluff, Ark.

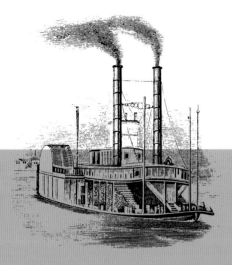

"Rollin' on the River . . ."

The first steamboat to ascend the Arkansas River from New Orleans was the *Comet*, which arrived at Arkansas Post about 10 p.m. on March 31, 1820. Despite the late hour, a "considerable number" of well-wishers were on hand to welcome Captain Byrne, who said the trip required eight days.

People had been traveling the river in handcrafted boats for a number of years previously. Bayou Bartholomew was a primary waterway for steamboats and other crafts as well. Arkansas River port traffic remains a viable commodity in the region.

This photo — by Glenn Crain — shows Bayou Bartholomew near Tarry, south of Pine Bluff.

"Neither snow, nor rain, nor gloom of night . . ."

In July 1829, U.S. Postmaster General William T. Barry, advertised in the *Arkansas Gazette* for proposals to carry the mail over ten routes in the state. Among the routes were a twice-monthly run between Arkansas Post and Villemont (Chicot County), a distance of about seventy miles, and a weekly run between Little Rock and Monroe, Louisiana, via Pine Bluff and Bartholomew (Desha County). A contract for a 120-mile route from Little Rock to Arkansas Post had been let several years earlier.

Main Street looking north from 4th Avenue in Pine Bluff. Horse-drawn wagons were once the major mode of transportation. The original photograph was taken by H. S. Dryfus on September 18, 1897.

The first mail road in Arkansas was approved by Congress on April 30, 1816. It started at St. Louis and continued southward to Arkansas Post.

Arkansas' First Road?

Major John Pyeatt, an early settler of Crystal Hill in Pulaski County, headed a project in 1807 to open a road from Crystal Hill and Cadron to Arkansas Post. The work party followed the north bank of the Arkansas River for about fifty miles from Crystal Hill, to a point at which they connected to an old Indian trail that led to Arkansas Post. Some say this was the state's first road. It later became a link in the military road from Memphis, via Little Rock, to Fort Smith.

Pine Bluff's Union Station celebrated its 100th anniversary in May 2006. The rail industry long provided a good share of the area's jobs, and the old Cotton Belt shops represented a major hub for the region. Related industries added to the regional economy. A number of companies, including one firm that still manufactures train wheels, profited from the railroad interests.

Railroad passes were common possessions in the early days of rail passenger service. These passes, from railways serving the area, were never issued.

Cotton Belt Steam Locomotive No. 819, below, is a grand symbol of the affection people of the region hold for railroading. The locomotive was manufactured at Pine Bluff in 1942 at a cost of $143,607 and ran the rails until replaced by diesel locomotives in 1954. The old locomotive was donated to the City of Pine Bluff in 1955 and displayed at Oakland Park until 1983, when a group of sentimental railroad enthusiasts decided to save it from neglect and vandalism.

The Cotton Belt Historical Society took over the engine's restoration, which cost $140,000, and the "old gal" began making trips again and became a major tourist attraction. Locomotive No. 819 is the shining star at the Cotton Belt Historical Museum in Pine Bluff.

"Cotton Belt Star"

PINE BLUFF, ARKANSAS TO
ST. LOUIS, MISSOURI AND RETURN
FOR THE
NATIONAL RAILWAY HISTORICAL SOCIETY
50TH ANNIVERSARY CONVENTION
JUNE 14-17, 1990

ORIGIN .... PINE BLUFF, ARK. .....

DESTINATION STUTTGART, ARK. .....

DATE .... JUNE 12, 1990 .....

PASSENGER RECEIPT
NOT GOOD FOR PASSAGE   N⁰   2185

VOID IF STUB IS DETACHED
VALID ONLY ON DATE STAMPED

"Cotton Belt Star"

PINE BLUFF, ARK.
ORIGIN ....

DESTINATION STUTTGART, ARK. .....

DATE .... JUNE 12, 1990 .....

VOID IF
DETACHED   N⁰   2185

GOOD FOR ONE PASSAGE

TICKETS PRINTED COURTESY
THE PERDUE CO., INC., PINE BLUFF, ARK.

Pine Bluff has long been a railroad town. Daily, the rails through downtown Pine Bluff haul commerce across the county. At left, clockwise, the lines of transport reflect on a summer sunset; a caboose nominated for the National Register of Historic Places; the train station in downtown Pine Bluff . . . now home to the Pine Bluff/Jefferson County Historical Museum; and, rusting, colorful train wheels.

She flew away

By the 1920s, air travel had taken hold in Southeast Arkansas.

In Pine Bluff, Mayor W. L. Toney was an aviation advocate and a member of the National Airport Association. The city's first municipal airport, completed in July 1927, and funded by a group of local businessmen calling themselves the Pine Bluff Landing Field Association, was named Toney Field in honor of the mayor. Legendary pilot Charles Lindbergh was among Toney Field's early customers and also visited other, smaller airfields in the region. Toney Field featured an administration building and a clubhouse as well as hangars and was considered one of the state's preeminent airports.

As an illustration of aviation's lightning-fast development during the era, Toney Field was declared inadequate in 1940, only 13 years after its creation. Toney Field quickly bowed to a new facility, Grider Field, which was constructed to serve the adjacent Pine Bluff School of Aviation. The first class of air cadets graduated in March 1941, just eight months prior to the Japanese attack on U.S. Naval forces at Pearl Harbor, Hawaii, and the nation's entry into World War II.

The state's first concrete highway — the 22.2-mile Dollarway Road — opened in 1914 and ran from near Pine Bluff to Little Rock. The road's construction cost was $1 per linear foot, thus the name "Dollarway."

As land and road travel evolved, ferries and bridges became more necessary.

Early Pine Bluff settler Dexter Harding constructed a sawdust bridge over a lake near his home in the 1850s. The unusual bridge was situated in the area of what is now East 10th Avenue and State Street. The lake, originally called Harding's Lake, is now Harding Drain.

On July 4, 1890, a 1,200-foot long pontoon bridge over the Arkansas River in Pine Bluff was put into service. Passage fees ranged from a nickel for a "man on foot" to a dollar for "vehicles" drawn by four horses or cattle or mules.

License plates from the past ran from city plates to those that at one point reflected a county's rank in population . . . 1-401 . . . Pulaski County, number one in population. Notice the Centennial plate from 1935 . . . issued to mark the state's 100th year of statehood in 1936.

Above, an ad from Smart Chevrolet in 1954.

Above right, the original leg of I-530 opened between Pine Bluff and Little Rock in the late 1960s.

Right, an ad for commercial trucking, "The trains don't stop in Star City, Arkansas anymore."

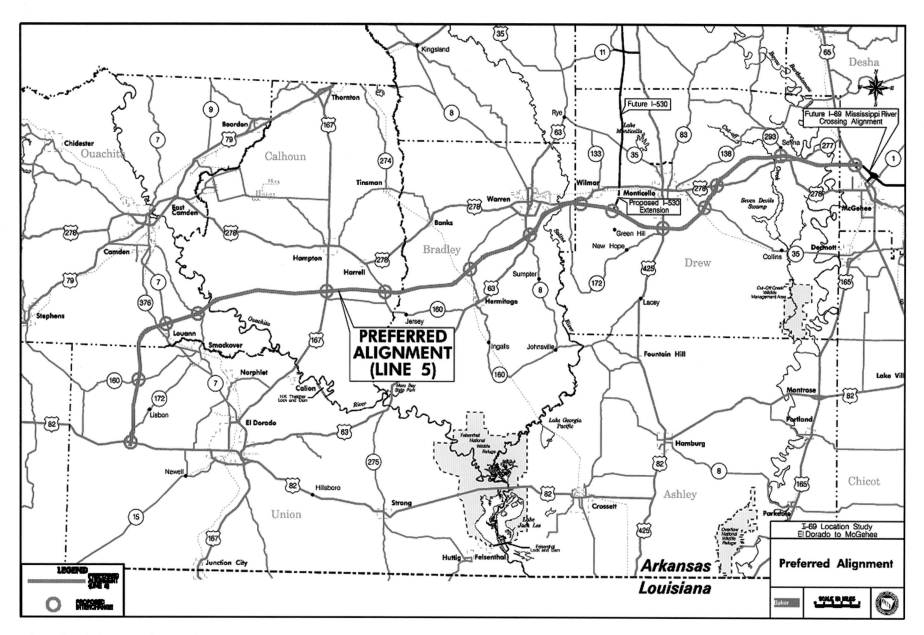

The preferred alignment of proposed I-69 across
Southeast Arkansas is shown above in this 2006 map.
Will construction happen in the years ahead?

The first Arkansas River free bridge was constructed near Pine Bluff and opened in 1915. It was demolished by dynamite in 1972. A new bridge, needed to better allow barge traffic resulting from the Kerr-McClellan Navigation Project, replaced the old structure.

Southeast Arkansas has lagged in automotive freeway service, but motorists of the future will enjoy Interstate 69, which will link the district with Texas, Louisiana, Mississippi, Tennessee, Kentucky, Indiana and Michigan.

Interstate 530 — the automotive expressway between Pine Bluff and Little Rock — has been, for nearly half a century, the only freeway in Southeast Arkansas. The northern 10 miles of the four-lane passage, originally U.S. Highway 65, date back to the 1960s.

But the roadway wasn't commissioned as Interstate 530 until August 2, 1999, the same day the twelve-mile Pine Bluff southern bypass was opened. U.S. 65 resumes at the end of the bypass, but a connecting extension to Interstate 530 is being constructed and will extend southward to between Wilmar and Monticello.

The idea for a bypass originated in the 1960s, and at one time the projected stretch was designated the Bayou Bartholomew Expressway, as it dissected the crooked waterway at several points. As many as three route plans were considered by authorities.

Freeway development has been both positive and negative for cities and towns along expressway routes. The old, downtown or primary trade communities along the once ruling but now less-traveled highways and roads have suffered from the decreased traffic flow, but areas near freeway exits have become profitable business locales. The convenience and speed of a freeway, however, have helped in reducing travel time, and many people will commute to a larger city to work while living in a nearby smaller town or rural setting.

So, populations have increased outside the bigger cities that have experienced declines in their residential counts, but many people motor to more substantial locales — with a fuller offering of goods and services — for most of their spending. A victim of the change in shopping habits is small, old-fashioned "mom and pop" grocery stores, which formerly dotted roadways and neighborhoods but have steadily yielded to chain operations.

Continuing construction and on-going renovations have become accepted facts of life for freeway users.

Above, this old steel bridge across the Saline River near Warren has been replaced with a concrete structure.

A computer rendering of the proposed Great River Bridge across the Mississippi River near Arkansas City. The bridge would be part of the I-69 project running from Canada to Mexico.

The future of Southeast Arkansas transportation is brighter because challenges of the past have led to a couple of major improvement proposals as the 21st Century began.

Neither the issuing agent or recipient of the pictured 1907 Pine Bluff two-horse wagon permit could have likely conceived the astonishing enhancements of road travel that would occur over the next century.

PINE BLUFF
2 H. WAGON
$10⁰⁰ № 16
1907

First, Interstate 69 — currently a $17 billion project — would give Southeast Arkansas its first automotive expressway. Interstate 69, once completed, would run from Mexico to Canada through nine states, including Arkansas, Texas, Louisiana and Mississippi.

U.S. Highway 530, which will eventually extend 38 miles from Pine Bluff to Wilmar, will serve as a connector to proposed Interstate 69. It is expected to be finalized by 2012.

Meanwhile, another leg of the project, from near Benoit, Mississippi, to near McGehee, would include the Great River Bridge spanning the Mississippi River. The bridge's cost will be $500 million — about $23,000 a foot.

A cable-stayed bridge, it will feature tall towers with cables grounded diagonally.

The bridge will serve as a gateway to Desha County's Arkansas City, now little more than a ghost town in comparison to the once-thriving river port's illustrious past.

Arkansas City, at its prime, counted around 15,000 residents. Today, less than 600 persons live there. Another bustling town, Napoleon, was located 15 miles northward.

Famed author Mark Twain wrote of Napoleon several times, but the city has since faded away and is no longer included on maps. Both Arkansas City and Napoleon were largely doomed by the monstrous Mississippi River flood of 1927, known in these parts simply as "The Flood" or "The Great Flood."

Could it be that the new bridge and Interstate 69 will miraculously result in a Napoleon and Arkansas City renaissance?

The geography around the towns isn't what it had been, but better times ought to be around the corner, thanks to Desha County movers and shakers Charlotte Schexnayder and Dorothy Moore and others whose persistence, devotion and energy over several decades have finally made the bridge a reality.

The bridge will be named the Charles W. Dean Memorial Bridge, in honor of the Mississippi civil engineer responsible for its design.

YOU CAN BE BAYOU-SELF ON THE BAYOU

Bayou Bartholomew takes a serpentine course through Southeast Arkansas originating north of Pine Bluff. The bayou is 375 miles long — the longest in the world — and crosses into Louisiana before joining the Ouachita River. The bayou is full of cypress and tupelo swamps, inhabited by alligators, turtles, and frogs and is visited by wintering waterfowl. There are more than 130 species of fishes found in its waters. Once, Bayou Bartholomew was a primary waterway for steamboats and other crafts. Today, the bayou is overgrown in spots, and has been polluted through several generations. The Bayou Bartholomew Alliance was established in 1995 by Dr. Curtis Merrell and others as a non-profit organization dedicated to restoring the bayou to its former glory.

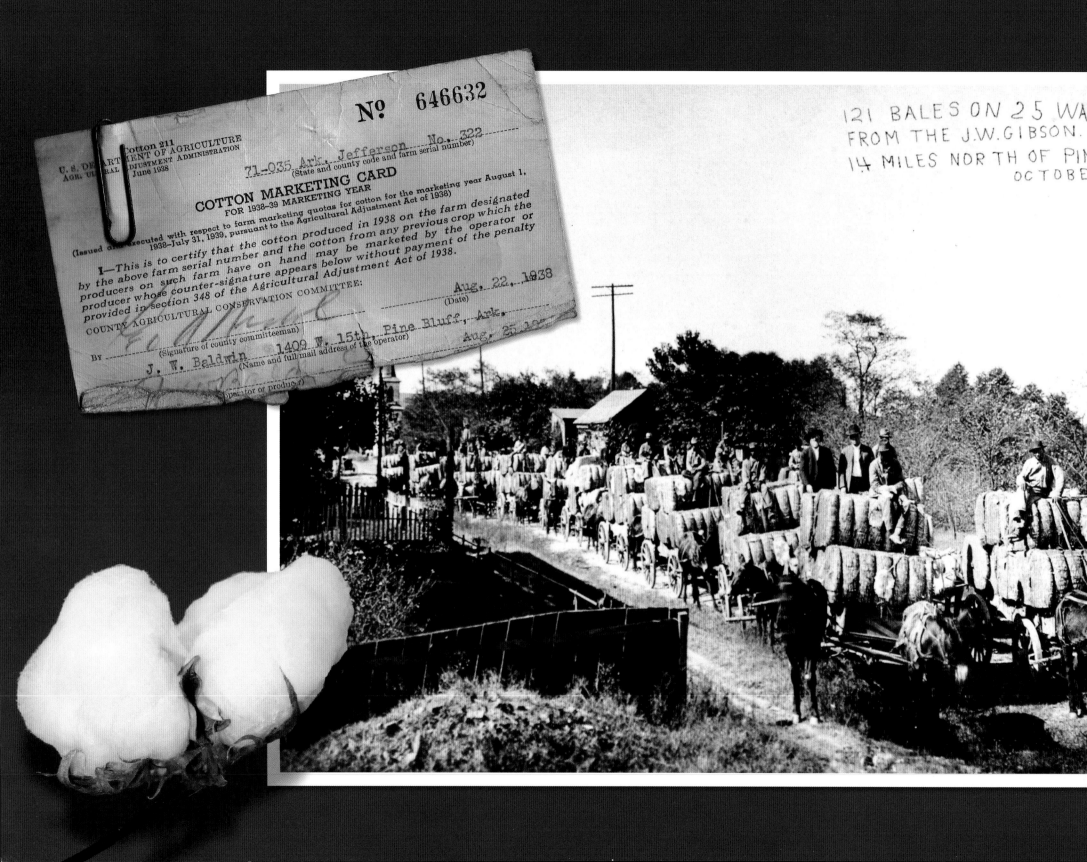

No. 646632

Cotton 211

U. S. DEPARTMENT OF AGRICULTURE
AGRICULTURAL ADJUSTMENT ADMINISTRATION
June 1938

71-035 Ark. Jefferson No. 322
(State and county code and farm serial number)

COTTON MARKETING CARD
FOR 1938–39 MARKETING YEAR

(Issued and executed with respect to farm marketing quotas for cotton for the marketing year August 1,
1938–July 31, 1939, pursuant to the Agricultural Adjustment Act of 1938)

I—This is to certify that the cotton produced in 1938 on the farm designated
by the above farm serial number and the cotton from any previous crop which the
producers on such farm have on hand may be marketed by the operator or
producer whose counter-signature appears below without payment of the penalty
provided in section 348 of the Agricultural Adjustment Act of 1938.

COUNTY AGRICULTURAL CONSERVATION COMMITTEE:

Aug. 22, 1938
(Date)

By
(Signature of county committeeman)

J. W. Baldwin   1409 W. 15th, Pine Bluff, Ark.   Aug. 25, 19
(Name and full mail address of the operator)
(Operator or producer)

121 BALES ON 25 WA
FROM THE J.W. GIBSON.
14 MILES NORTH OF PIN
OCTOBE

CHAPTER FOUR

Agriculture and Industry

Agriculture and industry . . . Why, that's just farming and manufacturing, right? Well, yes — and no.

One might lightly ponder each arena and reach such a simplistic conclusion. But a complete consideration would produce a much broader realization.

In totality, the relationship between the interests represents a deep and sometimes complex science, one that combines the assorted elements of the natural partnership that threads into virtually every aspect of our lives.

Agriculture is the world's oldest industry, and as it developed, industry grew to support not only improvements in farming, but also industry itself. If that seems confusing, maybe it should be restated as, "Needs generate needs, and progress generates progress."

One might compare the agriculture and industry affiliation to a never-ending circle.

Environment Is a Key Consideration.

The core of any area's agricultural abilities is within the region's environment. Climate, soil quality, landscape, rainfall, other water resources and geological features have been and remain the chief determining factors in defining an area.

Southeast Arkansas is easily one of the world's richest agricultural areas.

Long ago covered by water, the region, overall, possesses excellent soil. Meanwhile, Southeast Arkansas is truly "Bayou Country," as the Bartholomew and numerous other waterways —including the Arkansas, Mississippi, Saline and White rivers — help to energize the area.

A wide variety of crops have been produced here. Cotton, of course, was long the top money maker, but it also took an injurious toll on the soil. Production has been diversified and now includes rice and soybeans and multiple fruits and vegetables.

The region is also a pacesetter in timber production.

For many years, dairy operations were plentiful and livestock production was steady and profitable. Before subsidies were available to support farmers through periods in which soil was allowed to rejuvenate, the farmers had to devise different avenues to survive economically.

Requirements Give Birth to Support Activities.

Farmers needed supplies and equipment to do their jobs, and that essentially, sparked industry. There was money to be made in satisfying the farmers' requirements, and mass production meant lower costs and higher profits.

Of course, production firms needed certain provisions to achieve their purposes. Farmers and livestock and timber producers wound up having the capability of selling goods and services to the very concerns that supported them, and other entrepreneurs found livelihoods in meeting the widening demands.

Eventually, industry grew to be able to help in soil and water conservation and enhancements, further strengthening itself by empowering agriculture. As support needs increased, new businesses and industries

Clockwise, from left, a cotton-chopping crew from Lincoln County heads home after a day in the fields. Cotton pickers were paid by the total number of pounds they picked; wages were minimal. A two-story farm house with its windmill to pump water.

were born and, in due time, expanded in scope to include home and personal products.

The cycle is continuing as agri-industry explores avenues of creating and producing more-economical energy sources. This and other pursuits have been grouped under a new umbrella of endeavors classified as "alternative agriculture."

Many industrial improvements have resulted from shortcomings identified through unpleasant occurrences.

The Great Flood of 1927 illustrated a need for flood control as well as emergency preparedness and response. Before the event, the federal government had considered recovery from disasters to be a local responsibility, but the flood was such a widespread calamity that it delivered a lesson that some tragedies deliver problems too big to be handled by limited, area resources.

The flood also indicated a need for consistent navigation oversight on the Arkansas River. In 1971, the McClellan-Kerr Navigation System was enacted from the mouth of the Mississippi River to near Tulsa. The economic impact of the dam system hasn't been as profitable in river traffic as was anticipated, but it has aided in flood control and water quality, improvements that have led to greater population along the river.

The Pine Bluff area profited from World War II with the construction of the Army's Pine Bluff Arsenal, which has been nationally cited for its sensitivity to environmental and agricultural protection. Not only were new jobs created by the installation's construction and staffing, but also within associated businesses and industries.

Quality Hunting, Fishing Are Credited to Agriculture/ Industry Partnership.

Hunting and fishing are more than just pastimes in Southeast Arkansas. Outdoor sports in the area translate into a multi-billion dollar attraction.

As mentioned previously, agriculture gave birth to industry, and agriculture is dependent upon the environment. Thus, it only makes sense that both agricultural and industry leaders are devoted to protecting and enhancing Southeast Arkansas' natural resources.

John Brown Watson

John Brown Watson got his start in agriculture, so to speak.

He was born in Tyler, Texas, in 1869 to former slaves Frank and Crystal Watson, who apparently instilled in their son the lesson that wisdom is strength.

Watson had a desire for knowledge, which led him to significance as one of the nation's leading educators of his time. He touched the lives of hundreds who benefited from his leadership and vision.

Receiving his early education in the Tyler area, Watson became a county-licensed teacher in 1887. Even with the teaching certificate, however, Watson had only seven years of classroom education and wanted more.

In 1891, he entered Bishop College in Marshall, Texas, where he earned a high school diploma in 1898. After resuming his teaching career for two years, he enrolled at Colgate University in Hamilton, New York, and then transferred to Brown University in Providence, Rhode Island, in 1901. He earned a degree at Brown in 1904.

Watson began to receive admiring attention within education circles. An earlier Brown graduate, John Hope, who became the first black president of both Morehouse College in Atlanta and Atlanta College, was among those who took notice of Watson. Hope secured Watson's services as a mathematics and science professor at Morehouse from 1904–1908. During this span, Watson married. Meanwhile, Hope encouraged Watson to fulfill his potential by reaching for higher posts. Watson listened.

Over the next fifteen years, he worked in several influential business roles. In 1923, he returned to education as president of Leland College in Baker, Louisiana. Five years later, Watson was named president of Arkansas Agricultural, Mechanical and Normal College, now the University of Arkansas at Pine Bluff (UAPB).

His arrival in Pine Bluff coincided with the start of perhaps the most exciting period in UAPB's history. The institution had been a junior college for thirty-five years, but became a four-year institute and moved to its current site in 1929 as Watson settled into his command.

Because of the new campus' construction, Watson's inauguration service was delayed. The event was finally conducted in 1930, in conjunction with a campus dedication. John Hope — Watson's trusted friend and advisor of nearly three decades — was the guest speaker.

Under Watson's guidance, UAPB was reorganized into four divisions, including agriculture, the cornerstone of its founding as a land-grant college.

When Watson came to UAPB, enrollment totaled only thirty-six students and the college had just thirty-two faculty and staff members. Over the next fourteen years, his visionary vim brought big dividends. By the time of his death in 1942, UAPB counted nearly 500 students and its faculty numbered sixty-six.

Economic planners have long known that environmental preservation is a key to tourism, which is closely associated with agriculture, business and industry.

The White River National Wildlife Reserve provides a uniquely beautiful and enjoyable destination for visitors, and a wonderful home for fish and wildlife. The vegetation and landscape is undisturbed and completely natural.

Stuttgart and DeWitt are known for more than their world-leading rice production. The areas are considered the world's best for duck hunting. The rice industry is a perfect partner for the Arkansas County wetlands.

There are plenty of Southeast Arkansas locales in which deer thrive. In fact, there's an old joke that in New Edinburg, signs are posted on trees along roadways warning deer that the stretches of pavement are "human crossings." The practice is said to have decreased the number of collisions between deer and automobiles.

The many charms of Southeast Arkansas' natural resources are celebrated in a number of museums and centers that are outlined in the following chapter.

Timber Industry, Agriculture Are Stressed in Area Education.

As business and industry diversity moved farther from agriculture, awareness had waned that the area's two four-year educational institutions — the University of Arkansas at Monticello (UAM) and the University of Arkansas at Pine Bluff (UAPB) — were founded and remain rooted as agricultural colleges.

UAM is the only Arkansas university with a degree program in forestry. Various degrees are offered in forest resources, wildlife management and spatial information systems. The program has been hailed for its quality and depth of instruction.

Fish farming is a growing industry, and has been bolstered by studies conducted within the nationally-acclaimed UAPB fisheries program. UAPB is also recognized for its attention to rural development. Each year, UAPB conducts its Rural Life Conference that addresses developing issues.

Southeast Arkansas College in Pine Bluff is a two-year college with accelerating enrollment. It partners with UAPB in several areas.

The McClellan-Kerr Lock and Dam System on the Arkansas River, above, has had a tremendous impact on the economy of Southeast Arkansas. The system has helped in generating and maintaining assorted industries, supported area farming and enhanced river transportation. Efforts to continue development of an intermodal facility between Monticello and Warren would open other doors for shipping manufactured goods.

Okay; so those lug tractors were not the fanciest of all devices. They were still better than a mule any day; these Grand Prairie (rice producers) would testify.

The Stuttgart Rice Mill at left was a part of the rice industry that has made Arkansas County a leading player in the rice industry around the world.

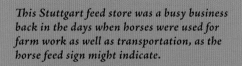

Various meats were sold and purchased at Dietz Meat Market, an early Stuttgart business.

This Stuttgart feed store was a busy business back in the days when horses were used for farm work as well as transportation, as the horse feed sign might indicate.

The Stuttgart skyline — "Castles of the Prairie."

The annual Rural Life Conference at the University of Arkansas at Pine Bluff has steadily grown into one of the area's chief events. Conferences have addressed all aspects of rural life, and the number of participants in the program increases annually.

Wildlife of many species abounds in Bayou Country.

Visitors to the Governor Mike Huckabee Delta Rivers Nature Center at Pine Bluff . . . many of them students . . . can learn about the fish and wildlife in Southeast Arkansas. Delta Rivers Nature Center was the first educational nature facility to open in the state, and relates to Arkansas' natural story.

Far right, a turtle along the banks of Bayou Bartholomew.

Business and Tourism

Sometimes forgotten as tools for entertainment, learning and actually experiencing the past are the assorted museums of Southeast Arkansas.

In Pine Bluff alone, interests ranging from art and musical bands to butterflies and the Civil War are addressed through displays and presentations.

The Arts and Science Center for Southeast Arkansas houses paintings, sculptures and modern art forms. It also features changing attractions, such as special collections, and its theater provides a stage for community productions.

Outdoor enthusiasts will likely enjoy the Governor Mike Huckabee Delta Rivers Nature Center. The facility has a butterfly garden, a welcoming pond inhabited by catfish and turtles, hunting and fishing displays, animal exhibits and various instructional programs.

Homegrown talents such as musicians Johnny Cash and Glen Campbell, actress Mary Steenburgen and actor Billy Bob Thornton are saluted in the Arkansas Entertainers Hall of Fame, which is located within the Pine Bluff Convention Center. The Arkansas Band Museum features instruments of famous band musicians, as well as rare instruments and equipment.

The Pine Bluff/Jefferson County Historical Museum, housed within the city's landmark rail depot, boasts a large doll collection, a Civil War flag of a local Confederate group, other military artifacts and scores of items of local interest.

For the area's many train enthusiasts, the Arkansas Railroad Museum is a must. It houses the restored Cotton Belt Steam Locomotive No. 819, originally built in 1942. Old passenger, freight and dining cars, cabooses and rail equipment are also displayed.

Local black heritage and University of Arkansas at Pine Bluff (UAPB) history are addressed in the Persistence of the Spirit/Keepers of the Spirit exhibit and the new UAPB Museum.

The nearby White Hall Historical Museum includes indoor and outdoor displays on past life in the area, including items related to the Army's Pine Bluff Arsenal. Children can play on a restored, old caboose. Fronting the museum is an impressive monument to World War II soldiers.

ARKANSAS' FIRST NEWSPAPER

Southeast Arkansas is the original home of the oldest newspaper west of the Mississippi River.

New York native William Edward Woodruff founded the *Arkansas Gazette* at Arkansas Post — then the state capital — in 1819, publishing his first edition on November 20.

He moved the newspaper to Little Rock when it was named the state's seat of government in October 1820.

Pine Bluff was the site of Arkansas' first radio station. Businessman Harvey C. Couch founded radio station WOK, which was housed in a Main Street building near Simmons First National Bank. WOK's first broadcast was aired on April 8, 1922.

Gordon Freeman literally grew up at the Pine Bluff Commercial. A young son of publisher E. W. Freeman and a grandson of former publisher Major Charles G. Newman, the young Freeman is pictured here in a posed newsboy shot made in the early 1900s. On the back of the photograph, he penned a loving inscription to his father.

CHAPTER FIVE

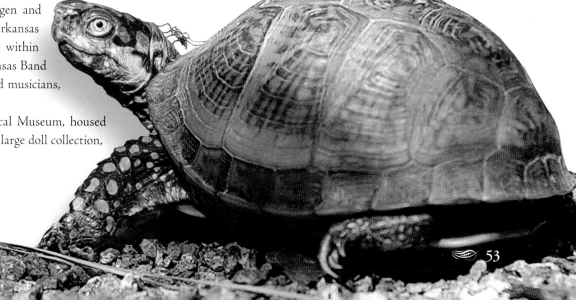

Left, the Pine Bluff/Jefferson County Historical Museum features a room dedicated to the county's rich military history. Below, an old honor token from Warren is pictured.

Other Southeast Arkansas museums include:

Arkansas City Museum — A restored 1850s log cabin is among the features. Arkansas City has a rich history, having once been a major Mississippi River port.

Arkansas Post National Monument — Arkansas Post was the original capital of Arkansas Territory. It was also the site of Revolutionary and Civil War battles.

Arkansas Post County Museum — Pioneer articles and Civil War artifacts are plentiful.

Arts Center for the Grand Prairie, Stuttgart — Local and regional artists are featured, and musical and theater entertainment are also offered.

Ashley County Museum, Hamburg — A carriage collection, Victorian clothing, rare glassware and county government archives number among the highlights.

Bradley County Museum, Warren — Housed in the county's oldest residential structure, the museum naturally includes a "Pink Tomato Room."

Dallas County Museum, Fordyce — Football and basketball fans will appreciate exhibits on legendary University of Alabama football coach Paul "Bear" Bryant and the Nutt (as in University of Arkansas football coach Houston Nutt) family, which has also produced noted basketball stars and coaches.

Desha County Museum, Dumas — One of the state's largest county museums, it includes several buildings representing pioneer homes and businesses. Farm implements, stone knives and Indian artifacts are also featured.

Drew County Museum, Monticello — Handcrafted toys, antique furniture, and Indian and war relics are only part of an interesting collection.

Grant County Museum, Sheridan — Widely acclaimed, this complex includes several old buildings, including an actual Masonic lodge, a 1930s café, a 1920s church, a World War II wooden barracks and a one-room schoolhouse. A variety of antique sporting goods are among the uncommon items displayed.

Museum Of The Grand Prairie, Stuttgart — Ducks and duck hunting are major themes. Antique agricultural equipment and a collection of old music boxes and radios are also available for inspection.

Pioneer Village, Rison — This replica 1800s settlement contains log cabins and a blacksmith shop.

St. Charles Museum — Focusing on a rich Civil War history, the facility also notes St. Charles' ties to the Arkansas and White rivers.

Turner Neal Museum Of Natural History, Monticello — Housed on the campus of the University of Arkansas at Monticello, this grand collection includes several mounted big-game animals, including an elephant and a polar bear. Local wildlife, plants and fish are also highlighted, and the facility features a small planetarium.

Early black leaders are remembered in displays at the Pine Bluff/Jefferson County Historical Museum.

Southeast Arkansas is hailed as the nation's best hunting area. The sport rates a large exhibit at the Pine Bluff/ Jefferson County Historical Museum. Nearby Arkansas County calls itself the "Duck Hunting Capital of the World."

MISS WILLIE K. HOCKER

Miss Willie Kavanaugh Hocker of Wabbaseka was the designer of the Arkansas state flag. Miss Hocker, a member of the Pine Bluff Chapter of the Daughters of the American Revolution, submitted her flag design to the Arkansas General Assembly in 1912. Her design was officially adopted as the flag of Arkansas on February 18, 1913. Miss Hocker, an author, poet and educator, taught in Jefferson County schools for 34 years. She spent most of her adult life as a resident of Wabbaseka. Miss Hocker lived in a home near this spot directly behind the Wabbaseka United Methodist Church, of which she was a member. She passed away on February 6, 1944 in Wabbaseka.

The designer of Arkansas' state flag . . . Willie K. Hocker of Wabbaeska is remembered in this display at the Pine Bluff/Jefferson County Historical Museum. At left, a historical marker recognizing her contribution to Arkansas history.

A collection of vintage wedding gowns is a popular attraction at the Pine Bluff/ Jefferson County Historical Museum.

Left, hats were a popular clothing item for ladies of all ages as evidenced by this photograph of workers and customers in Minnie Pierron's Hat Shop in Stuttgart in the early 1900s. The youngest girl isn't identified, but others pictured are (from left) Mrs. Phillip Schneider, Ester Scroggins Stuckey, Bertha Monitz, Pierron, and Clara Cassidy.

"Mr. Southeast Arkansas"

Louis L. Ramsay Jr. wasn't a big man because he was sociable with and kind and helpful to all persons, regardless of their status. He wasn't special because he possessed a remarkable business sense and knowledge of law. He didn't rate above others because of his leadership abilities and willingness to do whatever work was needed to achieve a positive goal. And he wasn't extraordinary because he was deeply devoted to education.

No, Ramsay was a big man because he was all of the above, and more. Named by readers as the city's "Most Influential Citizen" in a 1989 *Pine Bluff Commercial* poll, he was referred to by some as "Mr. Southeast Arkansas."

Born in Fordyce in 1918, he nearly wound up playing football at the University of Alabama, where his Fordyce friend Paul "Bear" Bryant was an assistant coach at the time, but instead donned a University of Arkansas uniform after accepting an offer of a scholarship to include law school.

At Arkansas, he lettered as a quarterback in 1940 and 1941.

After turning down a professional football offer and earning a pre-law degree, he served as an Army Air Corps pilot in the European Theater of Operations in World War II. Awarded the Air Medal with four Oak Leaf Clusters, he was discharged with the rank of major.

Above, Louis L. Ramsay Jr. gazes from the window of his office at the Simmons Bank Building. He is looking out toward the Jefferson County Courthouse and Lake Pine Bluff.

Right, The Jefferson County Courthouse stands facing Lake Pine Bluff.

In 1947, he received his juris doctor degree and moved to Pine Bluff, joining the law firm of Coleman and Gantt in what would become a life-long partnership.

He joined the board of directors of Simmons First National Bank in 1952 and was elected its president in 1970. He was chairman and chief executive officer of Simmons First National Bank and Simmons First National Corporation from 1973–1983.

Meanwhile, his influence grew to include membership on the Board of Trustees of the University of Arkansas system from 1970–1981. He was board chairman from 1978–1981.

He is, to date, the only person to have been president of both the Arkansas Bar Association and Arkansas Bankers Association.

Ramsay was listed in several publications as among the "Best Lawyers in America."

He was an active member and leader in an array of legal, banking, business, education and development groups and efforts, lending his skills to everything from highway improvements and health and insurance enhancements to science and technology evolution and employment opportunities.

Ramsay was appointed chairman of the Arkansas Sesquicentennial Commission by then Governor Bill Clinton in 1985.

The Louis L. Ramsay Educational Fund was established at the Arts and Science Center for Southeast Arkansas in 1989. He received the National Conference of Christians and Jews Humanitarian Award in 1989 and a Distinguished Service Award from the University of Arkansas Razorback Foundation in 1994.

Inducted into the Arkansas Business Hall of Fame in 2003, Ramsay was further honored when Simmons and Arkansas Blue Cross Blue Shield established a $250,000 faculty fund in tribute to him and his wife, Joy.

A devout Christian, Ramsay was always appreciative of salutes toward him, but typically downplayed his roles in the many successes he championed.

Diagnosed with cancer, he boldly fought the disease and continued a busy work and volunteer schedule until his death at the age of 85 on January 4, 2004.

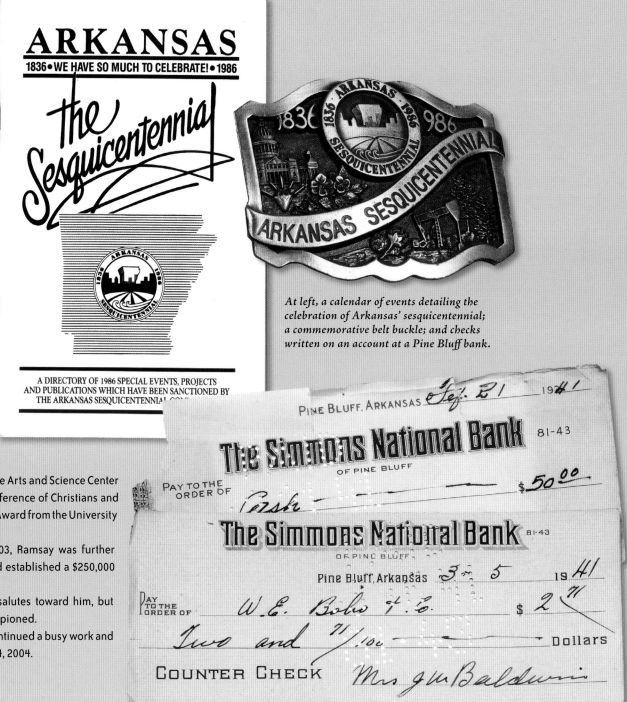

At left, a calendar of events detailing the celebration of Arkansas' sesquicentennial; a commemorative belt buckle; and checks written on an account at a Pine Bluff bank.

Now out of business, the Coca-Cola Bottling Company of South Arkansas in Pine Bluff, along with several civic groups, sponsored this welcome sign that greeted motorists in the 1950s.

Once common, this wooden Coca-Cola carrying case is now a rare antique.

Pine Bluff's Main Street, circa 1950, is pictured southward from the Jefferson County Courthouse and, on the opposite page, northward from the vicinity of the city's landmark Hotel Pines.

Hotel Pines, Pine Bluff, Arkansas

IC617-N

A postcard provides a moment in time at Pine Bluff's landmark Hotel Pines (above).

Left, is an old account file from the Cotton Belt Savings and Trust Company in Pine Bluff.

SAVINGS DEPARTMENT

Book No._____ Bank No._____

COTTON BELT
SAVINGS & TRUST CO.

PINE BLUFF, ARKANSAS

In Account With

TAKE CARE OF THIS BOOK

It must be presented when money is
Deposited or Withdrawn

If Lost or Stolen Notify the Bank at Once.

Above, Southern Mercantile Company in Pine Bluff, circa 1900.

Right, Dunk Goggins, Carter Wood, and Joe Gocio are pictured outside Gocio's store in Grady, circa 1915.

Below, a 1928 promissory note from Simmons National Bank in Pine Bluff.

Above, R. W. Teer General Merchant and Tie Contractor in Jefferson.

Right, the Grady railroad depot was well-organized for this 1907 photograph.

Grady was a busy Lincoln County city at the time these photographs were snapped in the late 1940s. Above, a trio of men converse outside a store. Above right, a couple of cars are parked in front of the city's movie theater. Obviously not a fun place to visit, the city jail at right, was already a decaying structure. Below, a wooden building housed the city's fire truck and firefighting equipment.

A sawdust bridge was constructed by early Pine Bluff resident Dexter Harding. A historical marker today marks the areas served by the bridge over what became known as Harding Lake.

SAWDUST BRIDGE

JEFFERSON COUNTY HISTORY COMMISSION 1976

Dexter Harding (1796-1862), a veteran of the War of 1812, in 1850 built a home and sawmill on the south bank of Harding Lake. He spanned this lake by a bridge of sawdust and mud. Both men and beasts dreaded to cross the spongy surface, especially at night, because of the strange lights, weird sounds, blasts of hot air, snakes and alligators. This marker fronts on the oblique stretch of modern State Street which follows near the path of the spooky Sawdust Bridge.

Each fall thousands of visitors are on hand to celebrate homecoming at the University of Arkansas at Pine Bluff. The homecoming parade through downtown Pine Bluff is a crowd favorite.

Above, Sixth Avenue School in Pine Bluff.

Right, school land deeds issued by the State of Arkansas in 1907.

PATENT FOR SCHOOL

—FROM THE—

State of Arka

TO

RE

Bo

Filed
this the
April 190

SCHOOL LA

Deed No.

From the State of

CHAPTER SIX

Education

Free public schools didn't exist in Arkansas until after the Civil War. Meaningful education had previously been a luxury, and a number of private schools — some for blacks, others for whites — had operated.

In 1867, the state legislature adopted measures establishing a public school system and levied a two-mill property tax to support it. In addition to the two mills, individual districts could vote up to an additional five-mill tax.

On March 1, 1869, Pine Bluff voters approved a one-mill tax and the district's first board. The first classes were held in the homes of two volunteer teachers. During the same year, the district purchased property between Laurel and Beech streets on the north side of West Sixth Avenue, where a three-story school with an 88-foot tall tower was constructed by the local firm of Bell and Bocage.

Called Pine Bluff High School, the facility — only the third of its kind in the entire state — opened in the fall of 1871 with Malcolm Currie as principal. He oversaw a staff of four women teachers.

The early years of the public education system were especially difficult. Revenue was scarce and private schools could compete for students by offering better teachers, books and supplies.

Nevertheless, the board of the public system pressed on and in 1870 purchased an American Missionary Association "colored" school at West Second Avenue and Linden Street. It became the public district's first black school. The Rev. M. W. Martin, who had been a teacher in the old school, was appointed as principal. He had but one assistant.

In 1875, the Pine Bluff schools closed due to a lack of funds, but the board allowed teachers to use the district's facilities at no charge in conducting tuition schools. The district would close again in 1934, when the Great Depression forced the district to charge students in order to keep schools open.

The 1877 hiring of sisters Mary E. "Minnie" and Ruth McBride greatly improved educational opportunities among the whites. Minnie McBride was principal until 1880. Ruth McBride, who had been her assistant, took over as principal when her sister married and gave up the post, and served until 1895 when Dr. John H. Hinemon was lured away from Monticello and named as Pine Bluff's first superintendent.

Before Hinemon's arrival, the district experienced growth due to the city's increasing population. More facilities were obtained and the district's staff was realigned.

The 1889 dismissal of a pair of supposedly unqualified black teachers by Marion A. Perry, the newly-appointed black principal, created discord within the black community. The disagreement resulted in a pair of arson fires — one at the original Merrill School on West Pullen between Linden and Mulberry streets and the other at the old American Missionary Association building.

A new Merrill School was built, but at 1 a.m. on January 23, 1890, the structure was leveled in yet another arson fire. Prominent black attorney S. J. Hollensworth was convicted of the crime but avoided a prison term.

A third Merrill School was completed in time for the opening of the 1890 fall term. The spacious, two-story structure served black students

Above, a group of young students at the Sixth Avenue School in Pine Bluff, in the early 1900s.

Right, a state issued deed for a Sixteenth Section of land for a school in Drew County, dated 1907.

Deed for Sixteenth Secti

HE STATE OF ARKANSAS,

To All to Whom These Presents Shall Come—Greeting

WHEREAS, Under the provisions of an Act of

Arkansas, entitled "An Act regulating the sale of the Sixteen

ection of all claims due the School Fund arising from the sal

for other purposes," approved March 31, 1885, and whereas

CERTIFICATE OF

ATE OF ARKANSAS,
County of Drew.

I J.W. Hambro Circuit Clerk and E
said, do hereby certify that the annexed and foregoing instrume
office on the 27 day of April A. D
and the same is now duly recorded with the acknowledgement a
8 page 124

In Witness Whereof, I have hereunto set my hand and affix
day of April 190 7

CHAPTER SIX

Education

Free public schools didn't exist in Arkansas until after the Civil War. Meaningful education had previously been a luxury, and a number of private schools — some for blacks, others for whites — had operated.

In 1867, the state legislature adopted measures establishing a public school system and levied a two-mill property tax to support it. In addition to the two mills, individual districts could vote up to an additional five-mill tax.

On March 1, 1869, Pine Bluff voters approved a one-mill tax and the district's first board. The first classes were held in the homes of two volunteer teachers. During the same year, the district purchased property between Laurel and Beech streets on the north side of West Sixth Avenue, where a three-story school with an 88-foot tall tower was constructed by the local firm of Bell and Bocage.

Called Pine Bluff High School, the facility — only the third of its kind in the entire state — opened in the fall of 1871 with Malcolm Currie as principal. He oversaw a staff of four women teachers.

The early years of the public education system were especially difficult. Revenue was scarce and private schools could compete for students by offering better teachers, books and supplies.

Nevertheless, the board of the public system pressed on and in 1870 purchased an American Missionary Association "colored" school at West Second Avenue and Linden Street. It became the public districts' first black school. The Rev. M. W. Martin, who had been a teacher in the old school, was appointed as principal. He had but one assistant.

In 1875, the Pine Bluff schools closed due to a lack of funds, but the board allowed teachers to use the district's facilities at no charge in conducting tuition schools. The district would close again in 1934, when the Great Depression forced the district to charge students in order to keep schools open.

The 1877 hiring of sisters Mary E. "Minnie" and Ruth McBride greatly improved educational opportunities among the whites. Minnie McBride was principal until 1880. Ruth McBride, who had been her assistant, took over as principal when her sister married and gave up the post, and served until 1895 when Dr. John H. Hinemon was lured away from Monticello and named as Pine Bluff's first superintendent.

Before Hinemon's arrival, the district experienced growth due to the city's increasing population. More facilities were obtained and the district's staff was realigned.

The 1889 dismissal of a pair of supposedly unqualified black teachers by Marion A. Perry, the newly-appointed black principal, created discord within the black community. The disagreement resulted in a pair of arson fires — one at the original Merrill School on West Pullen between Linden and Mulberry streets and the other at the old American Missionary Association building.

A new Merrill School was built, but at 1 a.m. on January 23, 1890, the structure was leveled in yet another arson fire. Prominent black attorney S. J. Hollensworth was convicted of the crime but avoided a prison term.

A third Merrill School was completed in time for the opening of the 1890 fall term. The spacious, two-story structure served black students

Above, a group of young students at the Sixth Avenue School in Pine Bluff in the early 1900s.

Right, a state issued deed for a Sixteenth Section of land for a school in Drew County, dated 1907.

until March 17, 1913, when it too was destroyed in a fire. Investigators blamed the blaze on defective flues.

Another Merrill School was built during the same year. Part of it remains in use today, but a large portion of the structure was leveled in a later fire.

Education Expands as Teachers are Restricted

Meanwhile, free public school systems had taken hold in other Southeast Arkansas locations. A number of rural schools had been developed.

Monticello had long had a reputation for quality education, thanks in large part to Hinemon and Professor Woodville Thompson, who is featured elsewhere in this section.

Many community schools were one-room structures in which all grades were taught. Up until the 1920s, only six to eight years of basic schooling were required to enter college.

In 1885, Hinemon founded Hinemon University at Monticello. He may have been the city's first public school superintendent as well.

Early-day teachers were terribly underpaid. And even worse, most teachers received the majority of their salaries in script, and there was no schedule for its distribution. Also, districts placed harsh restrictions upon their teachers and other employees. Such requirements wouldn't make it through a court challenge today.

Maurice Dean, who later became an English teacher at Arkansas State Teachers College (now the University of Central Arkansas) in Conway, started her teaching career around 1915 in the one-room Buzzard's Roost School between Stuttgart and Carlisle (in neighboring Lonoke County).

According to her contract, windows at her place of residence had to be covered at all times except for 11 a.m.–1 p.m. (she boarded with the superintendent and his family). Also, she was not to attend any public functions unescorted, but she could participate while in the company of the family of the superintendent or a "designated" chaperone.

She was disallowed from dating unless her prospective beau consented to a board interview and was then approved by the panel. At no time was he allowed to enter her home, they could not be out together after dusk unless accompanied by a "responsible" third party and any outward signs of affection — hand-holding, kissing or even writing an affectionate note — would result in her immediate dismissal.

Additionally, she could not ride in an automobile unless it was being driven by the district's male superintendent or another approved male. And she could not travel outside the district or receive guests at her residence unless she gave the superintendent advance notice and received his okay.

She was allowed to ride a horse, but only in a "proper manner."

Organization and Alignment Changes

In Pine Bluff and other cities with various schools, the period of 1900 until the start of World War I was one of expansion and rearrangement.

In 1902, Hinemon resigned as Pine Bluff's school chief and became the state superintendent of public instruction. He was replaced by University of Arkansas professor and former state superintendent Junius Jordan, who would steer the Pine Bluff district for 21 years. Jordan died on October 12, 1923, and was replaced by John R. Allen, who would serve until 1941.

In 1919, after districts had struggled through financial constraints caused by World War I, Pine Bluff adopted a 6–3–3 system — grades 1–6 in elementary school, grades 7–9 in junior high and grades 10–12 in high school. The 6–3–3 alignment became a norm, but has been altered several times throughout the years.

Schools in Southeast Arkansas encountered stiff challenges with the Great Flood of 1927, the draught of 1930, the Great Depression and World War II. The depression began in 1929 and diminished but continued into the era of America's 1941 entry into World War II. During the span, some smaller districts were financially disabled, at least for a time. Many one-school districts collapsed and merged with others.

Because of the presence of the Army's Pine Bluff Arsenal, Jefferson County schools fared well during World War II. The Korean War

OLD PALMYRA SCHOOL HOUSE

ELA BELL CHAMBLISS
FIRST GRADE TEACHER

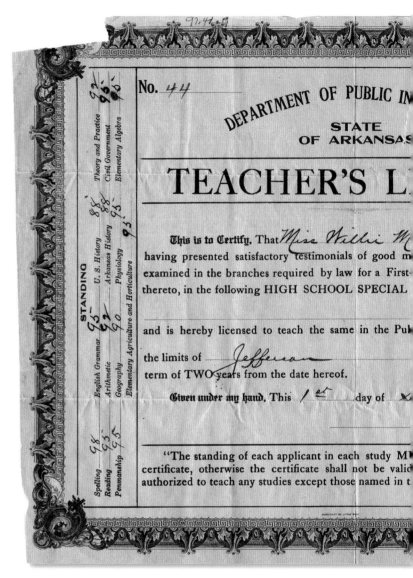

would bring another surge of prosperity to Pine Bluff and its growing school district. From 1943–1954, the district — under the guidance of Superintendent Henry F. Dial — constructed nine new schools.

Integration of the Pine Bluff School District did not occur until nearly a decade after the Little Rock Central High School crisis in 1957. It would occur even later within some of the area's districts.

Dr. C. B. Garrison — named Pine Bluff's superintendent in 1967 upon the death of Dr. John A. Trice, who stepped up when Dial retired in 1957 — did a good job during a difficult time of court-ordered desegregation. He also oversaw the construction of the current high school complex in 1968.

For the most part, integration is no longer a contended issue in the region.

A Bright Future

The future of public education in Southeast Arkansas seems bright at the time of this book's publication. In February 2006, Pine Bluff voters endorsed a $28.8 million package that will finance renovation of most of the schools in the district and restructure it.

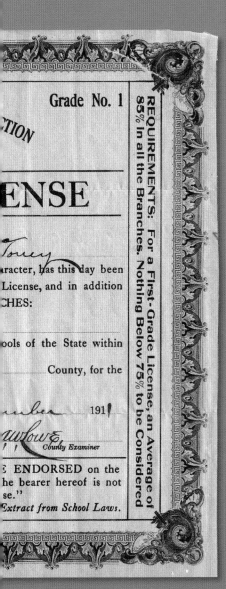

An Accidental Teacher

Professor Woodville E. Thompson refused to allow a series of setbacks in his early life to stop him from reaching what was seemingly his appointed destiny as a master educator.

Monticello and then the remainder of Arkansas greatly benefited from both his grit and firm but fair command.

He moved to Monticello in 1859 to commence his planned career as an attorney. But circumstances changed drastically, and Thompson instead wound up as the city's most revered teacher. He soon attained a statewide reputation and eventually served eight years as Arkansas' superintendent of public instruction, first by appointment of the state legislature and afterward at the desire of voters in three state elections.

Born in Maury, Tennessee, on September 30, 1834, Thompson was 12 when his father, James B. Thompson, died. The elder Thompson's widow, Ruth Davidson Thompson, was 40 and suddenly alone in caring for Woodville and his two brothers, James N. Thompson and John Franklin Thompson. Mrs. Thompson, however, possessed the same determined spirit that would define her sons. She managed the family's plantation and made certain her sons received quality education.

After earning a literary degree from the University of Mississippi in 1854, Woodville Thompson decided to pursue a law degree. Shy of money, he agreed to teach a year at the Chulahoma, Mississippi, Masonic School. Thompson's strength as an instructor and in dispensing and maintaining the discipline the school had previously lacked overwhelmed its patrons. Although he enrolled in the University of Mississippi Law School the following year, his performance as a teacher had been so impressive that his name began repeatedly surfacing in educational circles within the Mid-South.

Upon receipt of his law degree, Thompson married South Carolina native Harriet R. McGehee on August 19, 1858. Just over a year later, the couple established residency in Monticello.

Unfortunately, Thompson quickly fell ill with a severe case of feverish chills, apparently generated by a change in climate. He was unable to work the next three years, but his condition was improving when the Civil War began. Although he hadn't supported the South's secession, Thompson pledged his allegiance to the Confederate cause once the war started. His brothers immediately entered the Rebel army. James N. Thompson became a respected surgeon, assigned to the Little Rock Hospital Corps. John Franklin Thompson attained the rank of lieutenant in Owen's Battery.

Woodville Thompson longed to serve with his brothers, but his health problems disallowed his enlistment. Instead, at the request of a group of Monticello citizens, he took charge of the city's boys school. A year later, he left to join John Franklin Thompson's company, but fell ill with the measles before reaching the appropriate Confederate headquarters. Two months later, heeding the recommendation of Confederate physicians, he returned to Monticello and served until the war's end as a quartermasters clerk throughout the southern portion of the state.

The date of John Franklin Thompson's death in Cleburne, Texas, is uncertain, but there's reason to believe he perished in a Civil War battle there. Leaving a young wife and daughter, James N. Thompson died at Monticello in 1865. Meanwhile, Woodville Thompson had resumed his Monticello teaching career at the conclusion of hostilities. He was named principal of the private Monticello Institute, which was open to boys and girls. Respected across the region as an administrator and disciplinarian, he was admired for his personal character and ability to motivate students both individually and collectively. His pupils adored him, and many credited his caring counsel as having propelled them to their life successes.

In 1876, the state legislature appointed him to the Board of Trustees of the University of Arkansas. He continued his work in Monticello until 1880. He became the state superintendent of public education the next year, holding the post until declining health prompted him to step down in 1889. He retired to Little Rock, where he died on September 30, 1894 – his 60th birthday.

Thompson and his wife had 11 children, all born in Monticello. Those who survived to maturity were Claude, Earl, Fay, French, Guy, Hattie, Ione, Reola, Roy and William.

Callie Jones Private School students and faculty in 1900, in Pine Bluff, above. Right, an arithmetic book from the era.

An academy will be constructed on the high school campus, and two new schools will be erected. Six schools will be remodeled. The Pine Bluff District has long been considered one of the state's strongest.

Two other districts — Dollarway and Watson Chapel — exist in Pine Bluff.

In July 2006, Dollarway annexed the Altheimer-Sherrill Unified School District when the Arkansas Board of Education ruled that Altheimer-Sherrill was no longer fiscally solvent. The merger is expected to produce good results.

Watson Chapel has been hailed as one of the state's most progressive districts and consistently ranks high in teacher compensation.

The nearby White Hall School District, originally among the poorest in the area, is now one of the state's wealthiest and extends to Redfield and the Pulaski County line. The White Hall district has received acclaim in several categories.

In addition to Monticello, other districts within the area include DeWitt, Drew Central, Dumas, Fordyce, Hermitage, McGehee, Monticello, Rison, Sheridan, Star City, Stuttgart and Woodlawn.

Should one be searching for an example of a "self-made man" in Southeast Arkansas, it might be challenging to find a better model than Col. William H. Halliburton.

A Stewart County, Tennessee, native, Halliburton was 29 when in 1845 he moved to Arkansas, then in its infancy, having achieved statehood only nine years prior.

Despite having only eight months of formal education, Halliburton became a teacher and then an attorney, practicing law over 65 years before his death at age 96 on November

The dormitory at Richard Allen Institute at Pine Bluff in 1895.

18, 1912. He lived briefly in Jefferson County and Little Rock, but was a DeWitt-area resident of Arkansas County most of his life.

He witnessed the construction of three county courthouses in DeWitt. He not only practiced law in each structure, but also physically assisted in the building of the first – a log configuration. Additionally, he aided in planning the assemblage of the second and third.

He thought public service should be viewed as an honored duty, and put that belief to work as county clerk and tax collector and state legislator.

Despite his lack of traditional education, Halliburton never lost a lifelong thirst for knowledge. Said to have possessed a remarkable memory, he was an avid reader and book collector. He once donated a lot of over 2,000 books to Ouachita College (now Ouachita Baptist University) in Arkadelphia.

At the age of 17, Halliburton began clerking in a country store near his birthplace. Five years later, he married Catherine Alton, a daughter of a Tennessee Baptist minister. The couple had seven children.

Catherine Alton Halliburton died after the family's move to Arkansas County, where they had settled at Arkansas Post. Following a period of mourning, Col. Halliburton remarried there, exchanging vows with Hannah Jacobs, who bore him four daughters.

Unfortunately, unanticipated suffering again struck Col. Halliburton and his children when Hannah Jacobs Halliburton died. Although strained by sorrow, Col. Halliburton nobly pressed on in his professional pursuits to provide for his children, but also arranged his work

The Bell Tower on the campus of the University of Arkansas at Pine Bluff.

According to one account, Halliburton never carried a firearm in his tax trips from DeWitt to Little Rock. And, apparently, he didn't ever need one.

As it did with most, the Civil War created much change for Halliburton and his family.

Just six months before the war began, he moved to Little Rock and served as an aide to then-provisional Confederate Congressman and future Governor Augustus Garland. Jefferson Davis, president of the Confederacy, would eventually appoint Halliburton as Arkansas' war tax collector.

When Federal troops began closing in on Halliburton's Little Rock home, he loaded his family and possessions onto a flatboat, traveling down the Arkansas River to Jefferson County. He helped in putting together a log cabin for a temporary shelter, but the family stayed there only a short time before resuming their journey to their final destination, DeWitt.

After the war, Halliburton restarted his private legal practice and took on an increased role in public affairs. He was elected to three terms in the state legislature. He later worked in Washington, D.C., on occasion after receiving a federal assignment to clear titles to swamp lands in this region.

Halliburton was also recognized for his communicative skills. He was hailed as an outstanding orator and writer. He wrote a history of Arkansas County, the oldest of the state's 75 counties. The manuscript was described as a splendid work that not only gave an authentic, accurate account of the county's past, but also provided a valuable foundation for the region and state histories.

Halliburton was a noted collector, too. He accumulated an impressive number of rare coins and received a Louisiana Purchase Exposition award for his compilation of original papers relating to the Louisiana Purchase. Halliburton gathered the papers from various county archives.

He eventually retired as a practicing attorney, but never lost his amazing mental sharpness. In fact, his intelligence and alertness were so admired that only a few months before his death, he was asked to serve as a special judge during a term of circuit court.

requirements so as to allow himself to devote more time and attention to their parenting needs.

Halliburton later wedded Mary Belknap Patrick, who had migrated to nearby St. Charles from her native Boston.

Halliburton utilized teaching as a means of achieving his primary goal of becoming an attorney. After obtaining a teaching certificate upon moving to Arkansas, he rode horseback throughout Arkansas County to recruit students. Successful in his efforts, he established a small, private school.

Meanwhile, he began vigorously studying law on his own, utilizing his powerful memory in securing membership in the state bar. Giving up teaching, he was soon acclaimed as one of Arkansas' brightest and most gifted lawyers.

Serving as an Arkansas County sheriff's deputy, he supplemented his salary as an attorney while his private legal practice developed.

At the same time, he acted as county clerk and tax collector. He rode a horse from house to house in the county, collecting tax monies and storing the cash in saddlebags, venturing on horseback to Little Rock to deposit the funds in the state treasury.

What a difference nearly a hundred years can make. Here are two photographs of White Hall School in 1915, one showing Principal Fred Herrington with nine schoolboys and the other with Herrington and staff as well as the entire student body. The school house might have been nice for its time, but pales in comparison to today's White Hall schools, especially the newer junior high and high school facilities.

Halliburton accepted the invitation. And he was praised for his seemingly ageless judicial knowledge and demeanor.

In the process, he fittingly capped his life of remarkable experiences and achievements by likely establishing himself nationally as a record-setting arbitrator.

America was only 30 years old at the time of his birth, which followed the War of 1812 by only four years. He witnessed much of the country's early growth and then experienced its divide during the Civil War.

He saw two centuries of slavery end with the Emancipation Proclamation. He endured the assassination of President Abraham Lincoln and its lengthy, painful impact on a torn nation. He stood with his family, friends and neighbors and served them as their defeated homeland struggled through a postwar rebirth.

Along the way, he saw Indian wars that were finally ceded through government truces. He survived the years of the Old West, the wild era of Jesse James, Belle Starr, Wyatt Earp and Judge Isaac Parker.

He watched Americans, not yet fully reconnected from the split of the Civil War, merge into a united force against threatening foes from other countries. He observed the arrival of the train and the magnificent impact of railroads on the entire nation, and then was an eyewitness to the invention of automobiles and the advent of man in flight.

His many other personal accomplishments aside, it's Halliburton's lifelong exercising of his mental astuteness that may very well have netted him nationwide distinction.

If, at 96, Col. William H. Halliburton isn't the oldest person in the country to have served as a court judge, there's another interesting story somewhere, waiting to be told.

Above, an old postcard of the Administration Building what today is the University of Arkansas at Pine Bluff.

Right, a historical marker designating the site of Branch Normal School at Pine Bluff.

Clockwise from top left, Dumas Public School, 1929; arithmetic books used in public schools; Dumas Elementary School teacher Mary Ruth Henley in 1953; and a music "letter" from Dumas High School, 1962.

The John Milton Moore family of Drew County, early 1900s.

Hunting dogs were a measure of wealth among area residents for several generations. Below, a man in his Sunday best poses with some of his dogs, circa 1930s.

CHAPTER SEVEN

Home and Social Life

The old belief that times change but people remain the same is, as we say in Arkansas, a bunch of hogwash. Differences in home and social life come with each new generation.

Transformations are most evident in extreme comparisons. Thus, this article will carry its readers back to around 1900, about five generations ago. The differences between home and social life of 1900 and today are vast.

In 1900, agriculture dominated Southeast Arkansas. Men, especially those who owned large farms, were considered the movers and shakers of society, but the reality is that women silently contributed to commerce by successfully handling an array of demands.

At the time, men — whether sharecroppers or plantation owners — were seen as kings of their households, but only wealthy women with servants were able to enjoy a queen's status. Some planters were able to afford enough laborers to handle the chores of their farms, but most worked alongside their hired hands.

Women and children were expected to work in the fields and on other farm duties. Life was harsh and, too often, short. Thus, it was not uncommon for girls to marry by the time they were fourteen or fifteen. Some were only twelve or thirteen when they became wives. A single woman in her mid-twenties was generally looked upon as an "old maid."

Agriculture was such a powerful economic factor that school and social schedules were constructed around planting and harvesting periods. School schedules have changed little in the past century.

'A Woman's Work Is Never Done'

Most women of the time were the first to arise from bed in their homes each morning. Breakfast had to be made "from scratch," and that required much time and effort. Half an hour or so before roosters announced daybreak, breakfast — the most important meal of the day — was expected to be steaming hot and ready to eat.

Women figured to be too old to work in the fields helped younger mothers by babysitting children still needing care. It was simply the norm for young mothers to work in the fields along with their husbands, and children as young as five or six were often forced into picking cotton or performing other chores to help their families.

Wages were terribly low for sharecroppers, black or white.

Shortly after sunup, farm tasks got underway. But around eleven a.m. or so, the wives and some of the older, unmarried teenaged girls would trek back to their homes and prepare lunch. Work was halted for a couple or three hours around noon, so as to allow lunch and an afternoon nap to re-energize for additional work until sundown, and sometimes beyond.

Women would join in the afternoon and evening work, but break away again to cook supper.

Sometimes this routine would consume five days a week, but most often six. And at peak planting or harvest times, there was no such luxury as a day off. Somehow, along with her other chores, a wife had to find time to keep her home tidy, keep up with sewing needs for the family's clothing and help to attend to whatever other work might become necessary.

The homes of sharecroppers as well as owners of small farms were often bare of any extras. There was little electrical service and most people still depended on pumps and wells for their water. Nevertheless, the homes were customarily maintained with great attention and care.

Small "fancies" were big when money was scarce.

Women of Privilege Also Faced Extra Responsibilities

Wives and older daughters of wealthier planters weren't lacking duties beyond their standard household chores.

It was common at the time for financially-secure men to own hunting dogs, as attaining game meat to help feed families gave the men a chance for outdoor recreation and saved money on grocery bills.

A man's hunting dogs were highly valued. Wives and daughters were required to care for the dogs as if the dogs were family members.

Women of privilege — who many times operated or oversaw plantation "stores" — were also tasked with enabling their husbands to entertain guests, usually other well-to-do planters or businessmen and sometimes politicians who might be able to help enhance a family's social or financial standing.

No matter how many jobs a woman had to juggle, whether as a lady of wealth or the wife of a sharecropper, she was also expected to remain a "delicate" and "dainty" example of Southern womanhood.

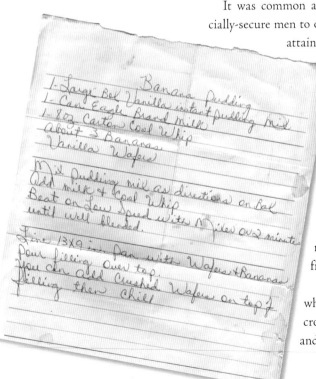

Right, an unknown woman holds up a baby.

Below, a banana pudding recipe.

Banana Pudding
1 - Large Box Vanilla instant Pudding Mix
1 - Can Eagle Brand Milk
1 - 8oz Carton Cool Whip
About 3 Bananas
Vanilla Wafers

Mix Pudding mix as directions on Box
Add Milk & Cool Whip
Beat on Low Speed with Mixer over 2 minutes
until well blended.
Line 13x9 in Pan with Wafers & Bananas
Pour filling over top.
You can add Crushed Wafers on top of
filling then Chill

Entertainment was often self-made. Especially on Saturday nights, community dances would be held with makeshift bands providing the music from the porch of a home. Partygoers would square-dance in the yard of the house.

Sometimes the festivities would stretch into the early hours of Sunday. With little other entertainment, many wanted to stretch fun as much as possible before returning to their rugged jobs and often-drab lives.

'Rain, Rain Come Today and Help to Wash the Dirt Away'

The old jokes about people sometimes bathing only on Saturdays weren't always in jest. Families had to conserve water for irrigation and cooking, and baths were often the major preparation for the Saturday night dances. Barrels were strategically placed around homes, barns and outbuildings to catch rainwater, which was employed for washing clothes as well as bathing.

Large, circular metal tubs were most often used for baths, and entire families bathed with the same water. Men and their sons washed first. Women and their daughters followed. Afterward, the water was often used to create mud for pigs.

Some farms had creeks or lakes in which clothes could be washed and baths could be conducted in the form of "skinny dipping."

Double Standards

Bathing was a vital tool in dating, which was then conducted much differently.

Courtship was a deliberate process, and public affection was a no-no. Kissing was regarded as an advanced activity among daters, and holding hands was enough to make one's heart beat faster.

But a double standard existed even then.

Above left, two women wash clothes
in tubs in front of their home.

Upper right, boxes of sewing thread.

Left, man's journal for salt,
coffee, and other items in the
early 1900s.

Right, A gathering of the Fraternity Club at the Hotel Jefferson, in Pine Bluff, 1908.

Far right, Owner O. C. Hauber stands in front of The Gem Theatre at Pine Bluff, around 1914.

Below, railroad workers and family members gather for a photo.

~FRATERNITY CLUB~
~BANQUET MCH. 12TH 1908~
~HOTEL JEFFERSON~
~PINE BLUFF~
~ARK~

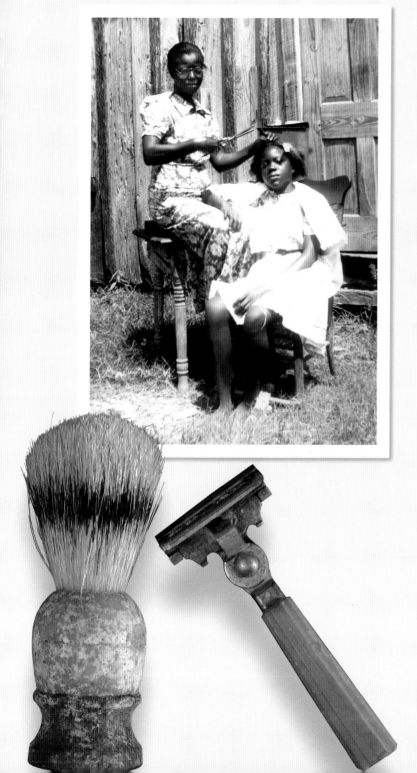

Left, women using a heated curling iron.

Below left, a soap brush and razor.

Below, A woman in her bridal gown.

AND, NOT A DROP TO DRINK

For Southeast Arkansas residents who liked to partake in the consumption of alcoholic beverages, 1917 was a bummer.

In January 1917, the Arkansas General Assembly adopted the "Bone Dry Law," which disallowed the transport, delivery or storage of liquor within the state. Talk about taking the fun out of a social gathering . . .

There were three exceptions, however — alcoholic beverages could be used for medical, religious and scientific purposes.

It's not known how many area consumers promptly declared themselves as doctors, ministers or professors, but it wasn't the first time that Arkansas lawmakers had outlawed drinking.

On several previous occasions, regulations were enacted that criminalized alcohol to some degree, but the 1917 measure was the strongest to date. There was a loophole in the measure — persons were not prohibited from bringing liquor into the state.

The U.S. Congress enacted prohibition in 1920. The federal ban was finally lifted in 1933.

But no matter how the prohibitionists tried or what evils they projected would take place should alcohol not be suppressed, they were never able to fully dispel drinking in the region.

Southeast Arkansas bootleggers devised many imaginative methods to produce "hooch" even under the close eye of the law, or "revenuers," as they were known.

Here's looking at you, kid.

THE GROWTH OF PUBLIC HEALTH AWARENESS

For many years, poor health was a major problem for home and public life not only in Southeast Arkansas, but also the remainder of the state.

Advances in personal hygiene and enhanced medical knowledge have greatly improved health. Before 1900, only the well-to-do could afford to see a physician, as insurance and social programs primarily did not exist.

In the early 1900s, most Arkansas children seldom had or wore shoes and often resided in dirt-floor homes and utilized unsanitary surroundings, such as dirt-floor outhouses. The state was still largely undeveloped with much of the land used for farming and in livestock production, and soil easily became infected with hookworms.

As a result, about half of the state's children acquired hookworms by walking barefoot in contaminated soil. An effort to eliminate the problem in Arkansas was empowered by the Rockefeller Foundation with a $1 million campaign in 1910.

Children were educated on the importance of wearing shoes and outhouses were made more sanitary. The drive proved greatly successful.

Another health issue that plagued Southeast Arkansas — malaria — was caused by mosquitoes, which have long thrived in the many wetlands of the region. Eradication projects and commercial anti-mosquito substances have helped to greatly reduce the threat of the dreaded disease.

Above, two Lincoln County midwives in the 1930s.

Right, a young, proud mother with her baby alongside a Lincoln County field.

It was largely accepted that men could not be faulted for yielding to their hormonal desires. People also thought that the more money, property or livestock a married man had, the more it should be understood — and accepted — that he might seek to relieve the stress of his "burden" in the arms of not his wife, but another woman.

Some thought it was helpful, if not necessary, for a man to be "experienced" in sexual concerns before marriage, so that he could better "lead" his wife. And the best wife candidates, meanwhile, were supposed to be "pure." The question then is the same as it always has been on such figuring — "If girls aren't to engage in such behavior, just how in the heck are boys to acquire their knowledge?"

Ah, isn't it nice to know that male chauvinism is an old and practiced art?

Just as depicted in movies and television programs, much courting of the era was conducted in the "parlor" of the girl's home, under the watchful eye of her parents and siblings.

"Stealing" a kiss was often the only opportunity for a dating couple to illustrate their mutual affection.

There were many social restrictions at the time. Interracial dating was, for all practical purposes, disallowed. Also, relationships between children of plantation owners and their sharecroppers were discouraged if not forbidden.

Racially-integrated social life was largely nonexistent, and division by monetary or "class" status was equally enforced. There were exceptions to the rules, however, as some interracial marriages did exist and — especially when more prominent planters anticipated a coming need for "natural" farmhands (children and grandchildren) — well-to-do young ladies were encouraged to wed strong and healthy sons of sharecroppers and other laborers.

Homes and Household Furnishings

A tradition of the time that isn't nearly as prominent today was "neighbor helping neighbor."

When big or small farmers, sharecroppers or farmhands became ill or suffered a calamity, their counterparts, as a whole, joined forces to bring the injured parties through their hard times. There were no welfare or subsidy programs in 1900, and people had to depend on each other in times of trouble. This compassion many times crossed racial lines.

The wealthy often hired carpentry crews to erect their grand homes, but their workers assisted one another in building their residences and outbuildings. And while the elite acquired expensive furniture from the day's leading American or foreign production firms, sharecroppers or tenant farmers shared their skills in constructing furnishings for their modest homes.

An unknown couple read the Bible on their porch.

Furnishings were sometimes somewhat primitive among the workers, but they made do with rather surprising craftsmanship. Not much material was wasted by farm workers. Even animal bones were utilized in furnishings or decor.

Eventually, farm workers were better able to acquire more and more professionally-manufactured furnishings, but they maintained their practicalities in meeting their home needs.

Not a Good Time to Be Black

Although some new opportunities were blossoming in the black community at the time, 1900 was not the best of times for most Southeast Arkansas blacks.

The wounds of the Civil War were still fresh, and blacks were held in low esteem or openly mistreated by many whites. There were few educational and cultural opportunities for blacks, and their social progress since the Civil War had been hampered.

But despite their hardships and the starkness of their lives as sharecroppers, blacks persevered and became stronger as proud partners in the region's progression.

Left, J. H. Hellums' cousin, Jim Sanders, became a partner at Hellums' Star City store.

Below, J. H. Hellums (left) oversees the Hellums Store in Grady in this 1904 photograph.

Top, Julius Hopwood Hellums, son of J. W. Hellums and Susie Carlton Hellums. Above, Lila Pearl Chapman married J. H. Hellums on January 5, 1898, in Georgia.

Docia Allen (second from left) and her family, relatives of the J. H. Hellums family, pose in an automobile in a photograph believed to have been taken in Pine Bluff, circa 1910.

ONE OF SOUTHEAST ARKANSAS' FIRST FAMILIES

The J.W. Hellums family has an interesting regional history that dates back to the Civil War era in the Grady, Monticello, Pine Bluff and Star City areas.

Hellums was born in Alabama in September 1836. His family moved in 1844 to Mississippi, where his father died a year later. His siblings and mother then relocated to Drew County, where she died in 1867. J.W. Hellums had joined the family there in 1858.

One of his brothers, Jacob P. Hellums, wound up in Star City.

In 1859, J.W. Hellums relocated to Pine Bluff and established a business. After service in the Civil War, during which he was taken prisoner but escaped, he migrated first to Drew County and then to Pine Bluff, where he closed his business before returning to Drew County.

He married Susie Carlton in 1864 and the couple had six children — Julius H., Clyde E., Cora, Jennie, Chester and Guy.

The family moved to Pine Bluff in 1889. Meanwhile, Hellums operated stores in Star City and Grady and also cultivated cotton on a farm that included over 1,000 acres.

Many of Hellums' decendants and relatives still reside in Southeast Arkansas.

The original Saenger Theatre burns November 11, 1922.

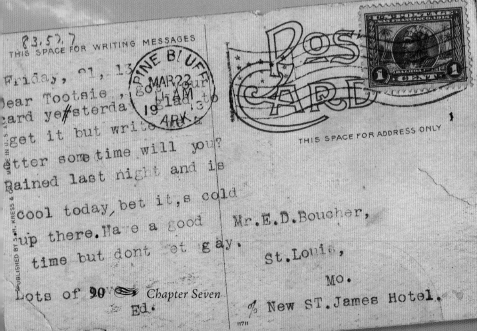

An unidentified Jefferson County couple, circa 1890.

A Lincoln County woman uses an umbrella to shield herself from the hot sun.

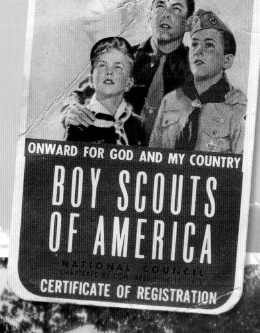

Left, young playmates share a wagon ride at Dumas.

Right, a Boy Scout membership card from 1953.

Below, a leather wallet from the late 1800s.

ONWARD FOR GOD AND MY COUNTRY

BOY SCOUTS OF AMERICA

NATIONAL COUNCIL
CHARTERED BY CONGRESS JUNE 15, 1916

CERTIFICATE OF REGISTRATION

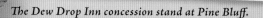

The Dew Drop Inn concession stand at Pine Bluff.

MT. PLEASANT
METHODIST CHURCH
KNOWN AS
"THE CAMP GROUND"
ORGANIZED — 1843
BY
REV. J. MILTON CARR
FIRST CHURCH IN DREW COUNTY
AND ONE OF THE OLDEST METHODIST
CHURCHES IN ARKANSAS
ERECTED 1962
BY
DREW COUNTY HISTORICAL SOCIETY,
MEMBERS AND FRIENDS OF CAMP GROUND

The First Methodist Church, Monticello, Ark.

Chapter Eight

Religious Life and Eternal Rest

Religion has been a staple of life within Southeast Arkansas since before the white man ever arrived.

Indians in the area believed in greater, controlling spirits. Some looked for guidance through animal sightings or signs in the sky, such as a shooting star.

Christian missions to the Indians probably started soon after the first whites arrived in the area.

Christians of different faiths worshiped together long before churches were constructed and newer denominations were formulated. Many organizations, such as the Order of the Eastern Star and Free and Accepted Masonry, are grounded in religious principles that date back hundreds of years.

Much of the history of organized churches in Southeast Arkansas traces back to Arkansas and Jefferson counties, simply because those counties represent the areas that were most heavily populated during the formative years of the region.

Many religious traditions were brought into the region by settlers who were still greatly influenced by the beliefs and customs of their ancestors from other countries.

Catholics, Methodists Were Earliest Groups

The majority of the earliest residents of Arkansas and Jefferson counties were Roman Catholics, who built the first churches in the area.

Methodists built the first church in Pine Bluff around 1840. The Reverend John A. Henry was the pastor. The church was the forerunner of today's First Methodist Church.

St. Mary's and St. Peter's were the first Catholic churches constructed in Jefferson County. St. Mary's congregation began meeting in 1834, and the church began a school in 1838.

Presbyterians organized in the region during the early and mid-1850s, about the same time as when Baptists, who had been active in the region since the 1820s, began to expand their building plans.

The Arkansas Baptist State Convention was created at Tulip in 1848.

The oldest Pine Bluff church building still in use today is Trinity Episcopal, which dates back to 1859. Construction was discontinued during the Civil War but resumed afterward. It's believed that the first service in the new sanctuary was held on Christmas Day 1870.

The church has been remodeled numerous times, but the original sanctuary is intact and in use.

Small churches were erected throughout the region as transportation of any measurable distance was sometimes difficult, and it could be miles between populated settlements.

The City of White Hall traces its birth to a settlement around a church, and the Watson Chapel community has roots related to organized religion.

Mt. Zion Presbyterian Church located between Star City and Monticello on U.S. Highway 425.

Left, a postcard shows the former First Baptist Church in Pine Bluff.

Slavery Issue Caused Church Splits

Even before the Civil War began, the question of slavery had created disagreement and disruption in many churches.

While many believed that "ownership" of slaves was a religious right and blessing, others fought against slavery and those who promoted and/or condoned it.

But even those who had slaves agreed that their servants should be introduced to Christianity. Many planters constructed church buildings for slaves, and a number of black congregations in the region can track their origins to such arrangements.

But surprisingly, there have been integrated churches in the region since long before the Civil War. The practice wasn't conducted at every church, but a number of slave holders allowed their servants to accompany them to and actually participate in church services.

Not surprising, however, is the fact that while blacks were allowed to attend religious services with whites prior to emancipation, segregation was usually practiced when seating arrangements were determined.

Following emancipation, blacks began to organize their own churches, even though integrated but predominantly-white churches were still common.

But whites sometimes attended churches that had mostly-black congregations. Such was the case in one Pine Bluff church, which was pastored by a black minister.

Organizations Supported Christians in Life and Death

Masons established a grand lodge in Arkansas in 1838 and grew rapidly in numbers and lodges.

The organization was viewed as an extension of organized religion, and it was not only fashionable for most men to be members of the organization, but membership was practically required in many circles.

Above, the First Baptist Church of Dumas, established in 1903.

Masonry gave Christianity a social status in interests outside the church, and it also gave much-welcomed opportunities for community events.

As entertainment was rare, Masonic parades were held for nearly any good cause, including funerals.

Although there were a number of black Masons, integrated lodges were rare. However, no one seemed to mind when black and white Masons celebrated together.

The more the merrier.

Masonic rites were established for funeral services, but those activities were almost always segregated.

For well over a century, Masons provided leadership for a wide array of public celebrations and festivals.

Temperance was always a popular topic at Masonic programs. Masonic groups saw themselves as moral guides for the areas in which they resided and worked.

Cemeteries Didn't Always Exist

In the early years of Southeast Arkansas, many areas did not have an established cemetery.

Typically, families buried their dead on family-owned property or in unincorporated, common locales. Cemeteries were started first within cities or areas with larger populations, but cemetery burials were typically held only for persons who didn't have any relatives in the area.

The first common cemeteries in the region were created around 1800. Church cemeteries would follow.

Eventually, authorities realized that economic development could be disrupted by burials outside of restricted areas. This and health concerns prompted laws against burial outside of designated areas.

Thus arrived the need for an "undertaking" profession.

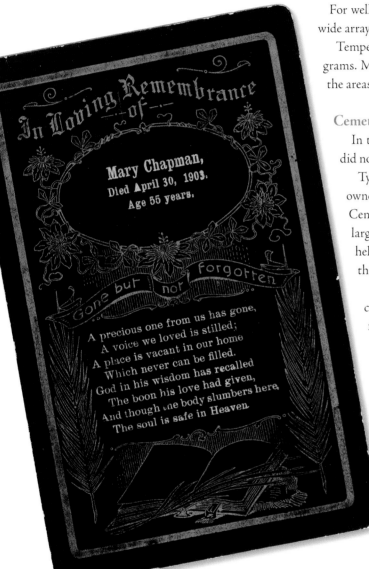

Above, a funeral remembrance card.

Bethlehem Baptist Church in Palmyra was organized on July 18, 1861. M.Y. Moran donated property for the building as well as a cemetery. The church pictured was constructed in the late 1880s or early 1890s. It was a replacement for the original structure, which was built with logs.

Left, First Baptist Church at Star City was organized in November 1873. The building pictured was constructed in 1926 and located in the second block south of the Lincoln County Courthouse.

Above, a postcard depicting St. John's Lutheran Church in Stuttgart.

Left this postcard shows the former Jewish Temple in Pine Bluff.

BATTLE OF PINE BLUFF

JEFFERSON COUNTY HISTORY COMMISSION 1976

During the morning and early afternoon of October 25, 1863, Colonel Powell Clayton commander of federal troops occupying Pine Bluff, successfully repulsed a three-pronged confederate attack of forces of General John S. Marmaduke. Cotton bales hastily placed around the courthouse and surrounding streets provided an effective barricade for union defenders. Confederate loss: 41 killed, wounded, and captured.

March 19. – 1863.

Three years ago today – I looked upon the last of my home treasures –, treasures, whose worth my own heart knows as priceless, and whose value has no estimate. I see that scene of parting yet, for memory faithful reminder of the Past, brings often to my troubled mind, the word, the look, the tone of parting, and I never can forget.

My Spirit-Sense, still feels my mother's dear embrace, my sisters' arms about my neck; still hears my brothers' wishes kind and true, and sees the children of my love & care, with all the kisses, tears & prayers, the parting tribute of affection given. Ah yes! I know it's true that I am separate from the friends of home and early days – and though I wander years, in every clime the whole world o'er – though I might tread on flowers – perennial 'neath my pathway – breathe the air of balmiest breath – where summer always reigns – I'd seek in vain to find the Spot that has the charm of home – for me. In strange captivity my heart is bound to her – and within its sanctuary lies treasured – Life's fondest memories of that dear place – whose hills are rugged & rockbound – & where the wintry winds blow cold & drear.

'Mid the voices of the many I have seen & known – I hear no voice with cadence sweet, like those which used to echo round my home –

The faces of the crowd tho' e'er so fair
Hath never charm for me –
Beside the one whose likenesses I keep
Pictured in memory.

And will this separation last without a hope of meeting? my Spirit trembles & my courage fails me, while I list for a reply. A ray of hope may linger, but no expectation cheers me, with the thought of a reunion with each parted one – till the grave shall cover the last of our number – and we meet each other again – with those who have gone before – in that Heavenly land, where – conflict & toil, sickness & death, separation & farewells – never come –

I pray God to prepare us all for a fairer, happier life than this, where strife cannot enter & where all is love.

H. B.

CHAPTER NINE

War and Peace

Much has been written on the Civil War and its impact on Southeast Arkansas, but it might be hard to argue against reasoning that World War II is the conflict that produced the most social changes in this area and all of America.

In July 1948 — just three years after World War II ended — President Harry S Truman ordered the complete integration of the nation's military. This monumental decision resulted from the war performances of blacks and other minorities as they fought side-by-side with white Americans. By the early 1950s, for the first time ever, many whites in the military found themselves under command of minority officers.

Women's "roles" were forever changed by World War II, and fears created by the war resulted in a shameful episode in which many Japanese-Americans were stripped of their homes and businesses and removed to scattered "relocation" camps, including fenced facilities in Jerome and Rohwer.

Before the Storm: Quiet Acceptance Among Women and Blacks

In the 1930s, most women in the area worked in agricultural or domestic endeavors. Their wages were lower than men's, even if the women workers were single and had to survive solely on their own salaries.

The plight was even worse for black women, who typically earned only 60–65 percent of what their white counterparts received.

Men typically received salaries that were up to 25 percent greater than women's. And to add insult to injury for women, American society had not progressed past a point at which women were considered as "secondary" citizens.

Some women were solely housewives and homemakers whose husbands' earnings were sufficient to house, feed and clothe a family. But the thinking of the era dictated that even if a woman worked outside her home, she was still responsible for housework and primary child care.

And she was to somehow maintain a soft, feminine grace throughout, from preserving a ladylike appearance and demeanor to wearing "proper" dresses. Women who wore pants were thought to be either "loose" or lesbians.

The war, however, would erase not only this "norm," but also serve to create new opportunities for blacks and bring about developments in integration that before appeared unlikely.

Nothing eases racial disharmony more than a common threat to liberties.

Hitler Stirs Support, Japan Brings Response

In the summer of 1941, America was boosting its military capabilities with a watchful eye on Germany's Adolph Hitler and his crusading Nazi forces. A measure of apprehension existed, but Americans felt strongly secure and possessed an

A Lucky Shot?

What many researchers figure was the most disastrous single shot of the Civil War occurred on Tuesday, June 17, 1862, when Confederate forces destroyed the Union ironclad gunboat *Mound City* on the White River at St. Charles.

Mound City, followed by the ironclad *St. Louis* and several smaller boats, was dispatched up the river for two purposes — to clear a new route for supplies to be delivered to Union troops in Batesville, and to uncover Confederate gunboats that managed to escape the Battle of Memphis.

Confederate Capt. and Lt. J. W. Dunnington merged their forces at St. Charles to ready for the Union advancement. It was soon determined by Rebel scouts that the Union had many more troops and gunboats than the Confederates.

Fry decided on June 16 to sink his gunboat and two transport steamboats and to station the guns along the riverbanks.

During the early morning of the following day, the Union fleet was seen approaching. A battle ensued, but neither side gained control until *Mound City* was positioned between a pair of Fry's guns.

Either a 32- or 42-pound (sources differ on the weight) shell from a Rebel cannon penetrated the casement of *Mound City*, smashing the ironclad's steam drum and generating an eruption of scalding water and steam. A number of Yankee soldiers died in the explosion. Others jumped into the river in a futile effort to escape injury — Confederate sharpshooters along the banks had been ordered to shoot those who departed the ironclad.

Despite their successful assault, Fry realized his Rebel troops were too thin to keep St. Charles under a Confederate flag, so he ordered a retreat.

The Union claimed a victory, but numbers might have indicated differently.

While only six Rebels perished and one sustained an injury, the Yankees counted over 200 dead.

Above, the ironclad Union gunboat Mound City.

Page background, the bombardment of Fort Hindman, Arkansas Post, January 11, 1863.

almost cocky confidence that the nation was largely isolated from the developing war.

Jefferson County Judge James P. McGaughy was advised by U.S. Congressman David D. Terry that President Franklin D. Roosevelt desired to place a military arsenal in Pulaski County, but a location satisfying Army requirements did not exist there.

Thus, McGaughy was invited to initiate efforts to bring the installation to Jefferson County. Meanwhile, officials in neighboring Lonoke County began a drive to bring the base to England, then the bustling center of an energetic farming region.

Lonoke County had some strong ties to Roosevelt, as it had been the home of powerful U.S. Senator Joseph T. Robinson, the Democratic Party's vice presidential nominee in 1928 and one of Roosevelt's most trusted advisors. But Robinson had died in 1937.

A few other communities forged campaigns to acquire the arsenal, but Pine Bluff and England wound up as the chief competitors. Various factors were weighed between the two, and the decision to locate the facility in Jefferson County may well have been finalized on immediate population numbers.

Jefferson County had a much larger potential workforce in closer proximity. The county's 1940 population was 65,101, including 21,290 in Pine Bluff alone. Lonoke County's population was 29,802, with only 5,000-6,000 living in the England area.

Some business and farm leaders in Jefferson County opposed the arsenal, fearing it would destroy the local economy by forcing salary increases that might push some concerns into bankruptcy. The Army ignored the fearful resentment.

On November 3, 1941, the Army allocated $10 million for the construction of Chemical Warfare Arsenal in an unincorporated area north of Pine Bluff (White Hall wasn't incorporated until over 20 years later). The installation was charged with manufacturing and assembling incendiary munitions for Great Britain.

The federal government purchased more than 200 parcels of land totaling about 15,000 acres at a cost of $250,000 — less than $17 an acre — and conducted a groundbreaking ceremony on December 2.

Five days later, Japan bombed the U.S. Navy's Pearl Harbor, Hawaii, base. Thus, America found itself at war and the Army commenced an accelerated construction schedule on its newest arsenal.

War Gives Birth to Unanticipated Boon and Changes

The influx of construction workers — estimated by one source at 16,000 — brought unexpected alterations to the Pine Bluff area.

Many of the city's graceful, old homes were dissected into apartments. One construction worker reportedly established residency in a rented chicken house just outside the arsenal grounds. There simply wasn't enough rental property to support the incoming laborers, so many lived up to 75 miles away and commuted to the arsenal daily.

Men of Arkansas at the Battle of Shiloh, April 6, 1862.

tar white phosphorus shells, smoke shells, hand grenades containing phosphorus or smoke, 100-pound white phosphorus bombs, mustard gas, lewisite gas, both liquid and gaseous chlorine, napalm, nerve gas and harassment gas.

At the peak of its World War II production in 1944, PBA counted about 9,000 civilian employees and 450 military personnel.

As Men March to War, Women Encounter New Challenges

The war didn't imprison women to an active support role. Rather, it liberated them from their long-standing economic and social restraints.

With many of their husbands, brothers and fathers in active military service, women showed they were quite capable of maintaining homes and families on their own during a time in which they were limited by decreased income as well as food and gasoline rationing.

They operated family businesses and farms or worked as sharecroppers. The lack of men pulled many into jobs that had once been almost forbidden among females, including jobs in assorted defense plants that were opening throughout the country and within the military itself.

As war demands increased, many blacks secured higher-paying jobs at PBA, which boasted one of the most integrated workforces of any American military installation.

Unfortunately, not all was positive.

Juvenile delinquency increased as mothers who found themselves alone departed their homemaking roles for jobs that often left their children without adult supervision.

In the private sector, decreased jobs and lowered salaries resulted in an increase in prostitution and other crimes among women. The state reported a jump in recorded cases of venereal diseases as ministers and school leaders bemoaned a moral decay.

Meanwhile, as soldiers returned home, most expected their wives to simply resign from defense jobs and return to their former lifestyles. Many women did just that, but others were not so willing to yield the

The facility's name was changed to Pine Bluff Arsenal (PBA) on March 5, 1942, and by the end of the month, it was headquartered on-site.

The hastened schedule and heightened mission caused installation costs to swell to $60 million from the original $10 million. The construction workers' spirited patriotism is still visible with the "V for Victory" signs that masons diligently mastered on walls of ceramic-tiled warehouses.

Production was started amid construction and in July 1942, PBA produced its first items — four-pound incendiary bombs for Great Britain.

Those bombs were later packaged into "papa bombs," which contained 110 of the small units. Production expanded to include 4.2 mor-

Pine Bluff High School graduates in WWII, Germany 1945.

Handwritten on photo: Pine Bluff Hi School Graduates + Long-time friends met up; Munich, Germany - Summer - 1945; Gentlemen; Elton Taylor; Jimmy Kalkbrenner; Jimmy Thompson

HEROES AMONG US

Injuries and deaths are inevitable at the battlefronts of any war, but can also tragically occur at support locations such as the Pine Bluff Arsenal (PBA).

While safety, as it is today, was stressed at PBA during World War II, hastened production activities at the time naturally increased the possibility of accidents.

As heroes emerged on the battlefronts, bravery and sacrifice were also evident at home. Sadly, 15 PBA workers gave their lives in service to their country while employed at PBA during the war.

Thirteen deaths came in 1943 alone.

Charles C. Lamphere perished in a February 9 scalding incident. A short time later, Geraldine Kinser was killed in another mishap.

Three fatalities were marked in October. Four days after sustaining severe burns in a fiery blast within an incendiary bomb production area, Ora Ella King succumbed. On October 23, Harvie Atwood died in yet another fire. And just five days later, yet another incident resulted in the death of Raymond Launius.

Two November explosions were especially harsh, as each claimed four lives.

Frieda Lyons, Doyne Howard Moore, Seigel Ramick Sutterfield and Susie Whiteside were fatally injured in a November 16 accident. A November 24 detonation resulted in the deaths of Winfield N. Anderson, Lloyd V. Ellison, Fred Lewis and Claudia B. Yancey.

The remaining two deaths occurred in 1944.

Neil Lewis died in an August 26 automobile accident on a parking lot where he was working with a carpentry crew. Later that year, William L. Wilson was killed when a large fan fell on him.

There were no shortage of heroes and heroines at PBA during the war, but one stood out.

Annie Young, a young wife and mother who joined PBA's workforce, became the first woman to receive the federal Exceptional Civilian Service Award — the highest citation for War Department-employed civilians. The honor was said to be the "civilian equivalent of the military Distinguished Service Award."

Young's valor was displayed not once, but twice.

On October 13, 1943, Young attempted to save King's life following a production area explosion. King's clothing was ablaze and Young tried to smother the flames with a security blanket. When that failed, Young disregarded her own safety by grabbing King and using her bare hands to rip off King's burning garments.

Young sustained second-degree burns on her hands and wrists, but returned to work the following day after receiving treatment at the PBA hospital.

Just over a month later, in the previously-addressed November 16 incident, Young witnessed Lyons — a former neighbor who had been a friend since the women's childhoods — running away from the scene, in shock as her clothing was on fire.

Young chased and caught Lyons and tried to roll her into a water-filled drainage ditch to douse the flames. Unable to achieve this initial rescue effort, Young again used her bare hands in yanking off Lyons' searing clothes. Once more, Young suffered second-degree burns to her hands and wrists. But on this occasion, Young returned to work the same day after being treated at the post hospital.

Young's action made news nationally. In late March 1944, Young and her husband were saluted at a PBA luncheon.

In a rare display of admiration and appreciation, PBA halted its production so that all arsenal workers could attend a ceremony in which Young was presented her award. Governor Homer Adkins took part in the ceremonies, along with Army officials. The 100-member Pine Bluff High School Band provided music at the event.

Emotions ran high when area Arkansas National Guardsmen activated from Pine Bluff returned home in 1991 after helping to liberate Kuwait from Iraq in Operations Desert Shield and Desert Storm. Happy but tearful reunions marked the occasion as helium-filled red, white and blue balloons filled the air.

WELCOME HOME 299th

STOCK NO. 2
DRESSING, FIRST AID
CAMOUFLAGED, SMALL
DYED STERILIZED DRESSING
Red color indicates back of dressing
Put other side next to wound
Calvine Cotton Mills, West New York, N

Two Army retirees — 1st Lt. Lloyd L. Burke of Tichnor and Col. James Lamar Stone of Pine Bluff — share a unique and proud distinction.

They are Southeast Arkansas' lone Medal of Honor recipients. Both were saluted for heroism during the Korean War.

A trio of antique planes from the Razorback Wing of the Confederate Air Force deliver an airborne tribute to area veterans of Operations Desert Shield and Desert Storm in a 1991 downtown Pine Bluff parade.

Left, World War II era first aid field dressing.

independence, authority and enjoyment they had found in their new activities.

Divorce rates swelled. Many women who remained with their husbands established new understandings with their mates, making it clear that a number of former traditions and expectations would be left in the past.

Area Is 'Home' to POWs and Relocated Japanese-Americans

From 1942-45, over 16,000 Japanese-Americans resided in relocation camps in Jerome and Rohwer.

Rounded up after Japan's attack on Pearl Harbor, approximately 110,000 "evacuees" from California, Oregon, Washington and numerous American military bases were removed to 10 camps, including the two Southeast Arkansas facilities.

Jerome "closed" in 1944 and its Japanese-American residents were transferred to Rohwer or other locations.

Meanwhile, the old Jerome camp became one of the nation's largest war prisons. Renamed Camp Dermott, the facility would house about 7,000 German prisoners.

Only about 160 of the Japanese-Americans remained in Arkansas after the war, and the number of former internees in the state has steadily declined.

Some of the German prisoners were actually put on "work release" prior to the war's conclusion. Farm laborers were in short supply in Southeast Arkansas, and many Germans joined with Italian prisoners from Camp Monticello in helping cotton growers.

Other prisoners assisted in constructing schools, hospitals and roads. Escape efforts were rare and never successful.

In 1988, President Ronald Reagan signed into law a measure that not only apologized to the Japanese-Americans who were placed in the relocation centers, but also granted a $20,000 cash payment to each of the then-60,000 survivors.

World War II Medal of Honor winner Maurice "Footsie" Britt, a former lieutenant governor, publicly discussed his war experiences for the first time at a Rotary Club meeting in Pine Bluff shortly before his 1995 death.

Left, Liaison Committee Medal.

CHEMICAL CLEAN-UP

A project to help make the world safer and, hopefully, more peaceful is underway at the Pine Bluff Arsenal (PBA).

The Pine Bluff Chemical Agent Disposal Facility (PBCDF) is scheduled to complete its mission of safely destroying over 12 percent of the nation's original stockpile of chemical munitions by around 2012.

When demilitarization in the multi-billion dollar project commenced on March 29, 2005, PBA housed the country's largest inventory of M55 rockets. Also in the PBA stockpile are land mines and ton containers.

The PBCDF site covers 26 acres. Construction began on January 15, 1999. The facility's closure — a process in which the incineration plant will consume itself — will culminate the project.

The project has created a number of new jobs, as dramatic growth in the population of White Hall, which borders PBA, reflects.

A worldwide treaty generated the demilitarization effort. PBCDF is one of eight demilitarization sites in the U.S.

The local project is overseen by a variety of local, state and federal agencies, including the Arkansas Department of Environmental Quality, Arkansas Department of Health, Arkansas Department of Emergency Management and the Federal Environmental Protection Agency.

A worker at the Pine Bluff Arsenal inspects a wall of gauges that are part of the incineration plant where the PBA stockpile is being eliminated. Disposal is scheduled for completion by 2012.

CHAPTER TEN

The Good, the Bad, and the Convicted

There is no greater sacrifice than that of one who gives up his or her life in service and protection of others.

In Southeast Arkansas, 17 law enforcement officers have given their lives while performing their duties.

The Arkansas Department of Correction (ADC) has lost three officers — Sgt. Scott A. Grimes, Lt. Ronald Opie McPherson and Correctional Officer Jackie Wayne Pierce.

An inmate serving a life sentence at the Tucker Maximum Security Unit in Jefferson County stabbed Grimes to death on November 29, 1995. The stabbing occurred after the inmate had escaped from his cell. ADC's Grimes Unit in Newport is named in the officer's honor.

McPherson died as a result of accidental gunfire during a May 2, 1979, training exercise at Cummins Prison in Lincoln County. ADC also named a Newport unit in his honor.

Pierce died in a December 31, 1997, automobile accident in Pine Bluff, moments after securing materials from the agency's central office to be delivered to a work release center elsewhere. The Pierce Administration Building at the Mississippi County Work Release Center in Luxora was named as a tribute to him.

Two Arkansas State Police members — Troopers Charles Michael Bassing and Herbert James Smith — have died in the line of duty.

Bassing perished in a July 24, 1986, helicopter crash. The Federal Drug Enforcement Administration was training Bassing, Jefferson County Sheriff's Office Criminal Investigator Kevin Brosch and Pulaski County Sheriff's Office Detective James Addison Avant as spotters in a marijuana eradication program.

The three had just refueled their helicopter when, after ascending only a short distance, the craft experienced a mechanical failure and crashed. It burst into flames, and the officers died in the fire.

Smith, who worked the Jefferson County area, died as a result of a February 4, 2001, automobile accident on Arkansas Highway 365 near Wrightsville in Pulaski County. Rushing to the scene of a medical emergency involving an infant, Smith lost control of his vehicle at 80 miles an hour.

The automobile overturned. Smith was severely injured, remaining in a coma until his death on February 14.

DeWitt Police Chief Robert Burbanks was shot and killed while responding to a disturbance call on September 2, 1954. He never saw his assailant, who shot Burbanks through a door as the officer knocked.

Two Grant County constables — Johnny Bratton and H. Lem Smith — were killed in an 1884 shootout with Mann Sneed of Grant County, who was on the run to avoid arrest in a beating and shooting death of another Grant County man. The constables took Sneed into custody, but Sneed broke free, produced a gun and shot both of his pursuers.

The Jefferson County Sheriff's Office has lost, in addition to Brosch, two other deputies — Lustachia Browder and Fortune Crowder.

Browder died on September 15, 1957, when he was stabbed and then shot twice in the chest with his own service revolver by a man who Browder was attempting to arrest after the man had evaded officers in a nightclub raid the previous night. Browder, 67, had had 30 years of experience as a lawman.

The entire Pine Bluff Police Department — along with a few guests and city officials — posed for this 1929 photograph in front of police headquarters at the time. Pictured are (front row, from left) Pete Lyon, T. Branson, T. Lyle, Chief Fiveash, Mayor H.I. Holderness, Assistant Chief Howell, Sid King, C.C. Culpepper, Cleve Huffstutler; (second row, from left) Bob Lea, Chris Dean, T. Gray, Pat Henry, unknown; (third row, from left) Walter "Duck" Mayberry, Ben Sandman, Dunlap, John Good, F. Mulligan and Bob Unsel. The scant identities were marked on the back of the photo.

The Pine Bluff Police Department has lost four officers — Patrolmen John R. Fallis and Claud Holt Pickett and Detectives C. C. Lynn and Homer C. Nuckolls.

Fallis was shot and killed on March 4, 1985, while investigating a noise complaint. He confronted two men who were occupying an automobile while playing loud music on the car's radio. As he attempted to radio in license plate information, one of the vehicle's occupants — who investigators would later discover was being sought in an out-of-state murder — exited and opened fire with a handgun.

Fallis was struck in an arm and the chest.

In a startling example of vigilante justice, Lynn's killer was shot down by local citizens on February 5, 1920.

Lynn was attempting to arrest a suspect in a prior shooting when the man shot and killed Lynn. The shooter tried to conceal himself within a group of residences, but angry citizens started a fire that burned three of the homes before the criminal ventured out and was promptly downed by an outburst of shots fired by the self-appointed posse.

Nuckolls was shot and killed on Christmas Day, 1926, while responding to a call at a residence at West 14th Avenue and Hazel Street. Another officer returned the fire, killing the assailant.

Pickett — on his first day as a Pine Bluff officer — died when he was shot on April 28, 1901, while on night patrol in the downtown area. He was shot in the face as he approached two suspicious men outside a business.

Two members of the Sheridan Police Department — Sgt. Otis Vernon Love Jr. and Patrolman Bobby Ray Watson — were killed on February 8, 1998, when a car being driven in the wrong lane by a legally-blind, intoxicated man collided with the officers' patrol car.

Love and Watson died instantly. The driver of the other vehicle was critically injured but survived.

PINE BLUFF CITY OFFICIALS

MET L. GALLIGHER
Chief of Police

GEORGE H. STEED
Mayor

GEORGE W. SMITH
Assistant Chief of Police

EDGAR POWELL
Patrolman

MELVIN JORDON
Motorcycle Patrolman

FRANCISE SHEPARD
Patrolman

D. B. CHESHIS
Patrolman

Pages from a directory of Pine Bluff city government and police personnel.

PINE BLUFF POLICE DEPARTMENT

ERNEST ALLRED
Patrolman

C. H. BOWDEN
Patrolman

J. D. BAIRD
Patrolman

J. O. SCHRATZ
Patrolman

JOHN E. TALBERT
City Detective

LEROY SMITH
Patrolman, Motorcycle

PINE BLUFF POLICE DEPARTMENT

J. L. WILSON
Patrolman

NORMAN YOUNG
Motorcycle Patrolman

FLOYD BURKHART
Patrolman

E. F. OLIGER
Patrolman

When the Civil War ended, individual thugs and bands of outlaws roamed Southeast Arkansas, looting and sometimes killing for whatever they desired.

Around Jefferson County, Captain Jonas Webb commanded a gang that terrorized freedmen and Union sympathizers. Captain William Dawes of the Freedman's Bureau was determined to put a stop to the activities of Webb and his ruffians.

At the time, Webb was described as about 32, sporting a mustache and billy-goat beard and having spots under his eyes. Having been in the area for several years, many knew him on sight.

Justice finally caught up with Webb, beginning on January 11, 1867, when he entered Pine Bluff, having already been drinking cheap whiskey. He was looking for trouble and found it.

Threatening to assault or shoot several persons, Webb finally fired a pistol ball into a lung of John Black, who survived. Webb was arrested and jailed on a charge of assault and battery.

An investigation into Webb's activities ensued. Soon, it became apparent that Webb had a passion for torturing and slaying blacks.

One black man had been shot twice — once by Webb and then, after he fell, by a Lt. Carr, one of Webb's followers. In another episode, Webb and his marauders raided the home of W.D. Whitmore in a black settlement at Simpson Creek, which was about 16 miles west of Pine Bluff. Whitmore was dragged from his home, shot to death and left for burial by his daughter.

On the same raid, S. Morris, a son of Thomas Morris, was slain.

The next day, Carr and Jake Anderson killed a black soldier who had been wounded at the Battle of Jenkins Ferry.

Webb and his charges also hanged a trio of blacks in the Saline River bottoms and were suspected of at least one murder in Dallas County.

Webb's band was standing by during his incarceration, prepared to take advantage of any situation that might result in Webb's escape.

Ku Klux Klan demonstrates circa 1922 at the Union Station in Pine Bluff.

A Deterrent?

Between 1880 and 1964, death sentences — by hanging or electrocution — were carried out by the state against 40 Southeast Arkansas men convicted of murder, robbery/murder or rape.

The criminals (by county in which they were sentenced), their offenses, dates of execution and means of execution are:

- ARKANSAS COUNTY — Ben Evers, murder, January 24, 1930, electric chair; Jordan Phillips, murder, May 22, 1896, hanging; James Yates, murder, May 25, 1945, electric chair.

- BRADLEY COUNTY — William Binns, murder, July 11, 1880, hanging; Howard Edmunds, murder, December 9, 1881, hanging; Abe Frazier, murder, November 28, 1884, hanging.

- DALLAS COUNTY — Wilson Wright, murder, August 1, 1952, electric chair.

- DESHA COUNTY — Stoney Allison, rape, November 11, 1942, electric chair; James Dillard, murder, December 13, 1940, electric chair; Lawrence Dunlap, robbery/murder, February 28, 1892, hanging; David Jobe, murder, February 28, 1892, hanging; Aaron Johnson, murder, June 22, 1917, electric chair; Anthony Johnson, murder, June 21, 1895, hanging; James Kitt, murder, July 25, 1902, hanging; Walter Owens, murder, March 19, 1915, electric chair; John Riney, rape, January 20, 1941, electric chair; Clay Simms, murder, March 19, 1915, hanging; Jim Williams, murder, September 9, 1903, hanging.

- DREW COUNTY — William Johnson, murder, January 12, 1883, hanging; Farlander McCormick, robbery/murder, December 11, 1936, electric chair; Willie Smith, robbery/murder, December 11, 1936, electric chair; Beverly White, robbery/murder, December 11, 1936, electric chair.

- JEFFERSON COUNTY — Henry Black, murder, June 28, 1892, hanging; Whit Brown, robbery/murder, February 24, 1882, hanging; Jack Buster, murder, January 26, 1925, electric chair; Robert Cox, rape, February 25, 1897, hanging; Jim Davis, murder, February 25, 1897, hanging; Charles Fields, rape, January 24, 1964, electric chair; Clifton Holmes, rape, January 10, 1947, electric chair; William Nail, murder, September 16, 1960, electric chair; W.T. Nichol, murder, June 7, 1912, hanging; Harvie Rorie, murder, July 22, 1949, electric chair; Andrew Thomas, murder, November 29, 1946, electric chair; Frank Williams, murder, August 1, 1884, hanging; Robert Williams, murder, July 15, 1894, hanging; Sylvester Williams, murder, January 30, 1939, electric chair.

- LINCOLN COUNTY — James Green, murder, March 20, 1903, hanging; Williams Ownes, murder, 1895, hanging; Fred Pelton, murder, March 28, 1914, electric chair; James Ruffin, murder, March 20, 1903, hanging.

The death penalty was declared unconstitutional in 1964, but that decision was reversed in 1976. Since then, only one Southeast Arkansas criminal has been executed. Clay King Smith, a murderer sentenced in Jefferson County, was administered a lethal injection on May 8, 2001. Smith had been convicted for the murder of five individuals.

Pine Bluff, and Southeast Arkansas, was still segregated when the photograph of a Ku Klux Klan march along West Fourth Avenue was taken in the early 1920s. Immediately after the Civil War, crimes against blacks and Union sympathizers weren't uncommon, but most whites opposed and worked against the shameful and divisive misdeeds, as the election of several blacks to political positions among a majority-white electorate here in the late 1860s and onward illustrate. Most of the post-war criminals involved also committed offenses against people of other races as well. Nevertheless, outward animosity over the failed Confederate cause in the Civil War lingered for the better part of a century, straining truly progressive race relations.

Carr and his cohorts intimidated potential witnesses against Webb. Prosecutors were unable to mount an effective case.

Meanwhile, Dawes — Webb's sworn enemy — was dispatched to New York to ensure his safety. William Hale, superintendent of the Freedman's Bureau in Arkansas County, assumed Dawes' responsibilities.

When Dawes returned, the first person he met in Pine Bluff was Webb, who had been convicted only on the assault charge and released after a $1,000 fine.

But the scrape with Dawes and his brush with a possible death sentence apparently gave Webb all the trouble he wanted. Webb faded from the public's eye and never caused any more commotion in the region.

In another crime of the era, a band of deserters kidnapped regional entrepreneur Creed Taylor. The thugs burned and cut him in an effort to learn the location of his vast amount of money.

In February, 1865, Will McCord — one of the larger landowners in Pine Bluff — disappeared after last being seen riding a mule from a nearby residence. About nine months later, a skeleton was found in a ravine on another Pine Bluff plantation. A skeleton of a mule was discovered in the vicinity.

McCord's remains were identified by clothing and boots. His skull had been pierced by a pair of bullets. A gang led by Antoine Descosa, of whom nothing more is known, was blamed for the killing.

The Rhodes-Sneed Feud: Father and Son, and Lawmen Killed

In 1867, wealthy planter Dr. Richard Rhodes was confronted by a gang of men and boys at his Grant County home. The pack demanded money, but Rhodes refused to cooperate. The ruffians responded by hanging him with a rope.

After the outlaws fled, Rhodes' slaves freed him from the rope's noose.

Soon after, the same band returned and hanged Rhodes a second time, using wire on this occasion. The gang left and Rhodes' slaves again saved him.

Unfortunately, the wire had severed Rhodes' windpipe. The wound became infected and Rhodes died.

Rhodes and his family had long feuded with the Sneed family, who were predominately Indian and the primary suspects in Rhodes' hangings.

The Sneeds, according to sources, resided in a Grant County settlement known as Moccasin Corner. The family had turned to crime after the Civil War and organized an outlaw gang that left a string of victims throughout Southeast Arkansas and other areas of the state as well as Mississippi, Oklahoma and Texas.

In 1884, the group was accused in the beating and shooting death of Jacob Rhodes, a son of Dr. Rhodes.

Three years later, reports were received by Grant County Sheriff W.C.C. Dorough that the Sneeds were hiding out in neighboring Pulaski County. Dorough dispatched a couple of constables — Johnny Bratton and H. Lem Smith — to arrest the bunch.

The constables took Mann Sneed into custody, but a shootout ensued and the constables were killed. Pulaski County deputies went into pursuit of Sneed and found him with a serious bullet wound to an arm. The deputies figured Sneed might be near death himself when they agreed to bring his father, who was in the state prison in Little Rock at the time, to the younger Sneed's cell so that the two could have what might be a final visit.

A surgeon amputated Mann Sneed's wounded arm, and he recovered. Several of the Sneeds avoided capture in the Jacob Rhodes case, but several were rounded up and brought to justice, serving abbreviated jail terms. Mann Sneed was imprisoned and later released.

Sneed later confessed to an 1865 murder of Mary White, who was gunned down in front of her Grant County home. Sneed told a relative that he was pointing a gun at the woman's husband, but as he pulled the trigger, she darted in front of her mate and took the bullet.

Texas Terror May Have Loved Area to Death

Cullen Montgomery Baker, a native of Tennessee, was a cold-blooded killer who favored whichever side best suited him at a particular moment.

When the Civil War broke out, Baker, who had already earned a reputation as a whiskey-drinking brawler, declared his allegiance to the Confederacy and served with Rebel forces in Arkansas. But as fortunes began to turn in the Union's favor, he suddenly claimed to be a Union loyalist.

But the truth was that Baker despised almost everyone, especially blacks and Union sympathizers.

After the war, he waged his own battles, headquartering in the Sulphur River bottoms near Brightstar in Miller County. Over the next four years, he terrorized Northeastern Texas. Over 30 murders were attributed to him.

Baker's style of delivering death was cowardly. All but a few of his victims died as a result of an ambush or a bullet in the back. Baker didn't like facing his targets.

Baker, at several points in his criminal career, would travel to Southeast Arkansas whenever he suspected lawmen or angry relatives or friends of his victims might be closing in on him. For reasons unknown, Baker was a respectable gentleman in this area, avoiding trouble and having little contact with others.

There are two versions on how Baker met his January 7, 1869, demise.

One has it that he was poisoned in Cass County, Texas, near the Sulphur River. But, in another account, he was shot and killed by a posse in Southeast Arkansas, the exact location unknown.

If the latter is true, his fondness for the region might have truly been a fatal attraction.

Search for Cheap Labor Nets Death and Dismay

In their zest to replace some former slaves who had migrated elsewhere after emancipation, some wealthy planters and businessmen in Jefferson County determined that bringing in Chinese workers would be a wise financial move. Chinese workers would accept as little as $10 — and a promise of a monthly ration of opium— for a five-year working agreement.

Hundreds of Chinese workers were brought in, but the scheme didn't work out as the investors had hoped. First, the price of opium increased to such a level that it was no longer affordable compensation. Secondly, the Chinese brought in to pick cotton wound up despising farm life and eventually drifted into jobs within the city, working in laundries, restaurants or stores.

In 1881, a Chinese laundryman, Lee Chow, became involved in a scandal when he married a local white woman, Estell Smith. The couple established residency in Pine Bluff, where the woman met a white doctor by the name of Rosenbaum.

Rosenbaum and Mrs. Chow allegedly began an affair. She reportedly left her husband and moved into Dr. Rosenbaum's plantation residence. Soon after, she returned to her husband and the Chows moved to Little Rock, supposedly with a healthy portion of Rosenbaum's money.

Rosenbaum is said to have followed the pair and encountered them in Little Rock, apparently greeting Mrs. Chow in an unflattering manner. He was arrested and fined $30 for his profane verbal assault.

Less than two weeks later, a shotgun blast left Rosenbaum dead in his home. Naturally, Chow was a suspect, but so was a black man who had recently clashed with Rosenbaum. In April, 1882, two black men — Ambrose Chinn and Alex Miles — were charged with the crime.

Also in 1882, an opium house in Pine Bluff drew the editorial ire of the *Pine Bluff Commercial*, although the place had been operating for some time previously. The *Commercial* bemoaned the opium den's "hideousness" and the fact that "young Americans" were frequenting the establishment and "fast becoming slaves to the seductive but fatal drug."

A year later, the newspaper again lashed out against the den, this time calling it "hellish" and issuing a blunt challenge, "If our city council

Arkansas' Most Wanted

Three of Arkansas' most-feared gangsters had their last taste of freedom in Redfield, where two met death.

Emory Connell, Eulos Sullivan and "Diamond" Joe Sullivan (the Sullivans apparently weren't related) were, according to an old source, "unequaled in Arkansas' criminal history for daring, resourcefulness and unconquerable spirit."

Connell and J. Sullivan were from Missouri. E. Sullivan was from Oklahoma. The trio formed a gang and staged several daring crimes, mostly jewel thefts.

In July 1923, Connell and J. Sullivan, while involved in a stolen diamond "fence" operation in Little Rock, were confronted by police officers and fatally shot two detectives, Luther C. Hay and George E. Moore.

The pair was brought to justice, found guilty of the slayings and sentenced to die in the electric chair. Connell reportedly boasted, "I will never burn."

About the same time, E. Sullivan was convicted in the Harrison murder of U.S. Marshall J. Walter Casey. Sullivan killed Casey when the officer was attempting to place Sullivan — captured after fleeing from incarceration as an Oklahoma jail escapee — into a cell.

Sullivan also drew a date with the electric chair. He escaped twice more before he was finally delivered to the state prison, then in Little Rock.

In the meanwhile, his father had been shot and killed by an Oklahoma police officer. So, apparently, violence and crime were family traditions for his clan.

On Friday, February 1, 1924, Connell — the leader of the gang — made good on his fourth escape attempt from the state prison. With a wooden pistol carved out of a toilet seat, he took the prison warden as a hostage and freed the Sullivan duo.

The three forced the warden to drive them in his own car through the prison gate.

The warden was released as authorities continued an all-out effort in trailing the fugitives. The posse caught up with the trio on February 5 in Redfield.

J. Sullivan surrendered after being shot by law enforcement officers, but Connell and E. Sullivan continued their flight. As the two tried to conceal themselves at the top of a tree, officers asked them to give up, but the pair refused, exhausting their pursuers' patience.

The posse filled the tree with hot lead, and Connell and E. Sullivan entered eternity before they descended to the ground.

"Diamond" Joe Sullivan recovered from his wounds, only to be electrocuted two months later in the completion of his sentence.

The three are still considered as the craftiest escape artists in Arkansas' criminal history. A Department of Correction spokesperson said the three were responsible for more trouble for state penal authorities that any other group of inmates since the prison system's inception.

"Diamond" Joe Sullivan was one of three Arkansas prison escapees involved in a bloody capture at Redfield.

Right, prison life was stale, uncomfortable and dangerous, as one might gather from this 1961 photograph of inmates in open barracks at Cummins Prison Farm.

will not give us relief let us form a committee to drive from our land these damnable Chinese dogs."

By the following week, the opium house was out of business, but for only a brief period. The Pine Bluff City Council, in 1886, finally outlawed local sale and use of opium and set a fine of $25 for each offense.

But the opium problem continued.

In October, 1890, a Chinaman's small building at Third Avenue and Texas Street was destroyed by fire. Investigators found the body of a black porter, Coolie Jackson, within the remains. The structure had been under suspicion as a gathering place for illegal activities, possibly including opium use.

Investigators also uncovered a large amount of coins.

Sam Ling, who had run a laundry in one of the building's four rooms, claimed the money was his, but there were whispers that Jackson had been carrying upward of $500 and was robbed and killed. Rumors circulated that the structure was then burned so that the murder might be hidden.

Opium dens operated at various locales throughout the city into the early 1900s.

It should be noted that the vast majority of Chinese here were law-abiding and hard-working citizens who took pride in themselves, their community and the city. They were sometimes victims of crimes committed by people of different races.

In May, 1896, Wiley Goode — a former police officer who had acquired a reputation as a bully — got into an argument with Qwang Wah at Wah's Chinese restaurant in the city. Goode began slugging Wah, who called for his

Right, a poster dated 1899 by The H.C. Miner Litho. Co., N.Y., celebrates the raid of an opium den.

partner, Hung Tom. As Goode continued the pummeling, Tom exited the kitchen, jumped into the fray and was shot in the arm by Goode. Meanwhile, Goode also shot and critically injured a customer, Frank Howe, who died a few days later.

Goode, who had been terminated as a police officer several months earlier after attacking Wah, drew a prison sentence as a result of Howe's death.

The Arkansas Department of Correction (ADC) — the state's prison system — dates back to 1841 and was originally located in Little Rock, but has been headquartered in Pine Bluff since 1973.

The state's first prison occupied what is today the site of the state capital building, which was later constructed with inmate labor, as were Cummins Prison in Lincoln County and Tucker Prison in Jefferson County.

Cummins has been occupied by inmates since 1902, the same year the land on which it stands was purchased by the state. The Tucker site was bought in 1916.

A second prison in Little Rock closed in 1933 and all inmates were moved to the Cummins and Tucker farms. Tucker housed the death chamber, although the facilities were racially segregated.

Facilities for female inmates were also segregated and had been located in Pulaski County before women's quarters were made at Cummins and Tucker.

Eventually, all sites within the system were racially desegregated.

Inmate "leasing" represents a dark chapter in ADC's history when crooked politicians and wealthy farmers and businessmen "rented" inmates as laborers, often neglecting and mistreating the inmates. Nearly 25 percent of the inmates died each year.

By 1902, public outcry against the practice had become so strong that the state decided to establish a self-supporting prison system.

Nevertheless, tales of inhumane treatment haunted the system for decades. In 1966, Governor Orval Faubus ordered an investigation into allegations of extortion (after reports that inmates' freedom could be purchased), misuse of state property and inmate drunkenness. The Arkansas State Police had to quell inmate riots at Cummins.

Two years later, state Prison Warden Thomas Murton, a reformer hired by Governor Winthrop Rockefeller to cleanse the system, alleged that human skeletons unearthed at Cummins were the remains of inmates beaten to death and secretly buried. The episode earned worldwide media attention.

Murton was soon fired, and Rockefeller ended his gubernatorial reign in 1970 by commuting the sentences of 15 death row inmates.

Also in 1970, the entire prison system was ruled unconstitutional, initiating a lengthy process in which assorted improvements were made so that the system could regain its legality.

The enhancements have included construction of new facilities throughout the state. Meanwhile, heightened standards and internal policing have helped ADC to gain a professional, progressive reputation and receive national acclaim.

PRISON RODEO

AUGUST 22, 23, 29 & 30, 1980
CUMMINS UNIT, VARNER, ARKANSAS
8 P.M.

SAW MILL SCENE, STATE FARM, CUMMINS, ARKANSAS

Overseen in part by trustee guards, inmates are seen here working in the sawmill at Cummins Prison Farm, circa 1915.

WHO SAYS CRIME DOESN'T PAY?

During the Great Depression, in 1939, 17-year-old Perry Williams of Sheridan decided he was going to rob a "rich man." He eyed a new automobile approaching him on Highway 167 just north of Sheridan.

Williams motioned for a ride, and the young driver, sporting a nice suit and tie, graciously stopped.

Williams pulled a pistol on the driver taking $63 in cash from him and then releasing him after taking command of the new Ford.

Williams was soon arrested in Hot Springs and promptly sent to prison . . . for a time.

Williams resumed his criminal activities after his initial release, robbing eight banks, escaping the electric chair after murdering a fellow convict, being shot during a prison escape and spending almost 50 years behind bars.

After his final exit from prison, he was given a job at Arkla Gas Company in Pine Bluff.

Who hired Williams?

The man he robbed in 1939 — future Arkla head and millionaire W.R. "Witt" Stephens.

Williams died in 1995, outliving the forgiving Stephens by four years.

One of the most well-known unsolved murders in Southeast Arkansas is the case of John Thurman McCool.

McCool's body was found in his car, which was discovered in Hardin Cemetery east of Sheridan following a January, 1962 snowstorm. McCool had been shot several times by a .45 caliber revolver.

A Grant County native, McCool at the time resided in Pine Bluff, where he had been a prominent businessman and politician.

Sent to prison on a forgery charge in 1956, he was paroled by Governor Orval Faubus in 1958.

Grant County Sheriff Vernon Hope investigated, but the crime, to date, remains a mystery.

Main, 1927 flood inundates Dermott, Arkansas.

Insets, flood waters cover streets in Pine Bluff, 1927.

East 2nd Ave. Pine Bluff Ark. Spring 1927

CHAPTER ELEVEN

Disasters

Southeast Arkansas has unfortunately had more than its share of disasters, encountering deadly and destructive floods, killer tornadoes, near-blizzard snows, crippling ice storms, catastrophic droughts, fatal heat waves and cold spells, disabling utility failures and even damaging earthquakes, in addition to detrimental fires and industry and transportation tragedies.

There is no rhyme or reason as to when such events may occur. Tornadoes have struck in every month, and Pine Bluff recorded the state's warmest February temperature with a whopping 93 degrees in 1918. Here are some brief accounts of some of the area's worst disasters.

Water, Water Everywhere: the Curse of River Flooding

In the summer of 1833, much of the state, including Southeast Arkansas, was devastated by heavy rains and Arkansas and Mississippi River flooding. If the state had been more populated, losses would have been much greater.

Most farms in Southeast Arkansas were under water, so crop damage and livestock losses were staggering. The financial setbacks were felt for a number of years.

Older Arkansans said they couldn't recall a worse flood. In some locations, water was three feet above previously-known high-water marks.

There are hundreds of thousands of photographs from the Arkansas River Flood of 1927, the worst natural disaster of the 1900s.

The flood impacted all modes of transportation, including boat traffic. In one Pine Bluff incident, a couple of men in a boat somehow managed to escape injury when they and their boat were tossed by a wave through a glass window of a downtown business.

The flood claimed 15 lives in Jefferson County and forever altered the federal government's disaster policies.

Minor flooding of the rivers, Bayou Bartholomew and other waterways was and continued to be fairly common, but occasionally flooding would be bad enough to cause injuries or deaths and costly property damages.

A 1908 Arkansas River flood prompted Jefferson County officials to wire President Theodore Roosevelt for assistance when high waters threatened the courthouse alongside the river. A number of nearby businesses and dwellings had already washed away when river banks tumbled into the waters.

But Roosevelt ignored the plea for help, and locals wound up taking the law into their own hands when waters began to lap within inches of the courthouse. Someone dynamited a nearby levee — an act that the Army Corps of Engineers had outlawed — a couple of days later, changing the river's course and saving the courthouse.

Federal authorities soon arrived in Pine Bluff to conduct an investigation, and lips suddenly stilled among townspeople.

For years, no one claimed involvement in the act, but after several decades of silence, a number of locals began taking credit for the event. Historian James W. Leslie believed the "culprits," or "heroes," were Abb S. Knox, Matt McGehee and a trio of unknown black men. All had

been promised substantial sums of money, but were never paid. Those behind the plot were never positively identified.

On January 31, 1916, floodwaters of the Arkansas River broke through a levee at Cummins Prison Farm in Varner and rolled over lowlands in Lincoln, Ashley, Chicot, Desha and Drew counties.

Three days later, former Lincoln County Clerk T.L. Purtius drowned in floodwaters at Dumas. The body of a second drowning victim, an unidentified black man, was found in Grady. On February 12, three unidentified black men, who were carrying emergency supplies to other flood victims, died when a current flipped their boat in Watson.

But no other flood here can begin to compare to the Great Flood of 1927, rated as the nation's worst weather disaster of the entire 20th century.

Arkansas was the hardest-hit of the seven states struck by the flood, which started on January 1 on the Mississippi River in Cairo, Illinois. The river had started rising in August 1926 following massive rains in Canada and several northern states.

Flooding spread to Missouri, Kentucky, Tennessee, Mississippi and Louisiana before waters finally began to recede on July 27. The calamity resulted in 246 confirmed deaths across the area, with another 250

persons who had gone missing never found. A disorganized response resulted in some persons actually starving to death as they awaited rescues from high land, attics, rooftops and even tree limbs.

About 162,000 homes were flooded and approximately 637,000 persons were displaced. Most persons at the time were employed in agricultural pursuits, and thousands of flood victims lost their liveli-

The Arkansas River Flood of 1927, was the worst natural disaster of the 1900s. The flood impacted all modes of transportation including boat traffic. In one Pine Bluff incident, a couple of men in a boat somehow managed to escape injury when they and their boat were tossed by a wave through a glass window of a downtown business. The flood claimed 15 lives in Jefferson County and forever altered the federal government's disaster policies.

High water at Avery, 1927 flood.

hoods as an estimated 27,000 square miles of farmland vanished under floodwaters.

About a fourth of Arkansas — including a third of the state's eastern portion — was flooded. The state's death toll varied in counts from 91 to 127. An estimated 143,000 Arkansans were displaced. Millions of acres of farmland were flooded.

Hastened by heavy rains, flooding began on the Arkansas River in Pine Bluff on the night of Friday, April 15. Over 150 residents of the city's lowlands left their homes to find safety elsewhere. By the morning of Sunday, April 17, another 50 citizens had abandoned their dwellings.

Around 50 Arkansas National Guardsmen began a watch on flooded areas in an effort to prevent looting.

Area levees along the river began breaking, and by nightfall, much of Jefferson County — including Pine Bluff's Main Street and a sizable portion of the city's east side — was flooded. Free Bridge Road was water-covered, as were roadways in other directions from the city.

When the Frenchtown levee below Pine Bluff gave way to the torrent at 10 a.m., about 200 feet of Cotton Belt Railroad track and a segment of the Missouri Pacific line south of the city were swept into the waters. Fairfield, Moscow, Noble Lake and Linwood were flooded.

The New Gascony levee yielded at 4 p.m. and the waters poured into Altheimer, Humphrey, Sherrill and Tucker.

Displaced persons were provided lodging at several locations, including Arkansas AM&N College (now the University of Arkansas at Pine Bluff) and various churches.

The area north of the river sustained the most damage in the county.

The U.S. Army Corps of Engineers-maintained levee close to the Free Bridge (near the current Highway 79 bridge) was the only point above water in the vicinity. Soon, a makeshift refugee camp was established on the Free Bridge. Meanwhile, many who had been unable to leave their homes took to their attics or rooftops.

Several heroes emerged during rescue efforts. Also, some boat owners employed their crafts to carry food, water and other supplies to refugees opting to stay on the Free Bridge, and to transport those who wished instead to stay in Pine Bluff until floodwaters retracted.

Fifteen persons perished in Jefferson County, including four persons who supposedly starved to death on the roof of a house on the north side of the river. Another victim, Ben Weil of Pine Bluff, drowned when his boat capsized in a drainage ditch southeast of the city.

On Thursday, April 21, levees in Desha and Lincoln counties bowed to the floodwaters' pressure. Arkansas City, Dermott, Lake Village, McGehee, Tillar and Watson — along with a sizable share of the remainder of Southeast Arkansas — went under in fast fashion.

In Arkansas City, the streets were reportedly "dry and dusty" at noon. But by 2 p.m., flooding was so intense that mules were drowning before would-be rescuers could unbind them from wagons.

By Sunday, April 24, the waters began to fade in Jefferson County. Unfortunately, high waters were slower to subside below Pine Bluff. Other levees continued to plunge south and east of the city.

Before the catastrophe, response to disasters had largely been a local concern. But the flood was of such great magnitude that it necessitated federal action, giving birth to the federal government's emergency relief, recovery and mitigation efforts.

Regrettably, relief and recovery efforts in the 1927 flood were blatantly discriminatory against blacks. The American Red Cross established 154 refugee camps, and all were segregated.

Aid was openly withheld from some blacks, who were left to fend for themselves or allegedly forced into dangerous situations while assisting white victims.

Perhaps the worst flood to strike the region in recent times occurred on December 15-17, 2001. The Arkansas River was already over flood stage in several areas of the region, and five days of heavy rains in Central and Western Arkansas were followed by some of the most severe flooding since 1950.

Killer Tornadoes: 'It Sounded Like a Freight Train'

Arkansas has consistently ranked high nationally in its number of killer tornadoes, although deaths have lessened dramatically as tornado-warning capabilities have improved.

Southeast Arkansas is no stranger to tornadoes and has unfortunately shared in several of the state's most lethal twisters.

TORNADO!

Jefferson County's most destructive tornado to date struck on June 1, 1947.

Along a 19-mile trek, it destroyed a number of homes and other structures while claiming 35 lives and leaving about 300 persons injured.

The tornado was especially strong in the old, rural Union community, where it leveled a string of residences and a couple of businesses, as these photographs show, and left several dead.

Survivors and, unfortunately, several victims — including an infant — were scattered among splintered remains that were carefully searched by responders.

These three photos of the 1947 tornado show damage and recovery efforts.

The state's deadliest single tornado of the 20th Century smacked Warren on Monday, January 3, 1949. The death toll was 55, which tied the mark for most fatalities in a single Arkansas twister. A Fort Smith tornado claimed 55 lives on January 12, 1898.

The Warren tornado resulted in 435 injuries. Property damage was estimated at $1.3 million.

During the evening of March 8, 1909, Grant and Jefferson counties were included in a tornado path that stretched over 85 miles, from Sheridan to northeast of Brinkley. The damage trail was 880 yards at its greatest width. Forty-nine persons were killed in the Brinkley area alone, and 58 deaths were confirmed overall. Also, several persons went missing and were presumed dead, although their remains were never located.

On February 20, 1912, about half of the town of Lanark near Warren was leveled by a tornado that left one person dead and several injured.

Just five days later, 15 persons were killed and 50 were injured when tornadoes slammed Arkansas, Jefferson and Lincoln counties. Many buildings were destroyed and a heavy loss of livestock was reported.

On April 28, 1912, a tornado caused heavy property damage in McGehee.

A June 5-6, 1916, storm system delivered 34 tornadoes statewide, resulting in 87 deaths, over 300 injuries and more than $1 million in property losses. Four people went missing and were never found.

Eight fatalities were marked in Stuttgart, where 20 were injured. Five were killed, three were injured and one went missing in Dalark, and a fatality also occurred in Arkansas City.

On December 8, 1916, three persons died in a Pine Bluff tornado. On December 26, a Stuttgart tornado killed 11.

Several persons died in a March 20, 1917, tornado in Dallas County.

On Thanksgiving Day, November 25, 1926, 52 persons died in tornadoes that struck Jefferson, Cleburne and Faulkner counties.

Moscow and an area near Sulphur Springs were especially hard hit. Ten fatalities were marked in Moscow alone.

Among the Sulphur Springs victims were young twin brothers who were home from college to celebrate the holiday with their family. The twins were pursuing ministerial degrees.

The state confirmed 27 tornadoes and 51 fatalities that day.

Jefferson County's worst tornado to date occurred on the afternoon of Pentecost Sunday, June 1, 1947. The tornado ripped a 19-mile trail that measured up to 1.5 miles in width.

Several people died as a string of homes in the old, rural Union community were demolished. Elsewhere, 11 teenagers perished in a Highway 15 meeting hall. Overall, 35 died and about 300 were injured. A utility worker was killed in an industrial accident while attempting to make repairs in the storm area a few days after the tornado.

Some pictures by part-time Pine Bluff photographer Thomas Watts, one of the first people on the scene after the tornado, were used in news coverage of the event.

One person was killed when a tornado struck a mobile home near DeWitt during a 1982 summer storm. The twister caused the trailer to flip over, and the man died when a refrigerator and other household items toppled onto him.

Arkansas saw a single-day record 56 tornadoes on January 21, 1999. Locally, the Pine Bluff Arsenal sustained the most damage. Also struck were Poyen, Tucker, White Hall and rural areas near Bunn, Pastoria and Princeton.

The twister that hit White Hall was on the ground for 16 miles. Luckily, there were no injuries or fatalities in Southeast Arkansas.

Also among the more recent tornadoes was a strong twister that swatted a section of Desha County on February 24, 2001. Parts of a downed farm building were found six miles away from the original spot.

Dallas, Grant and Jefferson counties had confirmed tornadoes on May 7, 2003.

Early Fires Caused Financial Losses, Suffering

Perhaps the area's most memorable fire of the past century was the April 28, 1976, blaze that destroyed much of the Jefferson County Courthouse. Surprisingly, only a few records were lost.

There were no deaths or injuries and some of the building was saved, but such good fortune hasn't always been the case.

In their infancy, fire departments were ill-equipped in fighting blazes that could quickly take a strong hold.

A Bit of History Goes Up in Smoke

The Jefferson County Courthouse in Pine Bluff, like many other government buildings, has long represented more than a mere structure or landmark.

Over time, the courthouse became a sort of silent sentinel within the public that it served. People appreciated the old building, but slipped into a lull and didn't realize the true depth of their fondness until the courthouse was almost lost forever in an April 28, 1976 fire.

In a dramatic statement of affection for their courthouse, voters overwhelmingly — by a margin of 7,531-733 — approved a bond issue and property tax to help save and remodel the building.

Of the 1856 courthouse, only the center portion containing the bell tower was retained in a new design. Completion of the $5,418,000 project arrived in time to be included in the celebration of the county's 150th anniversary. A program — with plenty of speeches — and a big parade highlighted the opening of the "reborn" courthouse on May 8, 1980.

These photographs show "before" and "after" comparisons. The photograph of the courthouse in all its previous glory was snapped earlier in 1976 for postcard purposes. The photos on the next page depict some of the damages caused by the blaze.

Nearly 50 years before the city would establish a fire department, Pine Bluff saw nearly all of its business district burned to ashes in a horrific September 20, 1850, blaze. Damages were estimated at about $40,000.

The fact that there were only two deaths in a February 13, 1907, Pine Bluff fire is a miracle. Fire engulfed a nine-block area of the city, destroying 150 homes and other buildings and causing $250,000 in damages.

An April 8, 1925, an inferno caused a staggering $500,000 in damages to the Breece White Manufacturing Company in Arkansas City.

Pine Bluff has experienced many destructive fires.

On October 10, 1876, two blocks of frame buildings were burned in a loss that totaled $150,000. The city's business district sustained $125,000 in damages in a January 2, 1883, blaze.

Several buildings on Main Street were lost in a November 19, 1891, fire. The financial loss was figured at $35,000.

On October 12, 1920, 54 homes were leveled in a fire that generated $300,000 in property losses.

The original Saenger Theater was destroyed by flames on November 12, 1922, with the damage registering $150,000.

There were significant early fires elsewhere within the region, too.

A huge fire in Monticello on December 13, 1890, flattened an untold number of homes and businesses. On October 2, 1905, Warren sustained $100,000 in losses brought on by a large blaze.

Damages were figured at $75,000 when a fire downed six businesses in Dumas on August 20, 1925. And a July 17, 1929, fire destroyed the Arkansas Rice Growers Cooperative in Stuttgart.

Arkansas Railroad Engine No. 150 following a 1956 fire at the roundhouse in Star City.

Right, an early fire in downtown Warren obviously did great damage. The Warren bank is clearly visible.

Blizzards and Ice: Breezin' and Freezin'

Snow isn't common in Southeast Arkansas, but when a near-blizzard covered much of the state on January 27–28, 2000, Drew County had the highest total with up to 18 inches in areas. Cleveland and Dallas had 14 inches while Lincoln County garnered 12. Eleven inches covered the ground in Desha and Jefferson counties. Bradley had 10 inches, Grant County counted eight and Arkansas County had six.

In an earlier, statewide snow storm on January 28, 1966, Pine Bluff had the most snowfall with 12.5 inches. Following the snow, an arctic outbreak carried strong winds into the area. The temperature slid to below zero in several locations. Sparkman shared the state's coldest temperature at -10 degrees.

Heavy snow was also experienced in the region in December, 1963 with measurements reaching 13 inches. A January 6–7, 1988, snowstorm dropped up to 10 inches in portions of Southeast Arkansas.

Ice storms have created havoc within the region a number of times.

A pair of ice storms crippled the area in December, 2000. On December 12–13, Pine Bluff and other locales in Jefferson County received as much as five inches of ice. Then, on December 25–28, another three inches fell.

Much of Southeast Arkansas felt the crunch as an estimated 100,000–150,000 homes, businesses and farms lost electrical power. Some power from the first storm had been restored but was lost again when the second bout arrived.

Some locales in the region had no electricity for nearly a month.

A January 7, 1979, ice storm was especially rough on McGehee, Monticello and Warren and nearby areas. Three inches of ice created woes that included a power outage for approximately 50,000 persons. Some residents were without electric service for two weeks.

Utility damages were figured at $5 million. Meanwhile, more than 3.5 million acres of timber sustained damages that created losses of $6.5 million for growers.

Ice storms of December 12–13, 1990, and February 9–11, 1994, were also oppressive.

The winter of 1917–1918 was one of the most severe. Northern Arkansas registered up to 30 inches of snow while ice and freezing conditions lingered in parts of Southeast Arkansas. In Little Rock and Pine Bluff, the Arkansas River froze to a depth that people walked across it, many recording the event with photographs.

A sharecropper of the time, L. E. "Brig" Moore, recalled years later that he and his family members and neighbors during a few nights of the season heard strange, loud popping noises. He said they eventually figured out the commotion was caused by trees so inundated with ice that they were "bursting" from the pressure of their frozen coats coupled with freezing from the inside, thus having no means of naturally "breathing."

The river froze, too, in 1912, 1940 and 1983, with the ice disrupting river traffic.

Harsh cold spells through the years have resulted in several deaths, either by exposure or fires generated by improper home-heating practices.

ARKANSAS RIVER FROZEN JANUARY 1912, PINE BLUFF, ARK.

THE BIG CHILL

The ice storms of December 12–13 and 25–28, 2000, crippled much of Southeast Arkansas as automotive and air travel was all but halted and an estimated 100,000-150,000 homes, businesses and farms were left without electrical power. In some locales, power was lost for almost a month. Power lines, trees and limbs were downed by the weight of the ice.

These Pine Bluff scenes are indicative of the woes created by the two ice storms, which carried a higher price tag on damages and corrective requirements than any other Arkansas weather disaster to date.

Those motorists who braved the roadways were often unable to drive beyond a snail's pace in order to avoid sliding off the pavement. Downed trees and limbs created havoc for home and business owners as they faced major cleanup chores.

A number of people were forced from their homes and wound up in emergency shelters, where conditions weren't always much better, but at least afforded better opportunities for warmth.

The second storm began in the wee hours of Christmas morning, and when many awoke to discover they had no electricity, they also realized that they were in for a much different type of Christmas than they had previously experienced.

Fasten Your Seatbelts, It's Going to be a Bumpy Ride

Although relatively few in numbers, transportation and industrial accidents have nevertheless occasionally created discomfort and despondency in Southeast Arkansas.

During the era when water travel was common, the area experienced several steamboat tragedies.

Among a number of steamer incidents was a January 29, 1866, explosion aboard the Steamer Miami about six miles above Napoleon. The initial estimate of deaths was over 100, but that number was trimmed as rescue efforts proved more successful than had been expected. An estimated 300 persons had been aboard.

The area has also encountered some railroad misfortunes.

On May 21, 1892, Cotton Belt Passenger Train No. 1 collided with a freight train on a bridge over a flooded Crooked Bayou near Humphrey.

The passenger train plunged off the bridge and into the water below. Several people drowned. The final death toll was 10.

At 1:15 a.m. on Valentine's Day 1945, Cotton Belt Passenger Train No. 1, this time out of Memphis, was southbound to Dallas when it entered a lengthy curve on tracks along the east side of Pine Bluff. The train was chugging along at a brisk 55 miles an hour.

The night was especially dark as the sky was covered by thick rain clouds.

The train's engineer, Walter J. Barrett, finally saw the sparkling glow of a flaming fuse and an outline of a freight caboose just ahead. But he didn't see it in time to avoid a collision.

The intensity of the crash resulted in the caboose's shredding into a splintered, unrecognizable heap.

Barrett died within minutes after arriving at the city's old Davis Hospital. Fireman J.B. Wilbanks, who had been standing on the front steps of the caboose, suffered severe wounds and died the following day.

Several other railroad workers and a passenger were injured.

A June 9, 1985, derailment in Pine Bluff of a St. Louis Southwestern train hauling toxic chemicals resulted in an explosion and fire and a sizable evacuation. The event was the lead story on national television news broadcasts for about three days.

During World War II, some residents around the Army's Pine Bluff Arsenal were surprised when, reportedly, a plane dropped small bombs onto their property. No injuries occurred, but at least one barn was damaged. An Army official said the bombs were being tested, but the activity was supposed to have been confined to installation grounds.

Shortly after World War II, several captured German rockets containing chemical agents were accidentally launched from the Pine Bluff Arsenal into the surrounding neighborhoods. Miraculously, there were no injuries.

Earthquakes and Droughts: Shakin' and Bakin'

Friday, March 31, 1911, started like most other days, but by noon, it would reach a climax as one of the most frightening in Southeast Arkansas' history.

An earthquake measuring 4.7 magnitude on the Richter Scale would strike with three separate, distinct shocks at around 10 and 11 a.m. and noon. The strongest was at 10:57 a.m.

The quake, centered between Rison and Warren, didn't result in any injuries or deaths, but left thousands of residents stunned and alarmed. The violent tremor was felt across Arkansas and into adjoining states.

In Pine Bluff, hundreds of terrified citizens rushed onto the streets from their homes or businesses. Persons within the Jefferson County Courthouse ran outside, fearing the structure might crumble into the nearby Arkansas River.

The *Arkansas Gazette* reported that plaster fell from the ceiling of the city's new "$100,000 high school building." At Sixth Avenue Elementary School, walls and ceilings split, dumping plaster onto students and teachers.

School was immediately dismissed for the remainder of the day.

In the city's stores, merchandise shook off of display shelves. Dishes were broken in numerous homes and eateries. In some settings, people were unseated when their chairs rocked or tipped over.

The current Cleveland County Courthouse was under construction at the time. Workers were erecting steel frames for the structure's roof and walls. They feared the building would topple when the quake caused the building to vibrate.

Rison-area residents were frightened when windows began breaking and several brick buildings developed cracks. Some area farmers observed plowed dirt in their fields twittering.

In Warren, the quake rattled that Bradley County Courthouse so violently that the building's tower bell rang during the second and third shocks. Officials evacuated the courthouse and surrounding vicinity, fearing the structure might tumble.

Schools shook strongly enough that terrified children dashed away. Books and other items were jostled from shelves and desktops.

Warren was less severely impacted by a 4.3 magnitude quake on June 4, 1967.

On May 5, 1960, a small tremor occurred in the old Dew Drop community, then three miles north but now part of Pine Bluff. Except for a few bottles shattering after slipping off a liquor store counter, there were no damages.

Sheridan and rural Grant County felt the effects of a series of three distinct quakes between 5:33 and 5:49 p.m. on February 15, 1974. The magnitudes of the tremors ranged from 3.3.–3.8.

Southeast Arkansas, according to authorities, would sustain light to moderate damage should a quake as severe as the 1811–1812 New Madrid Fault incident occur again. The quake was the country's worst-ever to date, and many scientists believe the fault is already overdue for a second major event.

Southeast Arkansas has also suffered from some of the nation's worst droughts.

Despite the fact that the region contains rich farming lands, the Great Flood of 1927 and the onset of the stock market crash and Great Depression were made even more detrimental by drought conditions that lingered from 1930–1939.

Several dust storms occurred during the decade, the worst ones in 1934. The summers of 1930 and 1934 were brutally hot as well as dry. The area has since endured several challenging but less-severe dry spells.

Heat waves and dangerously hot and humid summers have occasionally produced health disorders and deaths. The summers of 1953, 1954, 1980 and 2000 brought record-setting heat.

Left, railroad mishaps normally create little or no problems for the general public and most often occur without injury or death. But, as this photograph indicates, remedies to derailments can be costly.

CHAPTER TWELVE

Fun and Games

"Take me out to the ball game, take me out to the crowd. Buy me some peanuts and Cracker Jack. I don't care if I never get back. Let me root, root, root for the home team. If they don't win it's a shame. For it's one, two, three strikes you're out at the old ball game."
—Jack Norworth, 1908

Professional baseball long ago made a big hit in Pine Bluff. Before 1920, the city served as a spring training site for such major league clubs as Hall of Fame manager John McGraw's fabled New York Giants. In the 1940s and 1950s, the St. Louis Browns and St. Louis Cardinals held spring camps at Grider Field. Among the hundreds of major leaguers who participated in pre-season preparations in Pine Bluff were such notables as the Giants' Jim Thorpe, the first two-sport professional star, and Cardinal legend Stan Musial.

Pine Bluff itself also fielded several professional, minor league teams during the 1900s, traditionally enjoying more success on the diamond than at the ticket office. In fact, even though the city is noted for its appreciation and support of youth baseball, the leading reason for the assorted professional teams eventually striking out there was a lack of operating funds attributable to poor public support.

Here's a brief look at Pine Bluff's professional baseball teams.

This Budweiser Team's for You

Baseball was first played in Pine Bluff in 1867. But in 1900, a semi-professional crew, known simply as the Pine Bluff Budweiser Team, delivered organized baseball to the city.

There are a couple of big differences between semi-professional and professional baseball, however. Semi-professional teams may or may not be salaried for their play, and the clubs don't play regular schedules.

The local Budweiser brewery employed many of the Budweiser Team players, and they may have received no other compensation than paid time off for their practices and games. Other team members may not have collected any sort of payment.

But such details mattered little to a baseball-loving public that lived without radio and television and constantly hungered for entertainment. The team played other business and industrial squads as well as several, mostly loosely-organized city clubs.

Budweiser pitcher T. H. Slade was a favorite among the fans. Slade was a veteran player, well-respected for his pitching skills. He was employed at the now-defunct *Pine Bluff Graphic* newspaper.

Other regulars included outfielders J. L. Harrington, Clyde Vowell and Willie Vowell; infielders Charles Campbell, Ben Franklin, John Harris and Frank Reeves; catcher Louis Genevay; and substitutes F. Brewster and O. A. Brewster.

The team faded about as quickly as it had formed, but not before it served to illustrate Pine Bluff's interest in organized baseball. Three years later, professional baseball made its debut in Pine Bluff.

Before advancing on that subject, however, it should be noted that the city today boasts one of the region's most enduring and successful semi-professional teams – the Pine Bluff Braves. The historically black team has been fielding squads since the late 1940s.

Big-time Baseball: Joining the Cotton States League

In 1903, Pine Bluff joined the Cotton States League, then in its second year. Jefferson County Judge A. B. Grace directed a successful drive to compile a $2,500 franchise fee.

Without a team name, Pine Bluff played against squads representing Greenville, Natchez, and Vicksburg, Mississippi, and Baton Rouge and Monroe, Louisiana. Pine Bluff's original home was Jones Park at 17th Avenue and Main Street, but a move was soon made to Bell Park – later renamed Forrest Park — at 31st Avenue and Cherry Street.

George Blackburn was the original manager, but was replaced during the season by Frank Christian. Unfortunately, the change didn't improve the club's dismal performance and Pine Bluff wound up fourth in the standings.

Success, although short-lived, arrived in 1904.

A contest was held to name the team. Emma White received a season ticket for her winning entry — Lumbermen. Blackburn, a workhorse pitcher, was traded to Natchez. Christian departed and Bert Blue was appointed manager.

When Blue proved even more incapable as a skipper than his predecessors, the team brass soon secured George Reed as its new field chief, and Reed promptly turned the club around and guided it to a league championship.

Outfielder Howard Murphy was the circuit's top batsman with a .350 average. Infielders Harry Clayton and Lee Dawkins were Pine Bluff natives and, naturally, fan favorites.

Also on the Pine Bluff roster were pitchers Harry Berry, Walter Deaver, Bob White and Lee Vernucelli; infielders Fred Cavender, Herbert Grubb and Guy Sample; catcher Ed Lauzon; and outfielder Ollie Ofroerer.

The roster was largely the same for the 1905 season, but Reed moved on and Sample replaced him. The team experienced a horrible reversal of fortune and began losing. Lineup alterations were fruitless as the Lumbermen continued their downward tumble.

Attendance and revenue diminished. By July 17, the league was forced to revoke Pine Bluff's charter. Less than a year after having earned the Cotton States flag, Pine Bluff was without a baseball team.

A New Team, a New League and the Same Problems

After an absence of two years, professional baseball returned to Pine Bluff in 1908 when the city was awarded membership in the new Arkansas State League.

The local team was known as the Pine Knotts. Clubs in Argenta (now North Little Rock), Brinkley, Helena, Hot Springs, and Newport rounded out the confederation.

The Pine Knotts finished fourth with little public following, and professional baseball was finished in Pine Bluff a second time, but only for the next year.

Rejoining the group in 1910, the Pine Knotts franchise never had a real chance to gain any consistency. By July, the league itself was broke and the season was discontinued.

The bust left Pine Bluff fans bitter and disinterested, and although a number of business league teams performed during the drought, the city didn't have another professional crew for more than a decade.

Pine Bluff's White Sox: No Shame Here

The Chicago White Sox's fix in the 1919 World Series greatly damaged baseball's reputation, but Babe Ruth's monumental development as a then-unparalleled home run hitter saved the game by generating new, fervent interest.

The game's increased popularity resulted in a renewal of organized baseball in Pine Bluff in 1921. A semi-professional bunch, calling itself the White Sox, was formed.

Many baseball fans had remained loyal to the accused Chicago players who were banned from baseball by newly-appointed Commissioner Kenesaw Mountain Landis. It may have been that the organizers of the Pine Bluff White Sox were among those devotees.

After playing double-headers with assorted industry clubs and nearby city crews, the White Sox had obtained a regular audience here.

For the 1922 season, local businessman George Merrick became the team's manager. The squad enjoyed an excellent season, playing on a home field at Eighth Avenue and Oak Street. The site is now Jordan Stadium, Pine Bluff High School's football facility.

On May 22, the team traveled to Mississippi for an exhibition against Clarksdale of the Cotton States League. Pine Bluff won 5–1 and the White Sox earned big headlines in area newspapers.

Foy Hammons, who would eventually become a football coach at PBHS, was a team mainstay. Others who starred included future Jefferson County Judge Joe Henslee, 1914 PBHS state championship baseball team members Harlow Sanders and James H. Alexander, Guy Humphrey, Cotton Belt Railroad workers John "Shaggy" Graves,

Roy Holloway and Henry "Heinie" Shinall, and former PBHS and University of Arkansas football standout Monroe "Money" Perdue.

According to several sources, Perdue established his stardom as a Razorback by accepting a dare to head-butt a mule. Neither Perdue nor the mule were wearing a helmet, and after Perdue lined up opposite the mule, crouched and then met the mule in a head-on run, it brayed, stumbled and fell dead of a heart attack. Perdue survived with no noticeable injuries, but was depressed for some time over the mule's demise.

The White Sox celebrated Independence Day with a memorable double-header sweep of Wabbaseka. In the opener, Hammons tossed a no-hitter in a 6–0 win. In the second game, the White Sox strolled to a 12–1 victory.

With its reputation growing, the Pine Bluff collection wound up its campaign with a successful tour versus several South Arkansas and Louisiana teams.

In 1923, with Hammons as business chief as well as player/manager, the White Sox were granted a franchise in the South Arkansas League with Camden, El Dorado and Hope. The league established a 90-game schedule and a team salary limit of $2,000 per month.

Pine Bluff acquired the services of an impact player with its signing of Wild Cherry (Fulton County) catcher and power hitter C. R. "Doc" Roe, a 24-year-old with an impressive minor league background.

Pine Bluff was coasting atop the pack at the midway point of the season with a 7.5-game lead. But the Hope Gassers overtook the White Sox down the stretch and forced a best-of-five series for the league championship.

Hope rapidly claimed the title with three straight wins.

Sadly, the league – and the White Sox – faded into oblivion under the same financial pressures that doomed previous teams and affiliations.

1930: A Remarkable Return

Bolstered by the support of Jefferson County Judge R. H. Williams, a group of leading Pine Bluff businessman formulated the Pine Bluff Baseball Association and obtained membership in a revised, six-team Cotton States League in 1930.

The city was in desperate need of something positive, as the Great Depression had gripped the nation, and in Arkansas — especially Southeast Arkansas — recovery from the tragic 1927 flood of the Arkansas and Mississippi rivers had been delayed by the worst drought in state history.

The new baseball club was destined to deliver just the right medicine for a despaired city.

A baseball diamond with a wooden grandstand and wooden bleachers was constructed in a renovated Missouri Pacific Railroad Park at West Fourth Avenue and Plum Street.

Named the "Judges" in a contest, with the tag honoring Williams' dedication to bringing back professional baseball to Pine Bluff, the team was placed under the field management of Wray Query. A Texan, Query would, by season's end and however fleeting, be hailed as a managing genius.

The league featured a split-season. If different teams won the first- and second-half titles, a best-of-seven playoff would be held to determine the pennant winner.

In the first half, the Judges struggled and finished just one game out of the cellar. The story was much different in the second half, when Query began shuffling the lineup and making personnel changes.

Sparked by second baseman (and 1929 West Texas League homerun leader) Skeet Rawlins and centerfielder Stormy Davis, the Judges started making winning a habit, and the approving fans showed their appreciation with stout attendance figures.

The Judges stormed to a second-half title, and earned a playoff berth against El Dorado.

On August 29 at El Dorado, Pine Bluff erupted for four runs in the sixth inning, overcoming an early deficit and then hanging on for a 5–4 win. The next day, the visiting Judges took a 7–6 decision.

Back home on August 31, Pine Bluff survived another close contest by a 7–5 count with Rawlins providing the necessary offensive punch. Pitching ace Chick Galeria earned the mound victory.

The Judges secured the pennant in decisively easy fashion on September 1. Pine Bluff rolled to a 12–5 win, scoring seven runs on eight hits in the second inning and then tallying its remaining five runs on four hits in the third frame. "Smiling" Joe Berry was the winning pitcher.

For the series, Rawlins was 5 for 16 at the plate with four homeruns, a double, six runs and 10 runs batted in.

Other players contributing to the team's successes were hurlers Alvin Betts, Fuzz Douglas, Minor Formby, Jim Parker, Phil Schmidt and Lefty Vaught; infielders Dick Burrows, Toney DeFate and Emmitt Lipscomb; and outfielders Ralph Butler and Earl Persons. Query typically handled catching chores.

So admired was Query that the club hosted an "appreciation day" for him. The team management advertised that while its financial condition disallowed it from giving Query a monetary bonus, it felt the public should be granted an opportunity to thank him with donations.

It's not known just how much was raised, but the public was reportedly generous in expressing its gratitude.

Back to Bad Times

History would repeat itself, and the Judges vacated the league penthouse for what must have seemed like an outhouse in 1931.

First, Query left for bigger and better things. Then, a fire destroyed Missouri Pacific Park's grandstands and locker rooms on June 20. The team would prove to be as low-grade as most of the lumber donated for the park's rebuilding.

The squad's lone standout, pitcher Luke Gates, was sold to the New York Yankees at the end of the season for a then-amazing sum of $3,000.

Pine Bluff wasn't the only franchise fighting to stay alive, however. By July of 1932, the league was out of money and out of business. The association would fail in an attempted 1933 revival.

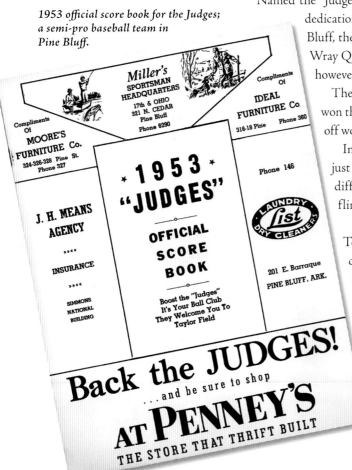

1953 official score book for the Judges; a semi-pro baseball team in Pine Bluff.

However, the Judges would field a team, but for only a portion of the 1933 season.

On June 16, the city was offered and accepted the defunct Waco, Texas, franchise in the new Dixie League. The circuit also counted teams in Jackson, Mississippi; Baton Rouge and Shreveport, Louisiana; Longview and Tyler, Texas; and El Dorado.

But by August 23, the Pine Bluff players went on strike because of an absence of pay. The team disbanded without finishing the season.

1934–1937: A Golden Era

The Judges, with crafty Lena Styles as their skipper, played a full season in the Dixie League in 1934. Pine Bluff won a second-half title but lost to Jackson in the pennant playoff.

Pine Bluff again reached the pennant series in 1935, only to bow to Jacksonville, Texas. But the highlight of the season was the arrival of one of Pine Bluff's most popular all-time players, outfielder Leroy L. "Cowboy" Jones, a McCall Creek, Mississippi, native and former member of the Washington Senators.

In 1936, the Cotton States League reorganized and Pine Bluff rejoined. Styles was traded away and Jones was named as his replacement.

Meanwhile, the Judges inked a working agreement with the St. Louis Cardinals. Branch Rickey, then president of the Cardinals organization, was saluted with a banquet in Pine Bluff.

The Judges failed to reach the playoffs, but the team's fans greatly enjoyed seeing Pine Bluff product Don Hutson play for the club. Hutson had just completed his All-American football eligibility with the University of Alabama and was waiting to begin his National Football League Hall of Fame career with the Green Bay Packers.

Jones remained on board for the 1937 season and steered the Judges to a league crown.

A New Park Is Spoiled by Old Troubles

Even though Jones returned as manager in 1938, the team stumbled as the Missouri Pacific Park fell into serious disrepair.

On July 17, Jones was swapped to Houston of the Texas League for .400 hitter Hugh Freah. Stanley Pintarell was named manager. Nothing seemed to help the club, which slid into the lower division.

For the 1939 campaign, Pine Bluff leader Pinchback Taylor donated land at East 16th Avenue and Kentucky Street. In appreciation, the site was named Taylor Field.

Mayor Jimmy McGaughy collected material from old buildings being razed in the downtown area and acquired an agreement for the federal Works Progress Administration (WPA) to construct a baseball stadium at Taylor Field.

Meanwhile, the Judges signed a new working agreement with the Brooklyn Dodgers, who brought in a new manager, Andy Cohen, after Pine Bluff got off to a slow start. But the Judges never recovered and the season was a flop.

Seeking a fresh start, the Judges dropped their working agreement with the Dodgers for the 1940 season. Club management made a bold move in attempting to lure Hall of Fame slugger Rogers Hornsby to manage the team, but he refused the offer.

Instead, Hornsby recommended 33-year-old W. Russell "Red" Rollings for the job. Rollings accepted the post. The Judges placed last in an eight-team race, and by season's end, attendance was so poor that professional baseball would not return to Pine Bluff until after World War II.

A New Beginning

In October 1947, the Pine Bluff Baseball Club was incorporated and stock was sold to the public. A developmental pact was made with the St. Louis Cardinals, and the local team was also called the Cardinals.

Left, Pine Bluff businessman Pinchback Taylor in 1940 deeded to the City of Pine Bluff property to be used as a baseball field. The federal Works Progress Administration constructed a stadium at East 16th Avenue and Florida Street. The field remains in use today, and in its 66 years has played host to major and minor league, semi-professional, college, high school and youth baseball.

The 1948 Pine Bluff Cardinals had some talented players, including future major leaguer Ted Lopat and Arkansas legend Ben "Rosie" Cantrell, but never learned to fly. The squad, first directed by Art Nelson and then Johnnie George, wound up sixth among eight teams.

In an expanded playoff system in 1949, the Cardinals managed to gain a post-season berth but were ousted in the first round. Underrated Harry Chozen was manager and Thomas "Lefty" Graham and Cantrell were key players and especially admired by the team's faithful.

Pine Bluff signed an agreement with the St. Louis Browns in 1950. The club dropped the Cardinals name and returned to Judges.

The Judges blended well with a good chemistry and won the regular-season crown before losing in the opening round of the playoffs. Chozen was obviously a wise manager and also contributed to the club's successes as a sound defensive catcher and .339 batter.

Cantrell and Graham were supported by outfielders Vic Fassero and John Ramm; infielders Harry Bollinger and Frank Scarpace; and Rinold Duren, a future New York Yankees World Series pitcher. Duren wore glasses that hinted of blindness and frightened opposing batters, often threw wide and wild pitches and unfortunately carried a passion for alcohol. All-in-all, he was downright scary both on and off the mound.

Cantrell was the lone returning player on the 1951 roster, and Chozen was succeeded by Bob Richards as manager. Centerfielder Freddie Boiko led the league with a .347 average. Bud Black and Don Harris were the top pitchers. Black would progress to the majors while Harris married Leah Hildreth of Pine Bluff and settled into the insurance business there.

The Judges lost in the opening round of the playoffs after finishing third in the regular season.

The 1952 season was a downer as Pine Bluff never made it out of the lower division. But the 1953 campaign saw a return to postseason play with a no-name lineup guided by new manager Frank Lucchesi, who would later direct the Chicago Cubs, Philadelphia Phillies and Texas Rangers. While with the Judges, Lucchesi married Mary Katherine Menotti of Pine Bluff.

The Browns became the Baltimore Orioles in 1954, but maintained the agreement with Pine Bluff. Lucchesi remained to manage a bland roster. The Judges missed the playoffs, tumbling to fifth.

The spiral continued into 1955, when Lucchesi left and was replaced by Bob Knoke. Attendance problems again struck the Judges, and on June 15, the Pine Bluff franchise was awarded to Meridian, Mississippi.

Four decades would pass before professional baseball returned to the city.

The Locomotives: Derailed Too Soon

Named for the city's long relationship with the railroad industry, the Pine Bluff Locomotives were organized in 1995 as a member of the Big South League.

The club, with Taylor Field as its home, assembled an impressive lineup that gave the city its first integrated professional team. As far as field management and player personnel were concerned, the Locomotives seemed on track from the start.

Regrettably, the team's business management was embarrassingly inept. The squad's initial field manager was fired despite a successful record. His sin? According to inside sources, team officials were upset because he was winning games more by defense than offense.

Late Pine Bluff historian James W. Leslie, who compiled an on-

going history of baseball here, couldn't bring himself to scribe on the Locomotives.

"Somebody else can write the history of that debacle," said Leslie. "If the management had been as good as the baseball players, the team might have survived longer."

Billy Bock didn't invent baseball, but he came mighty close to perfecting it. He was — and remains — Arkansas' most successful and well-known baseball coach. But he was recognized on a larger scale as well. "Collegiate Baseball" magazine declared him the National High School Baseball Coach of the Century (1900s).

Around Southeast Arkansas, honors like that fall into the category of "walking in high cotton."

The Pine Bluff High School (PBHS) legend was the American Baseball Coaches Association's National Coach of the Year in 1992, and his Coach of the Century award came after "Collegiate Baseball" had named him its National Coach of the Decade for the 1980s.

He came about those and many more achievements the old-fashioned way — he earned success. And along the way he imparted life lessons to his athletes, utilizing both imaginative ploys and straight-forward common sense

Left, Mr. Baseball —
Pine Bluff's Billy Bock.

in ensuring his brand of integrity and discipline would carry on to future generations.

When he died on July 8, 2003, many of those he had touched were unable to fight back their tears. It seemed as if activity within Pine Bluff was somehow draped. There was a real stillness, and a real air of sadness.

Billy Bock was a larger-than-life figure that one devotee described as "the most outstanding common man I've ever known." Off the baseball diamond, Bock was a warm, dedicated classroom teacher and an energetic community partner.

Bock was truly humble, and despite his many accomplishments, never adopted a superior attitude, although he certainly had an opportunity to do so.

He coached one or more sports a total of 44 years and never had a losing season. He taught baseball 30 years, winning a state-record nine state titles, notching 639 wins against 135 losses and amassing a state-record 38 consecutive victories. He won a record five consecutive state championships from 1982–1986.

During his 1983–2003 PBHS career, 90 of his PBHS players earned athletic scholarships. Several — including All-Star centerfielder Torii Hunter of the Minnesota Twins — became professionals. And from 1989–1991, the Texas Rangers of the American League had two PBHS products — John Barfield and Mike Jeffcoat — on their roster.

Bock, an outstanding athlete who excelled in team sports as well as boxing, was already a member of the University of the Ozarks Hall of Fame and Arkansas Sports Hall of Fame at the time of his death.

In January 2004, he was posthumously honored when he became only the 14th high school coach inducted into the American Baseball Coaches Association Hall of Fame.

Ezell Brown volunteered his coaching skills over the years.

Football in Bayou Country

Don Hutson worked for and achieved the status to which most others merely aspire before they surrender to and accept obstacles as limitations.

In his time, Hutson — who died in Rancho Mirage, California, at the age of 84 in 1997 — was, without question, foremost at his craft. He reigned so supreme above his challengers that he endures as a model to his successors, even though he retired just after World War II.

Hutson was professional football's marquee act during his 1935–1945 career with the Green Bay Packers. His impact on the game was of such power that it could legitimately be compared to the influence Babe Ruth spun on baseball.

Yes, Don Hutson was that imposing and that significant a figure. But the quiet Hutson's path to greatness was seemingly delivered at birth.

By his own admission, Hutson wasn't "that good a football player" at Pine Bluff High School. His early energies focused on baseball and Boy Scout activities. He excelled in the latter so as to become Arkansas' first Eagle Scout.

Hutson didn't play football as a sophomore in 1928 when the Zebras won a fourth consecutive state championship.

He joined the team in 1929, just as Fordyce started its renowned near-decade of state domination. The Zebras, meanwhile, began a decline with a lackluster 7–2–2 performance in which Hutson anchored the bench, failing to gain a letter.

The six-foot, 160-pound Hutson secured a starting berth as a senior, but he flashed only hints of the pass-catching ability that would finally erupt four years later at the University of Alabama and then carry him to charter membership in the National Football League's Hall of Fame.

Fordyce had no reason to fear Hutson and his PBHS teammates, however. The Redbugs, counting heralded left tackle Paul "Bear" Bryant in its star-studded lineup, thrashed the Zebras 50–12 enroute to a state title.

It was a friendship with Bryant that would present Hutson the opportunity necessary for Hutson to fulfill his promise.

Concluding an undefeated, national championship season, Alabama began recruiting several Fordyce and Pine Bluff players, centering on Bryant.

Hutson wasn't considered a prospect but wound up with an Alabama scholarship, along with Bryant and a handful of their teammates, in what might be best described as a "package deal."

Hutson was slow in impressing the Alabama coaches, playing sparingly as a freshman and sophomore. He didn't become a starter until late in his junior year.

His talent literally and unexpectedly exploded in 1934. Utilizing his deceptive 9.7 100-yard-dash speed to elude defenders, Hutson formed a feared, big-play combination with quarterback Dixie Howell. A "shuffling stride" earned Hutson a moniker as the "Alabama Antelope."

The Crimson Tide rolled to a Southeastern Conference championship at 9–0 and accepted an invitation to meet undefeated Stanford in the 1935 Rose Bowl.

Hutson caught six passes for 165 yards and two touchdowns as Alabama claimed the national title with a 29–13 triumph over the favored Indians (now Cardinal).

"I just ran like the devil and Dixie Howell got the ball there," said Hutson.

Certainly a late bloomer in high school and college, Hutson wasted no time in establishing himself as a professional.

On his first play as a Packer, he turned a quick over-the-middle pass from quarterback Arnie Herber into an 83-yard touchdown.

The NFL afforded Hutson a chance to showcase his skills package as he complemented his receiving talent by becoming a revered six-foot, one-inch, 180-pound tackler as well as a steady place-kicker and breakaway runner on end-around plays.

In his 11-year career, Hutson — who in 1935 and 1936 played minor league baseball in the Cincinnati Reds system — was All-NFL nine times. He led the league in receiving yardage, number of receptions and touchdown catches six, eight and nine seasons, respectively.

Hutson topped the NFL in scoring annually from 1940–1944 and amazingly tied for most interceptions in 1940. In a 57–21 Green Bay slaughter of Detroit in 1945, Hutson scored 31 points, including 29

No. 14 Don Hutson — simply the best in the business.

in the second quarter alone when he caught four touchdown passes and kicked five extra points.

He retired as the league's all-time leading scorer with 838 points. According to one source, Hutson, at one time or another, held over 100 single-play, period, game, season, playoff and career records.

His contribution to the Packer fortunes was immeasurable. With Hutson on its roster, Green Bay lost only 29 of 120 games and won five division and three league championships.

But Hutson's chief legacy may not be his success, but rather the conveyance of a simple lesson. In football, one is never more than a hundred yards away from his goal, but reaching it requires persistence.

Playing for Fun

They were known as the "Wandering Weevils."

From 1939–1941, the Arkansas Agricultural and Mechanical College (now the University of Arkansas at Monticello) Boll Weevils played football to such comical perfection that they were able to lose 30 of 33 games while not only pleasing their own fans,

An unknown football player.

"I want to be remembered by my players as a sort of fireside fool when they tell their children about the places they've been, the states they played in and the things they learned when they played football for Arkansas A&M. I want them to say, 'That Coach Ferguson was sort of a damn fool — didn't care much about whether we won, or lost. But, boy, the time we had!'"
— Stewart Ferguson

but while bringing laughter and enjoyment to football followers nationwide.

Stewart Ferguson was named coach at A&M in 1934, taking over a football program weakened by politics that resulted in the exit of long-time President Frank Horsfall.

The Weevils were downright pitiful, yielding 300 points while scoring just 13 and losing all eight of it games. In a stretch of six games, A&M was outscored 275–0.

Horsfall's replacement, Hugh Critz, kept Ferguson on staff as athletic director, dean of men, and a classroom instructor, but replaced him as coach with Eugene "Bo" Sherman, who was fired the previous year at Henderson State College (now University) in Arkadelphia after using ineligible players.

Sherman brought with him his philosophy that players need not be students, and when the program notched only four wins in three years, Sherman was shown the door by new A&M chief Marvin Bankston. The fact that Sherman's squad opened his final campaign with a 111–0 loss to Northeast Louisiana likely hastened his farewell.

The sport was on the verge of extinction at A&M. Trustees were tossing about a notion to drop the sport, but fate intervened.

Bankston figured Ferguson could, if nothing else, keep the program afloat for a while until it could stabilize. Ferguson had accepted a coaching post in Louisiana, but Bankston wouldn't stop his pursuit.

A&M Business Manager C. C. Smith was dispatched to Baton Rouge and charged with bringing Ferguson back to the Weevils. Ferguson refused, at least until he was offered a most unusual contract.

Ferguson was offered a $50 a month raise — quite a tidy sum at the time — and told he would be compensated not for coaching, but rather as an administrator and teacher. Furthermore, he wasn't required to win any games for three years, could do whatever he pleased within the athletic department and was advised that in lieu of coaching, all he had to do was "help out the football team when needed."

Ferguson couldn't refuse such an offer, but after accepting it realized he had been snookered a bit. "What was the difference in helping out the boys and actually coaching?" he later asked.

Ferguson took a conventional approach to the 1938 season. The result?

An 0–9 record in which the Boll Weevils tallied just 26 points while giving up 238. The team didn't score until its sixth game.

The future of the program was again at question. Football had become too expensive for A&M higher-ups, and Ferguson decided to make a bold move to save the sport.

First, he discontinued scholarships. Secondly, he dropped games with other Arkansas teams. Proclaiming his charges would perform simply for fun, he then scheduled contests with larger programs across the nation. The Weevils would receive bigger financial guarantees and the players would have travel opportunities they might otherwise never receive.

In the 1939 season, A&M played only two home games, losing to Louisiana College 29–6 and stunning previously-unbeaten Northeast Mississippi Junior College 26–6 for its only victory. The win angered some Weevil fans who had wagered against their team.

The Weevils traveled to Cleveland, Missouri, Philadelphia, Texas and West Virginia in gathering seven losses.

The following year, A&M played in California, New York, Pennsylvania and South Dakota while amassing a 2–9 record. The Weevils lost 79–0 at North Texas and 78–0 at Nevada-Reno in successive weeks and, just for good measure, surprised South Dakota Mines 26–7 and Northwest Mississippi Junior College 28–0.

The Weevils sported various uniforms, ranging from rainbow jerseys and pants to dress shirts, ties, overcoats and top hats. Substitutions would ride onto or off fields via a bicycle.

A&M players would leave a game to jam with the opposing school's band or enter the stands to flirt with girls. The Weevils would sometimes come within a yard or two of scoring, only to punt backward or create a play that allowed them to revert down the field with lateral passes.

The Great Depression had strained the outlooks of many Americans, but those fortunate enough to see the Wandering Weevils in action were able to forget their troubles for a time and enjoy the antics of the unpredictable Arkansans.

The team drew widespread media attention. A national magazine called the Weevils one of the "best attractions in college football."

For the 1940 season, Ferguson carefully planned the team's schedule so the team — which traveled in a tattered, green bus — could play within a mile of both the Atlantic and Pacific Oceans. Traveling over 10,000 miles, the team visited 17 states and over 100 colleges.

A&M players lunched with actress Constance Bennett and the mayor of Cleveland, met with Philadelphia Eagles football star Davey O'Brien and attended a World's Fair in New York. The Weevils also toured Hollywood and Las Vegas, walked across Revolutionary War and Civil War battlefields, saw the Grand Canyon and Boulder Dam, and met Roy Rogers and Betty Grable.

Along the way, Ferguson was involved in a bit of a scandal when he married his student secretary, 20-year-old Edna McAdam. Ferguson was twice her age.

Ferguson's Weevils were almost perfect in 1941, losing all of its 12 games, tallying just 25 points and yielding 513. Had A&M not scored in four contests, their performance would have been flawless.

A&M traveled to Alabama, North Carolina, New Jersey, Pennsylvania and West Virginia, bowing by such magnificent margins of 67–0 to Appalachian State and Bradley and 60–0 to Louisiana College and North Texas. Upsala scored only 19 points against A&M,

WANDERING WEEVILS

Among the players who comprised the Wandering Weevils were John T. Arnold, Boyd Arnold, Sam Bateman, Buell Bishop, Tunis Bishop, Coy Brown, Worth Bruner, Frank Carson, Pete Cheshier, Stanley Cheshier, Charles Colvin, Buddy Crook, J.R. Cubage, Oscar Dove, Terry Field, Beeny Gaston, Verl Gill, T.L. Godfrey, George Heroman, James Hill, Thomas Hooker, Eugene Jackson, Ira Jones, Collier Jordan, Lawrence Lavender, J.P. Leveritt, Robert Maskell, Ples McDonald, Teddy McKinney, Eddie McMillan, Loy Perry, Robert Potter, John Scritchfield, Paul Stegall, Ralph Stegall, Bix Stellwell, John Strange and George Tolson.

Southeast Arkansas' high school athletic teams have a winning tradition that has netted many state titles.

Here's an Arkansas Activities Association listing of the region's championship squads.

• FOOTBALL:

Dollarway — 1988, 1989, 1990, 1992 and 1993.

Fordyce — 1990 and 1991.

Jefferson Prep — 1981.

McGehee — 1969, 1984, 1987, 1988, 1989, 1998 and 1999.

Monticello — 1994.

Pine Bluff — 1951, 1962, 1963, 1977, 1990, 1993, 1994 and 1995.

Rison — 1950, 1970, 1982, 1990, 1991, 1995, 2000 and 2004.

Stuttgart — 1949, 1952, 1970, 1975, 1982 and 2002.

Warren — 2001 and 2002.

Watson Chapel — 1996.

• BOYS BASKETBALL:

Altheimer — 2003 and 2004.

Delta — 1987, 1989 and 1991.

Desha Central — 1969.

Dollarway — 2006.

Drew Central — 1975, 1978, 1983 and 1984.

Dumas — 1978, 1987, 1993 and 1994.

Grady — 1980.

Kingsland — 1992.

Monticello — 1963 and 1976.

Pine Bluff — 1923, 1924, 1926, 1928, 1933, 1934, 1935, 1952, 1977, 1979, 1990 and 2003.

Poyen — 2002.

Sheridan — 1958.

Star City — 1978 and 1990.

Stuttgart — 1914, 1915 and 1992.

Vaster — 1973.

Wabbaseka — 1986.

Warren — 1931.

Watson Chapel — 1999.

White Hall — 1966.

Wilmar — 1981.

• GIRLS BASKETBALL:

Altheimer — 1981.

Delta — 1993.

Drew Central — 1987.

Kingsland — 1990.

Pine Bluff _ 1995.

Star City — 1990.

• BASEBALL:

Pine Bluff — 1959, 1961, 1973, 1979, 1983, 1984, 1985, 1986, 1992 and 1995.

Warren — 2005.

Watson Chapel — 1988, 1991, 1996 and 2000.

White Hall — 1980.

• FAST-PITCH SOFTBALL:

Sheridan — 1999.

• BOYS CROSS COUNTRY:

Monticello — 1975.

Sheridan — 1993, 1994 and 1995.

• BOYS TRACK:

Altheimer — 1978.

Dollarway — 1990.

Dumas — 1953.

Fordyce — 1959, 1960 and 1967.

Gould — 1971.

McGehee — 1963, 1987 and 1988.

Pine Bluff — 1971, 1974, 1975, 1981, 1982, 1983, 1985, 1986, 1987, 1988, 1990, 1997, 1998, 2000 and 2001.

Rison — 1970.

Sheridan — 1995 and 1996.

Warren — 1994.

• GIRLS TRACK:

DeWitt — 1981.

Fordyce — 1984 and 1986.

Pine Bluff — 1981, 1982, 1983, 1984, 2001 and 2002.

Rison — 1979, 1980, 1981, 1985, 1986, 1987 and 2002.

Sheridan — 1994 and 1995.

Star City — 1987 and 1988.

Warren — 1992 and 1994.

Watson Chapel — 1996, 1998, 1999, 2001 and 2002.

• BOYS SWIMMING:

Drew Central — 1968 and 1969.

Warren — 1959, 1960, 1961, 1962, 1963 and 1964.

• BOYS GOLF:

Dollarway — 1960.

Dumas — 1959.

Fordyce — 1963, 1964 and 1965.

Jefferson Prep — 1985 and 1986.

McGehee — 1966, 1988 and 1998.

Monticello — 1953.

Pine Bluff — 1972 and 1983.

• GIRLS GOLF:

White Hall — 2004.

• BOYS TENNIS:

Fordyce — 1968 and 1971.

McGehee — 1968, 1970, 1980, 1985 and 1987.

Pine Bluff — 1971, 1972 and 1983.

• GIRLS TENNIS:

Drew Central — 2000.

Pine Bluff — 1971, 1976, 1979 and 1980.

Pine Bluff St. Joseph's — 2001, 2002 and 2003.

Warren — 1993.

---

but the Weevils averted complete embarrassment by posting just six points themselves.

What would be the final appearance of the Wandering Weevils occurred on Thanksgiving day, November 27, at Monticello versus Southern Arkansas. The Muleriders were victorious by a 25–7 count.

Less than two weeks later, Japan bombed Pearl Harbor and America entered World War II.

Because of the war, football was not played at A&M in 1942. Meanwhile, Ferguson departed for service in the Navy, and most of his players also entered the military.

In 1944, Ferguson returned to civilian life and settled in South Dakota, where he became coach at Deadwood High School. For the next dozen years, he never had a losing season. He suffered a fatal heart attack at the age of 55 on December 29, 1955.

Back in Monticello, football took a drastic turn when the program was renewed for the 1943 season. Because of the war, a Navy/Marine Corps officer training program was initiated at A&M, and some former big-time players from such universities as Arkansas, Oklahoma and Ole Miss found themselves in Monticello preparing for war duties.

In their opening game, the Weevils — who over the past nine years had won but seven games against 64 losses and scored just 311 points while surrendering 3,046 — traveled to Fayetteville for a date with the state's premier team, the Razorbacks.

A&M won 20–12.

A unknown player in position.

Right, the DeWitt Dragons 1959 football schedule.

DeWitt Dragons
1959 FOOTBALL SCHEDULE

Sept.	11	Dumas	T
Sept.	18	Forrest City	T
Sept.	25	England	T
Oct.	2	Stuttgart	T
Oct.	9	Jacksonville	T
Oct.	16	Helena	H
Oct.	23	Marianna	T
Oct.	30	Des Arc	H
Nov.	6	Batesville	T
Nov.	13	Brinkley	H
Nov.	20	DeQueen	H

HOME GAMES BEGIN AT 8:00 P. M. EXCEPT
NOVEMBER GAMES WHICH WILL BEGIN AT 7:30 P. M.

ADMISSION
Adults .... $1.00   Students 25c

JUNIOR DRAGON SCHEDULE

Sept. 12	Des Arc	H	Oct. 15	Dial (P. B.)	H
Sept. 17	Open		Oct. 22	Helena	T
Sept. 24	Dumas	H	Nov. 4	Forrest City	H
Sept. 29	Stuttgart	T			

R. W. DUDLEY HARDWARE
FRIGIDAIRE APPLIANCES

Metcalf & Carter Welding
Insurance Department DeWitt Bank & Trust Co.
DeWitt Hotel
Barnes Studio Photographers
The Domino Parlor Merle and Jess
Neal's Esso Station Phone WH 6-2271
New Theatre DeWitt and Gillett
Sportsman Stop Phone WH 6-2904
Phillips Petroleum Co. WH 6-5201 Pete Miller
A. R. Thorell Supply Co.
Ruddy's Welding Shop Phone WH 6-2803
Cockrum Motors Rambler — GMC Trucks Phone WH 6-2215
Rousseau Grocer Co. DeWitt, Ark.
J. C. Varnadore Dirt Moving
W. C. Merritt Esso Products
Davis Mobilgas Station Phone WH 6-5766
Harold L. Stephenson "Your Life Insurance Man"
Graves Electric Co. Telephone WH 6-2974
Rollison Elevator
Raines Star Cleaners Ph. WH 6-2131 DeWitt
Jim & Gladys Colvert
Hibbard Service Station We Honor All Credit Cards Phone WH 6-4201 DeWitt
OutBoard Motors Simpson Repair Shop & Lawn Mowers
Ted Danner Phone WH 6-4435
Johnson Machinery Co. Phone WH 6-4621 DeWitt
Adams Motor Co. Studebaker & Willys Phone WH 6-2812
Crow-Burlingame Phone WH 6-42 DeWitt
Trussell Plumbing Co. Phone WH 6-4411 DeWitt

LAYNE-ARKANSAS CO. Phone WH 6-5458 DeWitt, Ark.
HAMPTON DRUG CO. Phone WH 6-2381
ROSS ELECTRIC CO. Jewelry and Appliances Phone WH 6-4425
FIGHT 'EM DRAGONS
SCHALLHORN HARDWARE Phone WH 6-5111 DeWitt, Ark.
FERGUSON CASH GROCERY Phones WH 6-4291 & WH 6-2311
SIMPSON CHEVROLET CO.
ARKANSAS PETROLEUM INC. DeWitt, Arkansas
SMITH RICE MILL INC.

First National Bank Serving County and Community Since 1912
All-State Insurance W. H. Davis Jr.

DeWitt Bank & Trust Co. "Always At Your Service"
Cash-Way Grocery Backing The Dragons

C. W. Gilbert Colonial Bread Is Good Bread
Lelbrock Firestone Store
C. J. Shackelford Locker Plant
Scougale's
DeWitt Auto Supply Phones WH 6-5213 & WH 6-5351
DeWitt Cleaners Phone WH 6-2301
Chambers Machinery Co. Allis Chalmers Phone WH 6-4371
Gene's Palace
Busy Dept. Store Phone WH 6-2415
Gordon Motel & Coffee Shop Phone WH 6-6588
We Fit The Entire Family Young's Dept. Store Phone WH 6-4311
DeWitt Furniture Co. Phone WH 6-3301
Carroll & Chick Barber Shop On Little Broadway
DeWitt Publishing Co. Phone WH 6-3241
Baxter Brown Knit Wear Lorick's Store Phone WH 6-4163
DeWitt Bargain Store Phone WH 6-5590
McGahhey Hardware Phone WH 6-4487 DeWitt
Young's Market Phone WH 6-3325
Ruffin's Electric Service Phone WH 6-6193
Jones' Butane, Inc. Cities Service Products Phone WH 6-3161
FIBBER 5 & 10 McGHIE
Hamilton Radio-Television Phone WH 6-2351
First In Service Chas. L. Pattillo Ins. Agcy. Long Term Farm Loans
Dixie Drier
R. C. A. Television —See— Ed Mocry
Cities Service Station Phone WH 6-6976 Son Ellenburg
Zero Butane Lynn Burton
DeWitt Auction Co. Sale Every Saturday Phone WH 6-2392

L. A. BLACK HARDWARE Your John Deere Dealer
DEWITT REXALL DRUG STORE Phone WH 6-4221
DEWITT INSURANCE AGENCY Fire — Casualty — Marine Phone WH 6-3171
THE FARMERS CO-OP. ELEVATOR CO. Drying — Cleaning — Storage Loading — Storage Fertilizer Phone WH 6-2331 DeWitt
RICE BELT PRODUCE & FEED CO. Purina Chows
STEPHENSON FORD SALES, INC. Your Ford Dealer
DEWITT IMPLEMENTS, INC. Phone WH 6-2371 DeWitt, Ark.
J. W. PORTER LUMBER CO. Phone WH 6-2251

Once Upon a Time, There Was a Basketball Team . . .

The almost unbelievable story of the Vaster High School boys basketball team of 1972–1973 could easily be fashioned as a fairy tale.

Moscow, a tiny town about 11 miles south of Pine Bluff, then counted about 650 residents. Its population has since dwindled and the town no longer has any schools, but for a while Moscow was the home of Vaster High School, where the Pirate basketball team provided the area's primary entertainment.

In the 1971–1972 season, Vaster — coached by Herbert Pryor — had a young but deeply talented team that some figured might win the championship of the state's lowest school competition level, Class B.

The Pirates sailed to a conference crown, but wound up losing to Menifee in the semifinals of the Class B state tournament.

The entire team was back for the 1972–1973 campaign, and the Pirates and their fans in the one-sport town all but declared themselves state champs even before the season started.

Vaster — paced by Sam Biley, a reliable shooter and skilled floor leader — breezed to the Class B title game and won the crown with a 76–61 decision over Fountain Hill.

The championship tilt was almost an all-Jefferson County affair, but Wabbaseka had bowed to Fountain Hill 64–61 in a semifinal match.

In those days, the champion of each classification participated in a secondary tournament that determined an overall state title. As expected, larger schools had dominated the overall bouts.

But Vaster ignored tradition and nearly added a new chapter to the David versus Goliath story line.

In the opening round of the overall, the Pirates stunned Class AA champion Morrilton 73–64. Vaster trailed 50–44 after the third quarter, but out-scored the Devil Dogs 29–14 in the final period to take the comeback win.

Morrilton finished the year at 37–3.

In a semifinal, the Pirates pulled off a 62–61 upset over a strong Conway team that featured future University of Arkansas Razorback standout Marvin Delph. Conway, the Class AAA champion, settled at 28–6.

Next up for the Pirates was an overall title game against powerful Little Rock Central, which boasted of 6–10 scoring machine and defensive wizard Lanky Wells.

Central was an overwhelming favorite, but somebody forgot to tell the Pirates they weren't supposed to challenge the Tigers.

Vaster gave Central all it wanted and then some, as the Pirates staked a 36–31 halftime command.

Central, with a much deeper bench, wore down Vaster in the third quarter. The Tigers led 57–50 heading into the final round.

The Pirates, however, refused to yield. The Tigers were scared but averted embarrassment by hanging on for a 75–74 victory.

Central's final record was 29–6. Vaster finished 41–6. Sam Biley's chief teammates were Erick Biley, Carl Evans, James Evans and Homer Jackson.

Left, souvenir pin for Razorback Basketball 1980-1981.

Right, Pine Bluff Junior High School's 1935 team claimed the state championship.

..ler, Robt. Hutson, H. Rames, T. Leftwich, N. Langston, ... Young, C. Langley, B. Leftwich, R. O'Neil, —
J. Bush, Maurice McPhail, J.C. Piper, R. Silverthorn, T.D. Davis, Malcomb McPhail, Raymond Hutson, J. Stalworth —
W. Odgleen, ... Culpepper, R.C. Rivers, S. Eubanks, B. Palmer, J.D. Cunningham, M. Oden, E. Atkinson —
James "Red" King
State Jr. High Champions — 1935.

In 1984 the Arkansas basketball Razorbacks, coached by Eddie Sutton, came to the Pine Bluff Convention Center and upset the No. 1 team in the country, North Carolina. The win was considered by many as the biggest in the Razorback program until Arkansas won a national championship with a victory over top-rated Duke a decade later.

RAZORBACK BASKETBALL

ONE DOLLAR

ARKANSAS VS. NORTH CAROLINA
Feb. 12, 1984
PINE BLUFF C.C.

The Sport of Kings in Southeast Arkansas

Thoroughbred horse racing was an entertainment staple in the Pine Bluff area a full generation before Hot Springs' Oaklawn Park, long one of the nation's finest tracks, began operations in 1905.

The sport reached its zenith in Southeast Arkansas in the 1880s and 1890s. Possibly the best two racing locations in the region were Jones Park Track, within a 55-acre tract in the southeastern section of Pine Bluff, and a widely-hailed but nameless facility at Varner in neighboring Lincoln County.

The track owners respected one another as devoted racing partisans and also successful farmers and businessmen. Both were known for their civic involvement and political leadership.

But they also engendered a unique paradox, as one was born a slave to a black mother, impregnated by her white master, while the other arrived with privilege as a white son of a wealthy, white plantation owner.

Wiley Jones was born in Madison County, Georgia, on July 14, 1848. His mother, Ann, was a servant to his father, planter George Jones. Wiley Jones migrated to Pine Bluff after the Civil War, barely earning his keep as a barber and working for food as a waiter in a hotel eatery.

But Jones developed and put to practice a keen business sense. Some believe he was the state's first black millionaire. That figuring is likely a salutatory overestimation of his monetary worth, but nevertheless he was almost certainly Arkansas' richest black at the time of his death on December 7, 1904.

Jones initiated his financial climb by establishing a saloon at 207 Main Street. Under his management, the tavern soon became one of the city's most popular gathering places. Steady profits gave Jones the funds he needed to begin amassing his wealth through real estate and expanded commercial ventures.

He and a white business partner, Edward B. Houston, developed White Sulphur Springs, a profitable resort area southwest of Pine Bluff. Jones' moneymaking abilities netted him political influence as well, and he attended several national Republican conventions as a state delegate.

Wiley Jones founded a horse-drawn streetcar system in Pine Bluff.

After founding Pine Bluff's first streetcar line in 1886, he purchased the land for and constructed the park that bore his name and featured a racetrack complete with covered grandstands.

The park was later sold and cleared for the building of several housing subdivisions.

Jones, who never married, had but one hobby — breeding thoroughbred racehorses. He owned up to 25, quartering them in several stables and training them on pastures at his Pine Grove Farm on the eastern side of Pine Bluff. His favorite racer was Executor, a consistent winner that was considered one of the most well-proportioned thoroughbreds in the state.

Awaiting the start of a 1907 parade on Barraque Street are two Pine Bluff Fire Department-manned horse-drawn wagons and, accompanied by a well-dressed guide, two youngsters in a pony-drawn, flower-covered cart.

Robert Ritchie Rice II, born in the Lincoln County village of Auburn on December 27, 1849, built the Varner track. He married Medora S. Varner, a daughter of William Felix Varner, a Georgia native who was among Lincoln County's pioneer settlers and for whom the town of Varner was named. Medora Varner Rice was born on March 2, 1861.

The Rice and Varner landholdings were big and bountiful, so when marriage joined the families, the result was a plantation partnership that easily numbered among the state's largest and most lucrative agricultural enterprises.

Rice, who served as Lincoln County's sheriff from 1875–1876 and was a close advisor to Democratic Governor (1901–1906) and U.S. Senator (1907–1913) Jeff Davis, was a noted sportsman. He meticulously tended to a pack of hunting dogs that numbered over 100, and gained a reputation as one of the South's craftiest hunters of bears and deer.

But, as it did with Jones, racing rated as Rice's preferred pastime. Rice spared no expense in erecting an impressive track on a segment of his estate, and in July 1889, hosted a well-attended inaugural racing competition.

The track was described in news accounts of the time as "modern" and "well-constructed." Patrons appreciated the comfort it afforded spectators.

Rice put together a remarkably talented collection of racehorses that rightfully received some national regard.

According to one commentary, which may have been somewhat padded in its praise, Rice's chief stable stars were Wax Taper, "considered the greatest horse on the turf of his day," and W.B. Gates, which "won more races than any other horse ever won on the American turf, coming out first in 105 different races." Another of his charges, Francis Pape, gave Rice a Mexican Derby trophy.

Among Rice's other top performers were Chimes, Revenue and Ritful.

Robert Ritchie Rice II died on January 9, 1918. Medora Varner Rice died on December 26, 1949.

Daredevil Jumps to Re-finish

Garland "Buddy" Rhodes would always "jump" at an opportunity to entertain others.

The Stuttgart daredevil was admired and respected as an aerial acrobat who risked life and limb to please his gasping fans. A member of a pioneering aviation family, he started his career in 1921 with a Yates Flying Circus performance in New Mexico, and then returned to Stuttgart and worked with local pilots as a wing walker.

Before long, he was touring the country and headlining all sorts of events, expanding his act to include hanging by a leg from a plane as it flew over a mesmerized crowd. Then he would spellbound onlookers by climbing a rope ladder to another plane as it flew over.

Cheating death provided Rhodes with "pleasure" and he relished the uniqueness of his "art."

Constantly devising new stunts to thrill his followers, Rhodes decided to stage a record-setting performance at a March 15, 1931, air extravaganza at Little Rock's Adams Field. A then-record crowd had gathered and Rhodes was intent on being the star of the show.

He instructed the pilot of a bi-plane in which he was a passenger to fly to a level of 19,500 feet — the highest elevation ever achieved by a local plane.

Although the altitude dizzied Rhodes, he maintained proper circulation by slapping his fists against his chest.

As the pilot initiated an ascent, Rhodes' 20-foot auxiliary parachute accidentally opened. The pilot immediately began a maneuver for a descent to a landing, but Rhodes waved him off, holding true to the old entertainment adage of, "The show must go on."

Rhodes clung to the yet-unfurled parachute as he exited the plane, falling around 13,000 feet before finally allowing the parachute to fully activate so that it would ease his dive toward the ground just enough to keep him from injury.

Rhodes landed with a coarse stumble and roll in a field near the airport, but bounced up in sound condition and received a bouquet of flowers from Lois Hudson, Arkansas' first woman parachutist.

The audience's cheering was just the medicine Rhodes needed to soothe his bumps and bruises as he savored the moment — he had just completed the longest-known delayed parachute jump ever.

The ever-unpredictable Rhodes then did something totally unexpected.

He retired.

It was a smart decision, because he walked away from his profession not only while he was still able to walk, but also when he was at the absolute top of his business. And that's the kind of stuff from which legends are made.

He would soon become well-known and appreciated for his new livelihood — furniture refinishing. By the time of his 1987 death, he would be considered one of Southeast Arkansas' most skilled refinishers. Furniture refinishing certainly wasn't as thrilling as aerial acrobatics, but Rhodes managed to make the business every bit as much an art as his daredevil episodes had been.

Other Ways to Pass a Good Time

Readying for a 1917 parade are members of the Pine Bluff Fire Department with the agency's new, top-of-the-line fire truck. Although its attention is focused elsewhere, the department's dog — Timberwolf — is aboard, too.

Doug Mahle is behind the wheel and Lee J. MacDonald Jr. is his passenger as the two show off Stuttgart's first fire truck in 1916. The vehicle was proudly and frequently displayed in parades and other public gatherings.

The Stuttgart Ad (Associated Advertising) Club (of America) Band not only looked sharp and played well, but also was always ready to put some pizzazz into any function.

Buddy Deane, a Pine Bluff radio personality and businessman who promoted himself as the city's "morning mayor" during his daily radio shows, rides an elephant along Main Street during a Barnum and Bailey Circus parade on July 4, 1976. Later that day, the circus was the opening entertainment at the Pine Bluff Convention Center, which had an initial cost of nearly $6 million.

Harold S. Seabrook spent much of his boyhood involved in activities at Pine Bluff's Merrill Institute, a recreational facility for white youth. The Merrill Institute eventually became the Young Men's Christian Association. In 1957, Seabrook donated property at Ninth Avenue and Mulberry Street for a new Pine Bluff Boys Club. The facility later became the Seabrook YMCA, which is now located on Hazel Street and open to all youth.

Will Rogers, who visited Pine Bluff and other towns in Southeast Arkansas on several occasions, was a marquee entertainer, as this early 1930s photo of a Pine Bluff theater shows.

SOUTH BEND—*A Name Famous in Fishing*

No.40
ORENO

LEVEL
WINDING

CASTING
REEL

YOU RISK NOTHING

Take
Along
Some
FISH-OBITES

INSURED TO CATCH FISH

MOLDED OF
TENITE

INSURED
To Catch Fish!

A lazy day on Bayou Bartholomew is always good for fun.

Left, an old fishing reel.

CHAPTER THIRTEEN

Celebrities and Difference Makers

Edith Mae Patterson of Pine Bluff was blessed with an angelic face and a heavenly body. But after initiating the Hollywood movie career for which she seemed almost destined, she moved from in front of the cameras to behind a pulpit in a dramatic change of direction. And she remained devoted to her ministry, which largely defined the last 48 years of her life, until her death at age 71 on May 16, 1974.

The Country's Prettiest Girl

Born here on June 9, 1902, to Archie and Julia Denham Patterson, Edith Mae became a national celebrity overnight when she won a 1921 *St. Louis Globe Democrat* contest as the nation's prettiest girl. The competition was a prelude to the annual Miss America Pageant, which began the following year.

But Edith Mae did not enter herself into the event. Instead, a relative, without her knowledge, sent the newspaper a photograph of Edith Mae and placed her into a field of 7,000 hopefuls, according to a 1922 account.

The field was trimmed to 50 finalists, who traveled to St. Louis individually to appear before the contest's three judges (two paint artists and a sculptress). The panel unanimously selected Edith Mae for the title, plus a $3,500 grand prize. The announcement stirred a wave of pride across Arkansas.

Edith Mae's beauty drew comparisons to the exquisiteness of Elizabeth Patterson of Maryland. An ancestor of Edith Mae's father, Elizabeth Patterson had been hailed as perhaps the most beautiful woman in America at the time of her December 24, 1803, marriage to Jerome Bonaparte, brother of French leader Napoleon Bonaparte.

Instantly after winning the *Globe Democrat* contest, Edith Mae began receiving invitations to appear and sometimes speak at events throughout the state. Theater and movie agents dispatched telegrams expressing their interests in possibly signing her to entertainment contracts.

While such feverish fanfare would likely detract most from focusing on educational pursuits, Edith Mae's mother made certain her daughter remained on a timely and realistic course. Julia Denham Patterson had instilled in Edith Mae the values of Christian principles and the importance of continuing the integrity of the Denham and Patterson families.

Edith Mae appeared at a number of functions, but was never out of reach of her mother's guidance.

From Teaching to the Theater

After graduating from Pine Bluff High School, Edith Mae earned a degree at Rice University in Houston and returned to her hometown to commence what she figured might be a career as a classroom teacher.

But the public's interest in the beauty queen hadn't waned, and she was still inundated with appearance requests and theatrical and movie offers. She soon exited the classroom and developed an act, giving performances as an "added attraction" at 101 theaters throughout the country in just a year.

She received immediate status in the leading social circles of the era. Her activities were highly publicized and she was presented honorary citizenships in and ceremonial keys to a number of cities in welcoming ceremonies hosted by mayors and other politicians. She was honored by assorted interests with banquets and other gatherings.

And she soon longed for a change that would give her less demand on her time and more privacy and enjoyment in her personal life.

Onward to Hollywood

Edith Mae decided to leave the theater circuit and explore the Hollywood movie offers she had previously rejected. Her mother accompanied her on the westward venture.

Edith Mae was warmly received and movie opportunities came quickly. Directors found her to be a natural actress, and it seemed she might well be headed for stardom.

But her Pine Bluff, small-town attributes clashed with the lifestyles of many of Hollywood's leading performers, producers and directors. She found herself uncomfortable with and unable to accept the drinking, doping and sexual escapades that were common within the movie industry.

It was a particularly ugly period in Hollywood history.

A leading actor, Wallace Reid, became the first marquee star to succumb to a publicized drug addiction. Paramount Studios managed to keep Reid's morphine habit secret for some time, but finally leveled with fans when it became evident that Reid was nearing death.

Comic Fatty Arbuckle's trial in the sexually charged death of party girl Virginia Rappe received national media coverage, and even though the 330-pound, heavy-drinking Arbuckle was cleared of any wrongdoing, opposing public judgment ended his career.

William Desmond Taylor, a top director, was murdered in his sprawling home. Despite Paramount's best efforts to paint Taylor as a likely victim of a jealous boyfriend or husband of one of an untold number of rising starlets or established actresses supposedly among his conquests, the truth emerged. In reality, Taylor lusted for young boys. But, at the time, such subjects weren't discussed publicly and the media was slow in even approaching matters of the sort.

The blatant immorality disgusted Edith Mae, who began to see what she described as the fallacy of so-called Hollywood glamour. She wished for a more meaningful, satisfying and fulfilling life.

Finding Her Purpose

Edith Mae determined the time had come to find the contentment that had eluded her.

She fell in love with her business manager, Jesse Battle Pennington,

and married him in 1924. The following year, in a Pentecostal Holiness church in Oklahoma City, she made a public profession of faith, and following her baptism, announced she had accepted a call to the ministry.

On November 23, 1927, Edith Mae Pennington gave birth to her only child, daughter Edith Lorraine Pennington. In 1929, Edith Mae was licensed and ordained as a minister by the Assemblies of God denomination. Over the ensuing seven years, she served as an evangelist throughout the United States and Canada.

In 1936, she held a tent revival in Shreveport, Lousiana. She returned to the city in 1937 for another revival, and decided to stay. She believed God wanted her to establish and pastor a church there.

She soon founded the Full Gospel Tabernacle, which was renamed as the Full Gospel Temple in 1943. Her only sibling, brother Marvin Weber Patterson, joined the church as associate pastor, serving until his death in 1963.

Edith Mae remained affiliated with the Assemblies of God denomination until 1950, when she reorganized the church into the "The Plant of Renown," an interdenominational order focusing on "worldwide revival in the last days." Edith Lorraine Pennington assumed the ministry upon her mother's death.

The church was still functioning when this book was published.

Big Bill Was a Happy Man

William Lee Conley "Big Bill" Broonzy, who died in Chicago in 1958, was so content as a bluesman, drinker and womanizer that he provided specific instructions to those who might wish to write of his life and career.

"When you write about me, please don't say I'm a jazz musician," Broonzy, who established residency as a sharecropper near Pine Bluff in 1905 and first performed professionally there a short time later, wrote in notes eventually employed in a 1992 biography.

"Don't say I'm a musician or a guitar player," he continued. "Just write that 'Big Bill' was a well-known blues singer and player and has recorded 260 blues songs from 1925 up till 1952. He was a happy man when he was drunk and playing with women. He was liked by all the blues singers. Some would get a little jealous sometimes, but Bill would buy a bottle of whiskey and they would all start laughing and playing again."

Broonzy obviously took himself and his many musical skills rather lightly, but the fact is that his wide-ranging abilities as a violinist, guitarist, singer and songwriter that spanned across the gospel, blues, folk, rock and even country music genres have rightfully given him legendary status.

Broonzy, a native of Scott, Mississippi, claimed he was born in 1893, but the year is open to debate. His twin sister, Lannie Broonzy, said they were actually born in 1898. Most researchers figure Big Bill Broonzy added five years to his actual age, as it was common for black men to do in order to obtain better jobs or join the military during the era of his youth.

What is certain, however, is that Broonzy's appreciation of music began when he was a child, and he began developing his own musical talents when he arrived in Jefferson County. Broonzy — trained by Jerry Belcher, a maternal uncle — became a fiddler, or violinist. He was soon displaying his abilities at church and community gatherings as well as country dances here, gleefully discovering his new pastime could put cash in his pockets.

He received little formal education before quitting school to focus on providing for his family. He and Lannie were but two of the 18 children born to Frank and Mittie Belcher Broonzy.

Although his religious zeal would eventually fade, Big Bill Broonzy began combining preaching with his gospel music in 1912, a move that likely benefited him well as he immediately increased his opportunities to obtain financial offerings from his congregations. His earnings allowed him to purchase nice suits and a quality violin, further heightening his moneymaking potential in music as he continued to work primarily as a sharecropper.

After serving with the Army in World War I, he returned to Arkansas. He had decided farming wouldn't be his life's ambition, so he began expanding his music career by performing at clubs in Pine Bluff and Little Rock.

By 1920, he had left the farm for good and moved to Chicago, but still had to work as a janitor for almost a decade before he finally became able to attain a full livelihood as a musician.

It was in Chicago that Broonzy learned to play the guitar, under the guidance of highly regarded blues guitarist Papa Charlie Jackson. In 1928, Broonzy scored a hit with the signature tune "Big Bill's Blues," and only two years shy of a decade since arriving in the city, Broonzy was an "overnight success" in Chicago.

Broonzy's dedication and persistence had, at last, begun delivering big dividends.

Employing new electric instruments, Broonzy became a pioneer in the musical style known as Chicago Blues. He honed his own musical fashion, however, by combining Delta and Chicago Blues with jazz, gospel and folk music. He wrote a number of simplistic blues tunes that were uniquely conveyed with his unusual and often improvised guitar techniques.

Broonzy was credited with giving especially entertaining and memorable performances.

During much of the 1930s, he was a member of Memphis Minnie's traveling blues show.

In 1938, he played at New York's Carnegie Hall in John Hammond's famous "Spirituals to Swing" concerts. Broonzy remained in the show when it appeared in Africa, Australia, England, Europe and South America.

Broonzy continued touring until 1957, when throat cancer finally forced his retirement. Most of his late recordings were made in Europe, where he ventured into country music and also found fresh acclaim in blues circles as his star in America faded a bit behind a bevy of new performers.

During his career, Broonzy recorded over 350 compositions for the American Recording Corporation, Vocalion Records, Columbia Records and Mercury Records.

Inducted into the Blues Foundation Hall of Fame in 1980, he wrote and initially recorded the well-known "C. C. Rider." Another of his better-known songs is "Night Time Is the Right Time."

Broonzy was always fond of and sensitive to his Arkansas relatives and friends. Inspired by the Great Flood of 1927, which struck Southeast Arkansas extremely hard, he penned two songs, "Southern Flood Blues" and "Back Water Blues."

He later paid tribute to and recalled his association with the state with a song entitled "Back to Arkansas."

Mick Jagger of The Rolling Stones, the English rock band that began performing in the 1960s, has pointed to Broonzy as being one of the group's primary influences.

Jeremy Anderson

Notable Lives

JEREMY ANDERSON of Pine Bluff — A 1997 graduate of Watson Chapel High School, where his powerful bat helped lead the Wildcat baseball team to the 1996 state championship, he was an All-World Team performer for the Pine Bluff team in the 15-year-old Babe Ruth World Series in 1994. He was progressing toward professional baseball when he died in a tragic automobile accident in 2000.

HELON H. ARLITT of Pine Bluff — The first woman pilot in Jefferson County and one of the first in the state, she was known for her physical beauty as well as her skills as a flyer.

GILBERT ARONSON of Pine Bluff — Better known as Broncho Billy Anderson, he was the movies' first cowboy star, appearing in more than 400 movies. He was the headliner in the 1903 motion picture classic *The Great Train Robbery* and received an honorary Oscar in 1957.

M.L. BELL and **W.P. GRACE** of Pine Bluff and **W.T. WELLS** of Monticello — As three of Southeast Arkansas' leading pioneer attorneys, the trio attended the 1882 organizational meeting of the Arkansas Bar Association in Little Rock. Bell was elected president and Grace and Wells were picked as vice presidents.

LOUISE M. BOWKER of DeWitt — The first female member of the Arkansas Press Association (APA) and first female president of the National Press Association, she wound up serving 17 years as the APA's director.

LAWRENCE BLACKWELL of Pine Bluff — Pine Bluff mayor from 1940–1943, he led the city at the start of World War II and is credited with producing many positive changes, along with his efforts to secure Grider Field as a pilot training facility.

DR. AUGUSTUS LOUIS BREYSACHER of Pine Bluff — Born in Ohio, the chemist/pharmacist/physician practiced medicine in Pine Bluff for several years in the 1860s and 1870s. But it was in Little Rock on January 26, 1880, when he scored his biggest achievement, delivering a baby at the Little Rock Army Arsenal. The newborn was future General Douglas MacArthur.

PAUL "BEAR" BRYANT of Fordyce — After earning his nickname by wrestling — and defeating — a bear in a promotion at a Fordyce theater, he became one of the nation's most successful football coaches and won five national championships at the University of Alabama.

ROGER BURKS of Warren — A gifted musician, Burks roomed in Nashville with Waylon Jennings and Johnny Cash while considering a career in country music. He wound up returning home and retired as executive vice president and advertising director of The Mad Butcher food store chain.

HATTIE CARAWAY of Jonesboro and **HUEY P. "THE KINGFISH" LONG** of Louisiana — In 1932, Senator Caraway (she succeeded her husband when he died) became the first woman elected to the U.S. Senate, thanks in large part to Senator Long of Louisiana. Long joined Caraway, a decided underdog, for a successful, whirlwind campaign that included stops in Pine Bluff and other spots in Southeast Arkansas. Caraway would serve until 1945. Long would be assassinated in 1935.

JOHNNY CASH of Kingsland — During his remarkable career, the singer/songwriter/musician/actor/author had No. 1 recording hits in six decades. In 2003, Country Music Television proclaimed him the "Greatest Man in Country Music." During a 1969 concert in New York City, he performed a song entitled "Five Foot High and Rising," telling his audience that he was inspired to write the number by memories of his father transporting his family to "higher ground in Pine Bluff" during a flood at Kingsland.

Country singer Johnny Cash, who spent part of his childhood at Kingsland (standing) and his wife June Carter Cash (in hat) made a trip to Fordyce in 1982 to participate in a parade as part of the city's annual Fordyce on the Cotton Belt Festival.

EARL CHADICK of near Sherrill — A self-described "ruffian" in his younger days, he became a Methodist minister and then served as county judge from 1979–1987. Noted for his kindness, genuine concern and fast response to requests, he ranks among the county's all-time most-beloved public servants.

FLORENE OAKS CHADICK of near Sherrill — The wife of Jefferson County Judge Earl Chadick, she served in the post herself for 10 months following the March 18, 1987, death of her husband. She later served on the Jefferson County Quorum Court.

JANET CHANDLER of Pine Bluff — Born Lillian Elizabeth Guenther in Pine Bluff, she became a Hollywood actress in the early 1920s and continued making movies until the mid-1930s when a film accident prompted her retirement at the age of 24.

ELDRIDGE CLEAVER of Wabbaseka — A writer and convicted rapist, he was a leader in the radical Black Panther civil rights movement of the 1960s. Late in life, he became a conservative Republican.

DR. MOSES T. CLEGG of rural Jefferson County — In his brief life (he died at age 42 in 1918), he touched millions by first isolating the leprosy baillus around 1910, helping in the development of the modern treatment for the disease.

HARVEY C. COUCH of Pine Bluff — A business genius, he founded a Louisiana telephone company that counted 50 customers when he sold it to Southwestern Bell for over $1 million in 1911. Three years later, he founded Arkansas Power and Light Company in Pine Bluff. The firm is now known as Entergy.

LAWRENCE COUCH of Pine Bluff — Entering the business after serving in the Navy in World War II, he became one of the city's leading jewelers, working in the profession for 50 years.

JOHN W. CRAWFORD of Pine Bluff — The husband of Mattie Hudson Crawford, he practiced law in Pine Bluff over 40 years. A state senator from 1889–1891, he was regarded as one of the region's best quail hunters.

MATTIE HUDSON CRAWFORD of Pine Bluff — Devoted to the cause of public health care, she was a founder and long-time president of the Hospital and Benevolent Association of Pine Bluff. It required more than 15 years of her efforts, but her dedication finally reaped dividends when the city's first public hospital — Davis Hospital — opened in 1910. She was one of the city's most adored residents.

JOHN DAVID CROCKETT of Lincoln County — A great-grandson of legendary frontier hero Davy Crockett, he worked as a mail carrier on the Pendleton-to-Pine Bluff route at the tender age of 12 in 1870. Later, he became a farm manager and then a plantation owner in Lincoln County, where he served as president of the Bank of Gould.

BUDDY DEANE of Pine Bluff — A native of St. Charles, he gained fame as host of a rock-and-roll television program in Baltimore during the 1950s. He then became a popular radio executive and personality in Pine Bluff, often lending his talents to civic causes.

ISSAC FISHER of Pine Bluff — An 1898 graduate of Tuskegee, Alabama, Institute and a protege of Booker T. Washington, he became the second principal of Branch Normal School (now the University of Arkansas at Pine Bluff) in 1902. Under his guidance, the department of agriculture was formed.

IKEY FITZPATRICK of Pine Bluff — Utilizing his small paddle-wheel boat to carry emergency supplies to victims and evacuate refugees from north of the river into Pine Bluff, Fitzpatrick became a hero in the catastrophic Arkansas River flood of 1927.

IDA MAE GANDY of White Hall — A teacher and historian, she is credited with determining the early history of the White Hall area. Gandy Elementary School in the city is named in her honor.

JESSE GONDER of Monticello — Strictly a part-time performer, he won World Series rings with the New York Yankees in his first two seasons (1961 and 1962) of an eight-year professional baseball career.

GELEVE GRICE of Pine Bluff — The most prolific black photographer in the state to date, the Tamo native worked as a newspaper and private photographer for over half of the 20th Century.

GUEDETONGUAY of Arkansas County — A Quapaw Indian leader, he was a skilled communicator and diplomat and served as a key liaison between the Quapaw and French colonial officials prior to the Louisiana Purchase.

Mattie Hudson Crawford

IN THE PICTURES

"The desire of glory is not a sin," baseball great Ty Cobb once observed.

He was right, but the inability to learn to live with the realization that not all goals are met can be a deadly weakness. The demise of Pine Bluff's Peggy Shannon is a testimony to the perils of disappointment and disillusionment combined with a lack of determination. Born Winona Sammon in 1906, the leggy redhead joined the Ziegfeld Follies in New York City in 1923. Her name was changed and she was on her way to what seemed a promising entertainment career. She earned additional attention — and money — by posing partially nude in several "art" magazines of the era.

On her trek to "Movieland," she won a Miss Coney Island beauty pageant and appeared in a number of Broadway stage plays. She also married actor Alan Davis, (or Allen Davies, according to some sources) in 1926.

"Discovered" by Paramount Pictures executive B. P. Schulberg in 1931, she and her husband immediately relocated to Hollywood. Publicists declared her as another "It" girl, comparing her sexiness to that of the original "It" girl, Clara Bow.

Within days of Shannon's Hollywood arrival, Bow suffered a second nervous breakdown during filming of a movie entitled *The Secret Call*. Shannon stepped up to complete that production while working on a second film at the same time.

When *The Secret Call* held its world premiere in Pine Bluff in July 1931, "Peggy Shannon Day" was declared. Shannon's return to the city was a gala event, and movie writers' typewriters were humming as they wrote of her as Hollywood's newest sensation.

But her career began a downward tumble afterward.

Within just four years, her once-promising future had cooled to a fizzle, and she turned to alcohol to relieve her unhappiness. She attempted to conceal her drinking, but as she consumed more and more, her fondness for alcohol became evident within the movie industry and to the public.

By 1940, she had quietly divorced her first husband and married part-time actor Albert G. Roberts.

Her drinking worsened and she received fewer and fewer movie roles.

On May 11, 1941, her husband found her dead, slumped over their kitchen table. She had a cigarette between her lips and her head rested upon her crossed arms.

An autopsy revealed that Shannon had died of a heart attack. Her liver showed the strains of heavy drinking. She was only 35, but hard living had aged her and she appeared much older.

Two weeks later, Roberts could no longer bear the thought of being without Shannon. Sitting in the same chair in which Shannon had died, he committed suicide by shooting himself with a .22-caliber rifle. In a farewell note, he — for the last time — declared his love of Shannon.

In 2002, nearly a century after her birth in the living quarters of a business building on Barraque Street in downtown Pine Bluff and almost 60 years since she sailed into eternity on a sea of booze, Shannon was commemorated in her hometown when her face was included with depictions of other local celebrities in a historical mural that was painted on the side of a Main Street building.

Peggy Shannon was finally in "the pictures" again.

President Bill Clinton, the 42nd President of the United States, addresses a Democratic Political Rally at the Pine Bluff Convention Center. Clinton, serving in his second term, visited in November, 2002.

W. E. HOPE of Stuttgart — In 1901, he purchased some rice seed and planted it in a small garden plot at his home. Producing a healthy crop, he forever changed agriculture and agri-business in the Grand Prairie, giving birth to what would grow into a worldwide interest.

JOHN H. JOHNSON of Arkansas City — He founded Johnson Publishing Company in Chicago. The firm became the second-largest black-owned business in the nation, employing over 2,500 persons and recording more than $300 million in sales.

ROBERT WARD JOHNSON of Jefferson County — A powerful politician, he owned a huge plantation near Pine Bluff. In 1860, his holdings were assessed at near $1 million. He "owned" 193 slaves.

EMMA CLAYTON JONES of Pine Bluff — The daughter of John Middleton and Sarah Ann Clayton, she married Judge W. D. Jones. She was Pine Bluff's first (and, thus far, only) female postmaster, serving from 1889–1892. Noted for her work in charity causes, she was twice named the recipient of the City Federation of Women's Club Woman of the Year Award.

E. FAY JONES of Pine Bluff — The designer of Thorncrown Chapel near Eureka Springs, he became the first Southerner to receive architecture's highest honor, the American Institute of Architects Gold Medal. Jones received the award in 1990 from President George H. W. Bush.

GEORGE C. KEELER of Pine Bluff — An Illinois-born carpenter, he came to Pine Bluff in 1847 and formed a business partnership. He constructed the 1856 Jefferson County Courthouse on his own. He was a charter member of Jacob Brump Masonic Lodge No. 106 in Pine Bluff.

WILLIAM "BILL" KENNEDY JR. of Pine Bluff — A long-time Pine Bluff banking leader, he served on various city and county commissions, helping to net financial growth for the area with the attraction of new industries. He was a consistent volunteer in assorted civic endeavors.

BILL KERKSIECK of Ulm — A "righty," he pitched in 23 games for the Philadelphia Phillies of the National Baseball League. He lost in his only two decisions, gave up 81 hits in just 62.2 innings and yielded 13 home runs. Unimpressive, huh? Well, he made it to *The Show*. Did you?

JAMES W. LESLIE of Pine Bluff — A businessman, historian, journalist and author, he was a leading authority on Southeast Arkansas history. Respected for his researching abilities, the aviation enthusiast was a member of the Arkansas Sesquicentennial Commission in 1986.

THE RIGHT REV. J. M. LUCEY of Pine Bluff and **H. L. STODDARD** of Stuttgart — Reading papers on "The Historical Relics of Arkansas and Their Preservation" at a 1908 meeting of the Arkansas History Commission in Little Rock, the pair voiced displeasure with the fact that museums outside the state had removed a majority of Arkansas' most valuable relics.

JAMES SMITH McDONNELL JR. of Altheimer — Spending much of his boyhood in Altheimer, he grew up to become a partner in the aviation/aerospace firm of McDonnell-Douglas. He was inducted into the Aviation Hall of Fame in Dayton, Ohio, in 1977.

JOSEPH MERRILL of Pine Bluff — A New Hampshire native who attained wealth as a successful planter, he became a philanthropist, generously supporting black schools in Pine Bluff. He founded the Merrill Institute, a forerunner of the city's Young Men's Christian Association.

MARTHA BEALL MITCHELL of Pine Bluff — A one-time Pine Bluff Arsenal employee who wound up as the wife of John Mitchell, U.S. attorney general during the administration of President Richard M. Nixon, she was blamed by the president for much of the media onslaught surrounding the Watergate scandal, which led to his resignation. She never met a reporter she didn't like.

W. F. "JACK" MOODY of White Hall — The city's first mayor, he is credited with being the founder of the White Hall Chamber of Commerce.

CALVIN ATKINS NEWTON of Lincoln and Jefferson counties — At the minimum age of 25, he was elected in 1907 as a state representative for Lincoln County. Ten years later, after relocating to about nine miles south of Pine Bluff, he was elected as a state representative for Jefferson County.

JACK PALMATEER of Pine Bluff — A Colorado native who came to Pine Bluff to receive pilot training at Grider Field during World War II, he stayed and became a regional pioneer in public emergency management and disaster preparedness.

KEN PARSONS JR. of Redfield — A well-known radio personality, Parsons left that business, became a popular newspaper columnist and published the *Redfield Update* weekly newspaper for several years. He won several prizes for his "Along the Dollarway Road" columns, which often dealt with Redfield-area history.

HUGH PATTERSON of Pine Bluff — Educated in Pine Bluff, the Mississippi native served as publisher of the *Arkansas Gazette* from 1948–1986. His tenure included the 1957 integration crisis at Little Rock Central High School.

CLARENCE L. "PIER" PONDER of Pine Bluff — Executive director of the Miss Pine Bluff Pageant from 1988–1998, he also served as president of the Pine Bluff Little Theater and Community Theaters of Arkansas. He produced and directed several stage plays.

JOE PURCELL of Warren — Arkansas' attorney general from 1967–1971, he was lieutenant governor from 1974–1991 and acting governor for six days in 1979.

MARION DeWOODY PETTIGREW of Pine Bluff — A recognized genealogist, Pettigrew is regarded as the primary force in the establishment of a public library in Pine Bluff. She served as a vice president of the Arkansas Library Association and on the national board of the Library War Council in World War I.

ELVIS PRESLEY of Memphis — A frequent visitor to Pine Bluff during the early years of his phenomenal entertainment career, his September 7, 1976, concert at the Pine Bluff Convention Center was one of his final public appearances.

JACK ROBEY of Pine Bluff — A popular superintendent of Pine Bluff schools only a few years before his untimely death in a Hawaii traffic accident, he is remembered for engineering several education enhancements. The city's Robey Junior High School was named in tribute to him.

EMMETT SANDERS of Pine Bluff — Pine Bluff mayor from 1943–1947 and again in 1975, he was involved with nearly every phase of development in the Pine Bluff area during his lifetime. A state and national leader in flood control, a street in the Port of Pine Bluff area is named in his honor.

CHIEF SARACEN of Arkansas Post — The Quapaw Indian chief became a legendary hero around 1800 when he bravely rescued two white children who had been kidnapped near Arkansas Post by several Chickasaw Indians.

CHESTER A. SHIPPS SR. of Pine Bluff — A graduate of the University of Arkansas at Pine Bluff, Shipps founded his own electric service company in Springfield, Missouri, just after World War II. His dedication to hard work and customer satisfaction earned him the Missouri Minority Businessman of the Year Award in 1987.

CHARLIE MAY HOGUE SIMON of Monticello — One of Arkansas' most gifted writers, her works ranged from children's books to detailed, highly-researched biographies and studies. She received an Albert Schweitzer Book Prize in 1958. She was married to John Gould Fletcher, a Pulitzer Prize-winning poet.

EARL "OIL" SMITH of Sheridan — Over a 12-year professional baseball career, Smith had the uncanny good fortune to be a member of seven pennant and World Series teams. He struck gold with the New York Giants, Pittsburgh Pirates and St. Louis Cardinals.

HENRY MORTON STANLEY of near Varner — An English journalist, he gained international fame in 1871 when he found the missing and ailing Scottish missionary, Dr. David Livingstone, in Africa and exclaimed, "Dr. Livingstone, I presume!" He had previously resided and worked in a store at Varner, near the current site of Cummins Prison, where he was pressured by friends there into joining the Confederate Army during the Civil War.

JOHN ROBERT STARR of Pine Bluff — A proud member of Pine Bluff's fabled "Barraque Buckaroos" neighborhood basketball team, he grew up to become one the most colorful newspaper editors in Arkansas history. He directed the *Arkansas Democrat* in a successful newspaper war that ended with its takeover of the *Arkansas Gazette*.

CREED TAYLOR of near Pine Bluff — Moving his family to near Pine Bluff in 1821, he became one of the largest landowners in the county and his holdings became the system for the world's biggest cotton plantation system. He served as Jefferson County's first sheriff and later as a justice of the peace and county and probate clerk.

ADMIRAL JOHN SMITH THACH of Fordyce — Born in Pine Bluff, he became a highly-decorated World War II Naval aviation hero when he developed a maneuver that allowed slower U.S. planes to defeat Japanese flyers in their much faster Mitsubishi A6M2 aircraft. Thach's scheme became known as the "Thach Weave."

FRANK GLASGOW TINKER of DeWitt — A mercenary American pilot who shot down eight German and Italian fighter pilots during the Spanish Civil War in 1937, he wrote a book about his experiences. *Some Still Live* was published in 1938 and lauded by Ernest Hemingway. Tinker then committed suicide. He was only 29.

MARCUS R. TOWER of DeWitt —A leader in the modern development of the Arkansas River, he served on the Rogers County, Oklahoma, Port Authority Board of Directors almost 30 years. He retired as vice chairman of the Bank of Oklahoma.

DAVE WALLIS of Pine Bluff — A noted journalist, advertising executive, author, historian, World War II photographer and pilot, he was a member of the Jefferson County Quorum Court before serving as Pine Bluff mayor from 1979–1984.

CASEY BILL WELDON of Pine Bluff — A top blues music performer and writer in the 1930s, many of his lyrics were thinly veiled with sexual connotations. He was recognized as a master of the "bottleneck" or "slide swing" guitar.

GERALD "NICK" WORKS of White Hall — Becoming a coach and education administrator, he was a Dollarway High School football standout and regarded as one of the state's most rugged players. Fresh out of high school, he attended a Chicago Bears rookie camp, but was sent home with a knee injury.

Pine Bluff Mayor Dave Wallis, left, in a typical pose, making the rounds and catching up on the latest with County Treasurer Bill Ellis at the Jefferson County Courthouse, circa 1984.

Original press plate for Pine Bluff Commercial

THE PINE BLUFF C

TYPE

CHAPTER FOURTEEN

Pine Bluff Commercial – 125 Years

The *Pine Bluff Commercial* was born largely at the command of Major Charles Gordon Newman, a Virginia gent who fought for the Confederacy and returned to journalism after a 10-year career of "typically colorful" 19th-century journalism in Virginia and Northwest Arkansas.

Newman was also an unfulfilled actor — a frock-coated, striped trouser-wearing go-getter sporting a high collar, black tie and silk top hat. A sprig of lily of the valley plucked from his wife's garden always graced his lapel. But this was no dandy, this Newman, whose editorial blasts and love of community spewed forth in the first editions of *The Commercial*, which has now been in continuous publication for 125 years.

With the paper's debut, on April 18, 1881, Newman wrote, "With this, we begin the publication of the *Pine Bluff Commercial* as a business enterprise and to accomplish what good we can for a state and people whom we have so long and faithfully served by the potent agency of the press.

"We realize the opening of a bright day for our beloved Arkansas, under the application of advanced ideas and the intelligent use of God-given opportunities.

"The editor believes in progress. He has no taste for personal journalism, but does believe in a manly expression of opinion and he promises that with fairness and courtesy toward all, this paper shall labor for the common weal. It will be found that this paper is conducted by a Democrat of independent thought and action."

His statement held true. It would be 40 years after the major's death — 1952 — before the newspaper endorsed a Republican (Dwight D. Eisenhower) for the presidency

Newman died in 1911 and was succeeded by his son-in-law, E. W. Freeman Sr., much less a crusader than his father-in-law; more businessman than journalist, who spent the next 34 years modernizing *The Commercial's* production process.

In Newman's day, the process was at once simpler and slower. His editorials, for example, were written out in longhand, which was converted by the printer to print type by plucking metal and wooden letters from a tray and arranging them, laboriously, to reflect the Major's words.

Thousands of letters eventually spelled out two pages of newsprint, complete with ads put together the same way. The pages were then bound together in a frame and slid onto a flat-bed press, whose operator may have worn other hats, such as those of reporter and ad salesman. The pages were then inked and placed on the pages of type. With pressure from a hand-cranked roller, the ink was transferred from the letters of the type to the blank paper. Printing this way on both sides of the paper resulted in the four-page edition of *The Commercial*. It took many long hours to print the few hundred papers sold during that time.

The rotary press speeded things up — driven by electric or gasoline motors and, in the 1940s, the Linotype machine enabled the operator to set type at a rate of eight or 10 lines a minute. This jumped to 50 to 120 lines a minute in the 1970s with the advent of computerized photo-typesetting equipment. In the 1980s, reporters and editors were sitting in front of typewriters or what was called a VDT — video display terminal.

E. W. Freeman died in 1945 and was succeeded by his son, E.W. Freeman Jr., who, with the help of his sons, Armistead and E. W. III (Major Newman's great-grandsons), continued the legacy of the Commercial Printing Company and the *Pine Bluff Commercial*. They held to the newspaper until December, 1986, when the newspaper was sold to the Donrey Media Group, headed by Donald W. Reynolds. Donrey, at its peak, operated 52 newspapers in the U.S. Upon

Reynolds' death in 1993, the chain, including *The Commercial*, was sold to a Little Rock based investment firm, Stephens Inc., which continued operating the group as Donrey. In 1998, Donrey was moved from its headquarters at Fort Smith to Las Vegas, home of the flagship newspaper, the *Las Vegas Review-Journal* and Donrey was soon renamed as the Stephens Media Group. Currently, the company operates as Stephens Media, LLC.

The *Pine Bluff Commercial* today is one of only two newspapers in the state to have won a Pulitzer Prize, thanks to the editorial efforts of Paul Greenberg, a Shreveport, Louisiana, native and *The Commercial's* editorial writer starting in 1962. He won the Pulitzer in 1969 with his stunning collection of editorials dealing with racial issues, which focused on what was first expressed by Major Newman after a lynching 77 years before — a conscientious concern for racial harmony.

Today, the *Pine Bluff Commercial*, a member of the Arkansas Press Association, is the major newspaper in Southeast Arkansas utilizing the latest in technology. In 2002, it began publication of the weekly *White Hall Progress* and currently prints sister publications owned by Stephens Media, LLC.

— **By Judy Normand**

Keeping the Faith

Fall 2006

The Commercial's enduring agenda is to keep the faith and loyalty of our founders.

As always, *The Commercial* is a vigilant protector of our reader's right-to-know. We hope that we never fail our supporters. For you are our source of survival. Working for you, we have focused on the betterment of Southeast Arkansas. We have been successful — and on occasions have faltered, but our course of achievement and direction has not wavered.

We believe in the potential of Southeast Arkansas and pledge our efforts to see they are attained.

During the course of the last 125 years, *The Commercial* has worked for the good of the citizens of Southeast Arkansas and we hope the future brings more success to our region.

— **Charles A. Berry, Publisher**
Pine Bluff **Commercial**

Charles A. Berry

Other Southeast Arkansas Newspapers

The weekly *Gillett Reporter* was founded in 1914. It suspended operations around 1926. Soon after, the weekly *Gillett Record* was initiated. It ceased publication in 1936. *The Record* printed a short-lived weekly, the *Humphrey Headlight* in 1933.

The *Stuttgart Daily Leader* is representative of several newspaper merges, with its roots extending to the *Stuttgart Free Press*, which was founded around 1890.

The weekly *Jeffersonian of Pine Bluff* was founded by W. E. Smith in 1848. It was published only briefly.

The partnership of Luckie and Carter published the *Pine Bluff Republican* in 1850.

The weekly *Warren Watchman* was started in 1918. It ceased operations for a brief time in 1921, but resumed publication before permanently folding in 1923.

The weekly *Bradley County Journal* was founded in 1923. It went out of business in 1928.

The weekly *Warren Eagle Democrat* traces its beginning to 1885 with the *Bradley County News*.

The weekly *Cleveland County Herald* in Rison was established in 1888.

The weekly *Fordyce News-Advocate* resulted from a 1945 merger of two Dallas County weeklies, one which was originally established in 1894.

The weekly *Sparkman News* was founded in 1915 and ended operations in 1920. It was succeeded by the weekly *Sparkman Times* in 1923. *The Times* ceased publication in 1930.

There have been two weekly newspapers published in the old Dallas County town of Princeton — *The Princetonian* in 1890 and the *Dallas County News* in 1905. Carthage was also the home of a pair of weeklies — the *Herald* in 1909 and the *Dallas County Patriot* in 1912. The weekly *Dalark Dispatch* operated briefly in 1896.

The weekly *Arkansas City Democrat* has an uncertain past, but supposedly began in 1891. Believed to have absorbed several other newspapers, it discontinued publication in the early 1920s. The weekly *Desha County Journal* was founded in 1923 and endured only three years. The weekly *Arkansas City Star* was founded in 1927, but soon folded.

A pair of Dumas weekly newspapers — the *Dumas News* and the *Desha Democrat* — were both founded in 1897. They were succeeded in 1910 by the weekly *Desha County Democrat*, which was published until 1941.

Founded in 1929, the weekly *Dumas Clarion* suspended operations in World War II, but was revived in 1945.

The weekly *Desha County News* of McGehee, which was founded in 1910, was absorbed by the *McGehee Times* in 1927. *The Times*, established in 1925, ceased publication briefly in 1943 because of World War II, but resumed in 1944.

The weekly *Monticello Advance Monticellonian* is the product of a 1920 merger between two other weeklies — the *Monticellonian*, established in 1870, and the *Drew County Advance*, founded in 1892.

The weekly *Grant County News* was published in Sheridan from 1916–1928.

The weekly *Sheridan Headlight* was established in 1881 as the *Sheridan Spy*. Its name was changed two years later.

The weekly *Jefferson Banner* was published briefly in Pine Bluff beginning in late 1958.

The weekly *Star-Reporter* was founded in Pine Bluff in late 1953. It lasted only seven months.

The weekly *Pine Bluff News* was founded in 1964 and published as a daily for three months in 1970 and 1971 before reverting to a weekly. It went out of business in the mid-1990s.

A weekly, semi-weekly and daily publication at various times, the *Pine Bluff Graphic* was established in 1887 and continued operations until 1942.

Gould has had four weekly newspapers — the *Gazette*, *Advance* and *Journal* and the *Lincoln County Tribune*. The respective publication dates were 1922–1927, 1926–1929, 1949–1951 and 1929–1932.

The weekly *Star Ciy Lincoln Ledger* was founded as the *Lincoln Lance* in 1880. It absorbed the *Star City Democrat* in 1897 and merged with the *Lincoln County Enterprise* in 1909. Also operating at Star City is *The Lincoln-American*, established in 1995.

Pine Bluff's first newspaper, the *Jeffersonian*, was published in 1847.

The weekly *White Hall Journal* was founded in 1983. White Hall's largest circulation newspaper, *The Progress*, began publication in 2002.

The first newspaper in the state and the oldest newspaper west of the Mississippi River, the *Arkansas Gazette* (now the *Arkansas Democrat-Gazette*), was founded by William E. Woodruff in 1819 at Arkansas Post.

D.W. Shannon founded a weekly newspaper, the *Arkansas Sentinel*, at Napoleon in 1855.

Neil Clark founded the *Pine Bluff News* shopper and newspaper operation in 1964. The newspaper published daily for a short time before resuming as a weekly. Employees George Anderson and James E. Jones Jr. purchased the newspaper and a printing business from Clark. The newspaper operated successfully until the mid-1990s, when it failed under a pair of new owners.

S. W. Eichelberger Jr. founded a black weekly newspaper, the *Warren School Herald*, around 1912. It ceased publication in 1923.

A black weekly newspaper, the *Kingsland Progress*, was initiated by P. H. Green in 1900. It went out of business in 1902.

Fordyce has been the home of five black newspapers. A. G. McKinney operated the *Bradley District Herald* from around 1913–1915. W. G. McGowan oversaw Fordyce Publishing Company's *Evangel* from 1900–1902. In 1917, Milton S. Hampton founded the *Negro Advocate*, which ceased publication around 1922. J. W. McCrary edited two Star Publishing Company weeklies, the *Western Star* (1900–1909) and *Star Messenger* (1910–1913).

A black weekly newspaper, the *Messenger*, was founded in Dumas in 1900. It was out of business by the following year.

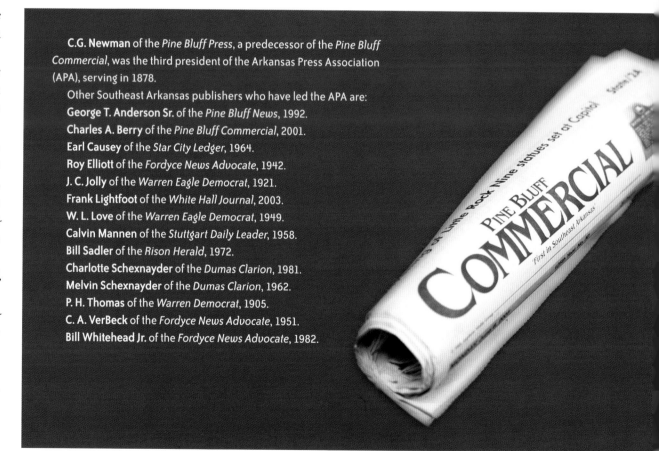

C.G. Newman of the *Pine Bluff Press*, a predecessor of the *Pine Bluff Commercial*, was the third president of the Arkansas Press Association (APA), serving in 1878.

Other Southeast Arkansas publishers who have led the APA are:

George T. Anderson Sr. of the *Pine Bluff News*, 1992.
Charles A. Berry of the *Pine Bluff Commercial*, 2001.
Earl Causey of the *Star City Ledger*, 1964.
Roy Elliott of the *Fordyce News Advocate*, 1942.
J. C. Jolly of the *Warren Eagle Democrat*, 1921.
Frank Lightfoot of the *White Hall Journal*, 2003.
W. L. Love of the *Warren Eagle Democrat*, 1949.
Calvin Mannen of the *Stuttgart Daily Leader*, 1958.
Bill Sadler of the *Rison Herald*, 1972.
Charlotte Schexnayder of the *Dumas Clarion*, 1981.
Melvin Schexnayder of the *Dumas Clarion*, 1962.
P. H. Thomas of the *Warren Democrat*, 1905.
C. A. VerBeck of the *Fordyce News Advocate*, 1951.
Bill Whitehead Jr. of the *Fordyce News Advocate*, 1982.

Heritage Sponsorships

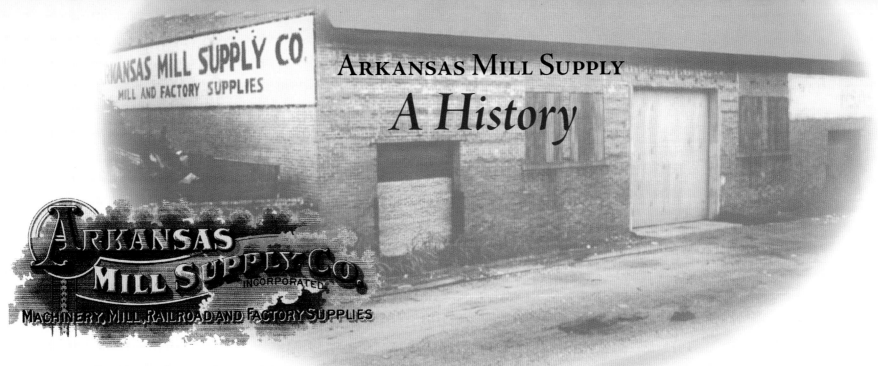

ARKANSAS MILL SUPPLY
A History

Arkansas Mill Supply's building (above) 1916–1969.

In 1905 Brown & Brothers Hardware of Camden merged with Camden Machinery and Supply Company to form Camden Hardware and Mill Supply Company. Among the original stockholders were Annie E. Brown, her son Edward M. Brown Sr., and W. Walter Brown. The new company was capitalized with $75,000.

This company re-located to Pine Bluff in 1912 with W. W. Brown as president. The name was changed to Arkansas Mill Supply Company and the logo that was adopted at that time is still in use today. Pine Bluff was a major railway center, which made it a more desirable location because salesmen rode the trains at that time calling on sawmills which located in towns along the rails.

Arkansas Mill Supply bought property on Main Street in Pine Bluff for which they paid $10,000.00 in cash and signed a 5-year note for $15,000 at 6 percent interest.

The property burned in 1916 and they leased a building at 3rd and Louisiana. The Great Flood of 1927 inundated this area and the business was closed for a month. A new office and warehouse facility was constructed in 1969 at 5th and Georgia. The present location, 701 Commerce Road, was completed in 1993 and serves as the corporate headquarters.

Other stores are located at Little Rock, Fort Smith, Rogers, and Texarkana.

After 100 years, the Brown Family still owns the majority stock in the company with the remainder of the stock being owned by the associates of the company. Pat Rhine Brown serves as chairman of the board, and David and Richard Brown are active in the business and represent the fifth generation of ownership. The company still sells mill supplies and is still dedicated to service to our customers in south, central, and northwest Arkansas.

Through their commitment to technology and to the business concept of "partnering" both with vendors and customers, they anticipate being a viable force in the business community of Arkansas for a long time. They have enlarged their customer base from predominately railroads and sawmills 100 years ago, to industrial and manufacturing plants and paper mills today. They do not resist change, they embrace it.

Corporate headquarters are located at 701 Commerce Road, Pine Bluff.

Grand opening day 1970 at the company's headquarters on Fifth Avenue at Alabama at Pine Bluff.

The board of directors, from left, are: Bobby Wade, Richard Brown, Pat Brown, Cliff Cheatwood, John Dobbs, and David Brown.

Early officers of the company were W. Walter Brown. W. W. "Buck" Taylor, L. T. "Louie" Rucks, Lev Goodrich (secretary-treasurer 1920-1963), Edward M. Brown (1916–1978), John Chidester (1919–1980), J. W. Bigham (1936–1997), Edward E. Brown (1949–1987). More recent officers were Cliff Cheatwood (1970–Present), Edwin Fuller (1953–1995), Richard Thompson (1957–1989), and Bobby Wade (1972–Present).

All smiles — E. M. Brown, left, and Edward E. "Ed" Brown are not disguising their pleasure upon being awarded recognition of eclipsing $1,000,000 in sales of R/M products.

BANK OF STAR CITY
The Secret is Out

The Bank of Star City's White Hall location.

For many years, the Bank of Star City was one of the best kept secrets in Southeast Arkansas. Chartered in 1926, it began as a hometown bank with assets of $156,272.43. Today, it has branch locations in Pine Bluff, White Hall, Watson Chapel, and Gould, and has accumulated assets of more than $98 million, all while maintaining the personal service that residents have come to expect.

Where did the inspiration for such growth begin? From the people of Lincoln County. The first stockholders meeting of record was on April 8, 1925, followed by the first board of directors meeting on May 4 of the same year. In attendance were A. B. Banks, J. L. Putney, W. A. Trussell, C. K. Nichols, J. D. Cogbill and A. J. Johnson. The Board elected A. B. Banks as president, J. L. Putney, vice president, W. R. Alsobrook as cashier and A. J. Johnson, secretary of the board. In 1930, Mr. Alsobrook purchased the entire interest of A. B. Banks in the Bank of Star City and Alsobrook was promptly elected president.

Data entry has changed over the decades.

The Bank of Star City has served its community for several generations, with much time spent in the building pictured above.

Robert O. Trout bought the interest in the bank and took over as president in 1969. Bennie Ryburn bought control of the Bank of Star City in 1982 and became president and chief executive officer. In 2006, Ryburn remains CEO and Mark Owen serves as president of the Bank of Star City.

Today, the Bank of Star City offers a wide variety of financial services to meet the needs of the 21st century customer including regular checking accounts, senior accounts, IRAs, debit and ATM cards, telephone banking, safety deposit boxes, and loans. Interest bearing accounts include regular savings accounts, certificates of deposit, investment money market accounts, Hy-Fi money market accounts, One Accounts, and Super Now Accounts.

The Bank of Star City's financial growth was followed by the need for physical expansion. In 1998, a new bank facility opened at Star City and the board of directors voted to donate the old headquarters to the city for use as a new municipal building, In 2002, the bank's success was recognized by the Chamber of Commerce, which named the Bank of Star City the Business of the Year. Looking to the future, the Bank of Star City strives to continue growing and serving Southeast Arkansas, as both a financial institution and a good neighbor.

JEFFERSON REGIONAL MEDICAL CENTER
100 Years of Care

With a rich history and a bright future, JRMC is a treasure tucked away amid the tall pine trees of south Pine Bluff.

Established in 1908, JRMC is quickly approaching its 100th anniversary as a leading provider of healthcare and medical technology in Arkansas. With 471 beds, JRMC is the fourth-largest hospital in Arkansas and consistently introduces new technology and programs that show the way in the healthcare community.

Beginnings

The story of Jefferson Regional Medical Center began in 1893 when a group of Pine Bluff women started raising money for construction of a hospital. In 1908, its dream became a reality with the opening of Davis Hospital at the corner of 11th Avenue and Cherry Street as the first hospital in South Arkansas.

The hospital's operation was taken over by the Arkansas Baptist Convention in 1919 and by the City of Pine Bluff in 1941. Eighteen years later, the hospital became a non-profit entity and its mission of community healthcare was in full swing. In 1960, Jefferson hospital opened on a sprawling 30-acre site on 42nd Avenue and in 1981 its named was changed to Jefferson Regional Medical Center with a mission to become a referral center.

Today

With more than 1,800 employees and 150 physicians, JRMC plays an important role in the South Arkansas community as an employer and healthcare provider. As the referral center of choice in Southeast Arkansas, JRMC is also preparing for the future. In 2005, JRMC purchased 11 acres of land in the growing White Hall community. The property presents a great opportunity for JRMC, which could place doctors offices, an imaging center or even a satellite hospital on the property.

JRMC takes seriously its role as a community leader and strives to provide leading care, to strengthen the community and to care for the individuals who choose its facilities and resources for their medical care.

Leading Care

JRMC is the first hospital in Arkansas to install a true 64-Slice CT Scanner. The revolutionary piece of medical technology provides physicians with precise images that capture the heart while it beats. As well as adding new technology, JRMC has also added new programs like a Hospitalist Program that focuses on hospitalized patients, the JRMC Weight Loss Program and a Smoking Cessation Program.

To increase flexibility and dependability, JRMC has also upgraded two of its most important recording systems — the Picture Archiving and Communication System and the Eclipsys Patient Care Management Systems, which make medical record keeping easier and more dependable than ever.

JRMC recently expanded to include a new medical office building that was constructed on the JRMC campus. The building will accommodate many of the new physicians who join the JRMC medical team each year.

Strengthening the Community

JRMC works hard to improve the healthcare of Southeast Arkansas by offering grants and scholarships, maternity fairs, support groups, childbirth classes, health screenings, the Jefferson School of Nursing, and other philanthropic efforts.

One of the recent successes is the Heart Safe Community Program, which provides grants for Automated External Defibrillators to community businesses, schools, churches and civic organizations. The program has provided more than 100 community groups with AEDs and the training they will need to use them in life-saving situations.

Caring for the Individual

JRMC remains dedicated to caring for each patient on an individual basis and providing opportunities for patients to improve their health and their lives. JRMC's Pastoral Care department is staffed with full-time pastoral care professionals to help patients of all faith backgrounds. JRMC offers a variety of fulfilling volunteer opportunities for adolescents and adults to give back to their community through offering their time and work to their community hospital.

GOVERNOR MIKE HUCKABEE DELTA RIVERS NATURE CENTER
The Nature of the Arkansas Delta Explained

The Governor Mike Huckabee Delta Rivers Nature Center was the first of four environmental education facilities to be built with proceeds from the one-eighth cent conservation sales tax, Amendment 75. Located in Pine Bluff's Regional Park, the center is framed by Black Dog Bayou and Lake Langhofer. The facility exists for the enjoyment of the general public, and admission is free.

The facility's primary theme focuses on the rivers of East Arkansas and the integral role these ageless waterways have played in the creation of today's Arkansas Delta region. A goal is to show how plants, animals, and human culture have adapted to river cycles.

The main building houses various interpretive and interactive exhibits and displays that include a Delta Rivers Flyover exhibit providing a birds eye view of the area's distinctive landscape. Visitors to the main building will also enjoy an object theatre that takes them through the history of the region from its "discovery" by DeSoto up to the modern day. A multi-use auditorium seating up to 100 people and a laboratory for special projects and field studies are also housed in the main building.

Attached at the rear of the building is one of Arkansas' largest freshwater aquariums. Holding a whopping 22,000 gallons of water, dozens of species of fish can be seen lurking beneath the surface. Feeding time is always a treat for fish and visitors alike.

Outdoor enthusiasts of all ages will marvel at the items found in the center's 800 square foot gift shop, where one-of-a-kind novelties, books, and conservation related educational items are available.

On the Arkansas River Discovery Loop trail, travelers encounter easy wildlife viewing opportunities in a variety of areas. Boardwalks invite visitors to explore the wetland forest, with blinds and a wildlife viewing tower provided to enhance the experience.

Outside the main building wild animal displays include various birds of prey, alligators, alligator snapping turtles, and a large butterfly and hummingbird garden. Attractive wildflowers and native plants are also found in abundance on the grounds.

Educational programs are offered regularly to the public at no charge. A few examples are nature quilting, plant swaps, outdoor photography seminars, falconry and flint-knapping classes, canoe outings and hunter education and boating education classes. More information can be had on the various classes by contacting the center, or getting on its newsletter mailing list. Organized groups (schools, scouts, church or civic groups) are encouraged to visit and schedule programs or guided tours. With advance notice, a program or presentation can be organized on just about any subject related to the wildlife or environment of the area: from amphibians to water quality.

While at the center, visitors can stop by the Nature Store for fun and interesting nature related gifts and souvenirs. The store offers a selection of books, educational items, bird feeders, and more. The center is open Tuesday through Saturday from 8:30 a.m. until 4:30 p.m. and Sunday afternoons from 1 until 5 p.m. During the summer months (from Memorial Day to Labor Day) the center stays open late on Fridays and Saturdays until 7:30 p.m.

Inside the Nature Center students get an up-close view of fish in Southeast Arkansas.

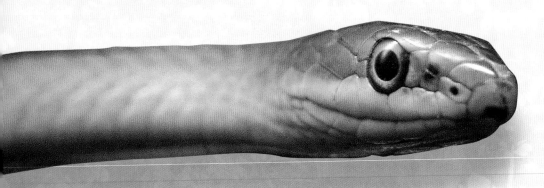

A green snake swims through the tank.

Outside the Nature Center in the spring . . . wildflowers in bloom.

Working the water for fish. Students get training on fish in Southeast Arkansas.

For more information or to get on the mailing list, call (870) 534-0011.

Governor Mike Huckabee Delta Rivers Nature Center
1400 Black Dog Road Pine Bluff, Ark. 71611
Telephone (870) 534-0011 Fax (870) 534-4422

History of Pine Bluff

The earliest settlers of the Pine Bluff area were French and Spanish. Many married Quapaw Indian women, and some of their descendants still reside in Jefferson County.

The first white settler here was Joseph Bonne, who migrated to the place that would later be named Pine Bluff, the first bluff above the mouth of the Arkansas River. The bluff was covered by towering pine trees.

Bonne and his wife, Mary Imbeau, lived in a lean-to cabin that he constructed. Their home also served as a tavern and had lodging accommodations for travelers.

The settlement initiated by Bonne was officially named "The Town of Pine Bluff" by the county court on October 16, 1832.

A key factor in the early growth of Pine Bluff was the arrival of steamboats on the Arkansas River.

During the Civil War, the Battle of Pine Bluff was fought on October 25, 1863, when Confederate Gen. John Marmaduke led 2,500 men in an attack on 550 federal troops under the command of Col. Powell Clayton.

Fighting from behind a breastwork of cotton bales erected by 300 former slaves, or freedmen, Clayton warded off the rebel attacks for five hours. Marmaduke withdrew rather than risk heavy losses. A number of stores and other buildings were burned — along with the bulk of the federal army's supplies — during the battle.

Reconstruction after the war included a three-year period of martial law. Afterward, a public school system was initiated.

With the arrival of the railroads in the 1870s and '80s, Pine Bluff's population grew from 2,081 in 1870 to about 10,000 in 1890. An agricultural boom resulted as planters could easily transport their cotton markets in New Orleans and St. Louis.

The turn of the century brought a flourishing lumber industry. Pine Bluff's two railroads opened lumber markets nationwide.

The city made its contribution to the World War I effort.

The Great Depression of the late 1920s and the '30s was brought to a close by World War II, in which Pine Bluff served as the site of a primary flight school and an Army arsenal that produced munitions.

The flight school was located at today's Grider Field, and what began as the Army's Chemical Warfare Arsenal is now the Pine Bluff Arsenal.

The post-war period was also witness to continued growth for Pine Bluff. The city's population increased from 20,000 in 1930 to 55,000 in 2000.

Pine Bluff Convention Center

Important dates in the history of the Pine Bluff Convention Center include:

+ **November 7, 1967** — Paul Bates and Fred Waymack met with interested citizens and discussed the need for a public facility for trade shows, meetings and entertainment events. Bates advised the group to form a non-profit corporation to serve as an applicant for federal assistance.

+ **April 12, 1968** — The Southeast Arkansas Convention Center Inc. was formed. Officers elected were W.H. Kennedy Jr., president; James Rogers, first-vice president; Willard

Burks, second vice president; Gail Cross, secretary; and Buck Sadler, treasurer.

+ **January 21, 1971** — U.S. Sen. John McClellan announces the Pine Bluff Convention Center has been approved with a federal Economic Development Agency (EDA) grant of $4.2 million.

+ **November 19, 1971** — After disallowing the monies, the EDA decides to reinstate the grant for the amount of $2.3. The grant is directed to the City of Pine Bluff, which became owner and operator of the facility.

+ **March 1, 1973** — Bids were taken and Baldwin Construction Company was approved for the construction of the facility.

+ **May 2, 1974** — Groundbreaking ceremonies were held.

+ **June 2, 1975** — Pine Bluff Mayor Charles E. Moore appoints Howell N. Davis, Emmett Sanders, Dr. Bill Owen, Dr. Vanette Johnson, Dr. Grace Wiley, Fred Waymack Jr., and Paul Lewey to a commission charged with overseeing the center's construction.

+ **June 27, 1976** — The Convention Center's construction is completed, and the official opening and dedication of the facility is conducted.

The total time from conception of the idea through the planning phase and construction was eight years and eight months. The final cost of construction was about $8,524,727.

Arkansas Entertainers Hall of Fame

Located in the Pine Bluff Convention Center, the Arkansas Entertainers Hall of Fame opened on October 2, 1998. It honors such notable Arkansas entertainers as Johnny Cash, Glen Campbell, Charlie Rich, Tracy Lawrence, Floyd Cramer, Al Green, Mary Steenburgen, Billy Bob Thornton, Jerry Van Dyke, Conway Twitty, William Warfield, Julie Adams, Freeman Owens, Broncho Billy Anderson, Ronnie Dunn, John Grisham, Levon Helm, Collin Raye, Jim Bridges, Lawrence Hamilton, Patsy Montana, Dick Powell, and Elizabeth Williams.

The 9,100-square-foot facility includes a life-size animatronic statue of Cash, stage wardrobe costumes of assorted artists, gold and platinum records and albums, musical instruments, original screenplays and television scripts, Broadway stage costumes and playbills, and motion picture-making equipment.

The Hall's first induction ceremony was held in Little Rock in 1996, but there was no facility in which to display memorabilia donated by the inductees. The Arkansas State Parks, Recreation and Tourism Commission thus initiated a competition among Arkansas cities to house the Hall of Fame.

A local committee was formed with Jerry Horne, Eva Marie Pearson, Renee Borchert, and Steve Arrison. The four visited similar facilities in other states and utilized their findings in successfully landing the Hall for Pine Bluff.

The Murals of Pine Bluff

Among Pine Bluff's more popular features is its historical murals, which represent the dedication of many interested citizens and continue to be coordinated through Pine Bluff Downtown Development (PBDD) Inc.

PBDD has overseen the completion of 13 murals. Nine additional murals are planned.

Providing the leadership in the project have been PBDD directors Montine McNulty, Renee Borchert and Joy Blankenship. The project stemmed from the interest of Jim Caldwell, Clark W. "Pinky" Curry, and Buck Sadler.

The initial project committee, a history panel, included Pat Brown, Jimmy Robinson, James W. Leslie, Lynn Gaines, Janice Kearney, Lillian Johnson and Dave Wallis.

"Main Street. 1888" became the first mural, when it was painted in 1992. The mural is an actual representation of how the street looked in 1888 and was drawn from an old photograph archived by the Jefferson County Historical Society.

Another mural depicts early Jefferson County Judge J.W. Bocage and Wiley Jones, who was born a slave but grew up to become one of Arkansas' wealthiest blacks.

A tribute to Quapaw Indian Chief Saracen, a legendary hero credited with saving the lives of two area children kidnapped by a band of Chickasaw Indians, is shown on another mural.

Among the nationally-known artists who have painted the Pine Bluff murals are Robert and Douglas Dafford, David and Susan Kelly Frye, Dan Sawatzky, Michael Wojczuk, Alan Wylie, Donald Genslet, and Benny Graess.

Downtown Revitalization

The Economic Development Alliance of Jefferson County, the City of Pine Bluff, Jefferson County and Pine Bluff Downtown Development received in 2003 a downtown framework plan designed by a team of urban developers hired to form a master plan for the central business district.

George Whittenberg, an architect and professor of urban studies and design, led the University of Arkansas at Little Rock planning team.

The plan addresses the following three questions:

Why is downtown important to the community?

What is the big idea for downtown?

What projects can jumpstart downtown revitalization?

Also in 2003, Simmons First National Bank celebrated its 100th anniversary in part by granting $100,000 to the City of Pine Bluff to help upgrade the Farmers Market. The gift was then parlayed into a $3.5 million project that has become known as "Saracen Landing" along the shore of Lake Pine Bluff.

This project has become a great example of public and private partnerships as funding has come from Jefferson County, the City of Pine Bluff, the State of Arkansas, the federal government, private foundations, and the public.

Pine Bluff's rich history centers on agricultural commerce and the Arkansas River. To honor this heritage, citizens are attempting to construct the 10,080-square-foot, open-air pavilion that will become the new Farmers Market.

Jefferson County Judge Jack Jones and the county bridge construction crew have built three bridge panels over the southern bank of Lake Pine Bluff on which the pavilion will stand.

The Farmers Market will be open three days each week, and on other days, the facility may be used for family reunions, art exhibits, musical entertainment and other gatherings. The Arkansas Game and Fish Commission will utilize the pavilion area for use in conjunction with the Delta Rivers Nature Center for courses in fishing and boating safety.

Two other buildings will accompany the pavilion. One will be built over the road near the pavilion and used for parking by farmers and excess parking on busy days at the market. The other structure will house a multi-purpose room that will be used by Pine Bluff's Parks and Recreation Department and house a classroom and a kitchen.

Enchanted Land of Lights & Legends Lighting Display

The popular Pine Bluff tradition of the Enchanted Land of Lights & Legends drive-through lighting display in the city's Regional Park began in 1997 when the Pine Bluff Festival Association evolved to create the attraction.

Local businesses, civic groups, organizations and individuals teamed with the Pine Bluff Festival Association to sponsor the displays as a gift to Pine Bluff and its holiday visitors.

The experience has become an award winner.

The Enchanted Land of Lights & Legends was cited by the Arkansas Festival Association in 1997 for being the best new festival idea and was runner-up for the honor of best new festival. In 2000, the event was named "Festival of the Year."

The extravaganza is an overwhelming success, as it's visited by over 100,000 people annually and is now the largest lighting drive-through in Arkansas and surrounding states.

Affiliated events that now occur each year are Randy's Reindeer Run, the Memorial Star Campaign, Tree Decorating Party for Kids, Lights and Legends Home Lighting Contest and Christmas for the Birds.

SEARK
Southeast Arkansas College

Southeast Arkansas College was created by Act 1244 of the 78th General Assembly of the State of Arkansas, which was signed into law by the Governor on April 17, 1991. As contained in Act 1244, "The purpose of this Act is to serve as legislative charter . . . for the establishment, organization and administration of a system of educational institutions throughout the state offering courses of instruction in technical, vocational and adult education programs, industry training and two-year college transfer programs. The system established under this Act shall provide educational programs which are easily accessible by all segments of the population to benefit from training, retraining or upgrade training for employment and which is highly responsive to individuals needing to achieve basic, general and specialized education to meet the needs of the workplace."

The Act further states that "technical college means an institution of higher education established under this Act dedicated primarily to the educational needs of the service area offering a comprehensive program including, but without limitation, vocational, trade and technical specialty courses and programs, courses in general adult education and courses comparable in content and quality to freshman and sophomore courses which may carry transfer credit to a four-year institution in a chosen course of study."

The above act re-designated and redefined the mission of 11 existing postsecondary vocational-technical schools located throughout the State to technical colleges. Similarly, state authority for these institutions was transferred from the Arkansas Coordinating Board of Vocational-Technical Education to the Arkansas Board of Higher Education. The latter serves as the state coordinating agency for all public universities, community colleges and technical colleges in the State of Arkansas.

The predecessor of Southeast Arkansas College was Pines Vocational-Technical School, which began offering postsecondary vocational-technical programs as Arkansas Vocational-Technical School on September 21, 1959. With the enactment of Act 1244, on July 1, 1991, all land, buildings, equipment, and personnel associated with Pines Vocational-Technical School was transferred to Pines Technical College. In October of 1991, the Governor appointed the Charter members of the Pines Technical College Board of Trustees. The College's first president was appointed by the Board of Trustees effective December 1, 1992. In order to better reflect the College's service area, the College changed its name from Pines Technical College to Southeast Arkansas Technical College on July 1, 1996. The word "Technical" was removed from the College's name on July 8, 1998.

The mission of Southeast Arkansas College is to provide comprehensive community college education and services, with an emphasis on technical education and workforce development, for the citizens of Jefferson, Cleveland, Desha, Drew, Grant, and Lincoln counties. These educational programs and services include: technical career education, workforce development, university transfer education, general education, adult education, continuing education, and community services.

SEARK College is committed to serving the educational and cultural needs of its constituency. The dedication to quality fosters our commitment to excellence in our administrative leadership, faculty, staff, and programs.

Dr. Phil Shirley is the president of Southeast Arkansas College.

SIMMONS FIRST
A Unique Vision

On March 23, 1903, Simmons First opened its doors for business in Pine Bluff.

The two paid employees had first day deposits of $3,338.22. Today, Simmons First is an eight bank financial holding company, with over 1,100 associates and assets of $2.5 billion.

Our founders had a unique vision and it has grown to become the largest publicly traded financial institution headquartered in Arkansas with over 80 financial centers in 46 communities.

Over the past 100 plus years, Simmons First has seen two world wars, unimagined scientific discoveries and medical breakthroughs. And we have played a key part in Arkansas history by helping countless Arkansas families buy homes, start business, invest in education and save for retirement.

Simmons First has grown from a small community bank to a multi-bank holding company serving the entire state of Arkansas. Our network of eight community banks with local management and boards provides our customers with the highest possible level of customer service and complete statewide access to Simmons First.

Our goal is simple: To be the premier community bank in Arkansas. Our strategy is to have the best people actively involved in the communities we serve and offering the very best in quality customer service and competitive products to our customers. This strategy has worked well for Simmons First and for our shareholders in particular.

With our statewide access, quality customer service and state-of-the-art products and services, Simmons First continues to put out customers first. And while we are proud of our growth and history of record earnings, we are most proud that Simmons First has been serving Arkansas for over 100 years. Our name has not changed and we have a remarkable record of earnings and dividends — in modern banking, that is quite an achievement.

Like the past century, the next hundred years will hold many challenging and exciting discoveries. We look forward to being there. For our customers, our community, our state and our country.

Simmons First is the largest student loan lender in Arkansas.

Simmons First credit cards have consistently been nationally recognized as one of the best bargains in America.

You can bank from home or phone with Simmons First Access and internet banking with Simmons First Bank Anywhere and Simmons First Bill Payment.

SISSY'S LOG CABIN
Life's Too Short for Ordinary Jewelry

Since 1970, Sissy's Log Cabin has been a family owned and operated jewelry store. We pride ourselves on quality and customer service. Our staff of experienced professionals has received numerous awards on both the state and national levels. Sissy's Log Cabin has evolved into Arkansas' largest independently owned jewelry store with 12,000 square feet of showroom filled with diamonds, jewelry, estate jewelry, fine gifts and fabulous antiques.

The story of Sissy's Log Cabin began on an afternoon in 1970 when Sissy Jones noticed a log cabin that was for sale as she was driving down U.S. 79. Sissy, who is an avid collector of antiques, pulled into the doughnut shop across the street and called the number. She then began renting the cabin for $50 a month and stocked it with antiques from her attic and home. Soon word began to spread about the wonderful finds that could be found at Sissy's Log Cabin, where Sissy made her living by appraising and selling her antiques.

As the word got out and people began to come to the little log cabin, they would bring all manner of things to sell or trade, including jewelry. Jones was once quoted as saying, "Jewelry, I didn't know anything about jewelry. I decided to get a little education. I bought two pairs of pliers, a pair of cutting pliers, some O-rings and I am a jeweler." She is credited with the creation of the watch slide bracelet and has won many awards over the years.

Sissy Jones never does anything halfway. When she decided to change her focus from antiques to jewelry she wanted to study it at the best schools. She has attended the Gemological Institute of America in California, McCarthey Jewelry Design School in Mena, Trenton

Today's location at 2319 Camden Road.

The original Sissy's Log Cabin

SISSY'S
LOG CABIN

RULE #1
THE CUSTOMER IS
ALWAYS RIGHT

RULE #2
IF THE CUSTOMER
IS EVER WRONG
REFER TO RULE #1

From left, Bill Jones, Ginger Cheatham, Sissy Jones, and Murphy Jones.

Jewelry/Goldsmith School at Memphis, and the University of Arkansas at Monticello. Sissy is also a licensed appraiser of antiques and antique jewelry.

Sissy's Log Cabin has always been a family owned and operated business. Sissy calls all of her 30-plus employees her "working family," not to mention that her husband, Murphy Jones, son Bill Jones and daughter Ginger Jones Cheatham have all worked for the company. Murphy Jones joined the Sissy's staff in 1988 and serves as the company's secretary/treasurer. He has been instrumental in the expansion of Sissy's Log Cabin and helped to shape it into what it is today. Murphy is also the designer of the new log cabin. Bill Jones joined the staff in 1984. He had planned to become a chemical engineer and attended the University of Arkansas at Fayetteville and Little Rock. After helping out in the store during his college days, Bill has since become the president of

the company and has been named one of the top 40 Arkansas Business People under 40 by Arkansas Business. Daughter Ginger Jones Cheatham joined the Sissy's Log Cabin team in 1984 after working three years as a registered nurse. She served as the executive vice president and the CEO of Sissy's Images until 2006.

In 1991, Sissy's business had finally outgrown her original little log cabin. So the day before Thanksgiving of that year, the entire store's contents were moved from the old log cabin into three newer buildings. Eventually the old log cabin was torn down to make room for the 12,000 square foot log cabin you see today.

Sissy Jones credits her success on hard work, family, good friends, wonderful customers and of course, the help of a few angels.

Potlatch in Arkansas

Between 1850 and 1880, America's population soared from 23 million to over 50 million, driving demand for lumber to new heights. Homesteads and farmland began to replace wild forests around the Great Lakes, and lumber companies set their sights beyond the Midwest to the yellow pine forests of the South. Arkansas had particular appeal. Not only was 96 percent of its land forested, the state offered the additional incentive of a newly laid 2,200-mile rail network that provided access both to timber and major lumber markets in the United States.

In 1882, these assets attracted two Midwestern lumbermen — Charles R. Ainsworth of Moline, Illinois, and James E. Lindsay of Davenport, Iowa — who established the Lindsay Land and Timber Company near Warren, Arkansas. The cost of maintaining some 40,000 acres, however, proved burdensome, and over the next two decades the pair welcomed new investors: David N. Richardson, a Davenport newspaperman, and the Weyerhaeuser and Denkman Company, a thriving Minnesota lumber business. In 1902, the partners incorporated the Southern Lumber Company in Warren, with F.E. Weyerhaeuser as its first president. This enterprise was the nucleus of what is today Potlatch in Arkansas.

From the start, the residents of Warren assumed that the businessmen from the Midwest would follow the usual "cut out and get out" pattern of other pine lumber mills in the state. Indeed, a survey done in the 1930s showed that 90 percent of the 22 million acres of forestland in Arkansas had been cut over. The future of commercial forestry in the state looked grim, but Southern Lumber Company made it clear that it had no intention of moving on. Adopting the latest forest management concepts, the company formed a woodlands department in 1937 and began implementing progressive reforestation initiatives. As a result of these early efforts, third- and fourth-generation softwood forests now thrive on Potlatch's Arkansas lands.

The company's commitment to the region was put to the test on December 27, 1939, when a fire virtually destroyed the Southern Lumber mill. Warren residents braced themselves for a pullout, but the company immediately announced it would rebuild. New general manager W. R. Warner, who moved to Warren from Cloquet, Minnesota, just after the fire, recognized that getting the company back to profitability would be no easy task. Building a state-of-the-

art facility would require that Southern Lumber's operating expenses exceed its operating income for a number of years. Rather than sink the company deeper into debt, Warner asked the board and shareholders in January 1940 to forego dividends for ten years so the money could be used for operating capital. Warner won their support, and within ten years, Southern Lumber was not only on a sound financial footing, its lumber mill was viewed as a model for the industry. In the rebuilding, Southern Lumber introduced a number of manufacturing innovations, including the first pneumatic debarker in North America.

Even so, the company realized that becoming a significant player in the forest products industry would require expansion of its technical expertise and capital resources. It began looking for a partner that shared its vision. In November 1956, it merged with what was then called Potlatch Forests, Inc. Southern Lumber brought to the merger a modern manufacturing plant in Warren, two smaller lumber mills, a finger-jointing lumber operation and approximately 137,000 acres of forestland.

In 1958, Potlatch moved into the hardwood business with the acquisition of the Bradley Lumber Company. Also located in Warren, the Bradley mill produced lumber and a range of specialty products from a variety of hardwoods and pines. Two years later, the company expanded its hardwood capacity with the purchase of the Woods Lumber Company in Clarendon. (The Woods mill burned down in 1975.) During the 1950s, Potlatch's forestland base in southern Arkansas had also grown to 350,000 acres.

The company went on to acquire the Ozan Lumber Company, which operated a pine lumber mill in Prescott, in 1966, and a mill in Stuttgart that made prefinished hardwood plank paneling under the name Townsend® in 1970. By the end of the 1970s, these and other acquisitions brought Potlatch's softwood and hardwood forestland ownership in Arkansas to more than 500,000 acres.

Age and changing industry economics led to the closure or sale of some of the mills. Since the mid-1990s, Potlatch's lumber manufacturing in Arkansas has been concentrated at pine mills in Warren and Prescott. The company implemented a modernization program to ensure these mills would be competitive well into the future. The lumber mill in Warren has been completely rebuilt, and major upgrades have been made to the mill in Prescott. These improvements have resulted in better resource utilization, higher product quality and lower operating costs. Annual capacity has more than doubled to 230 million board feet at each location. Potlatch's lumber operations are now regarded as the South's most efficient.

From its initial entry into Arkansas in the 1950s, Potlatch envisioned a fully integrated forest products operation, using residual lumber mill byproducts as economical raw material for a

bleached kraft pulp and paperboard mill. As early as 1955, Potlatch representatives began scouting appropriate sites for such a mill. An area called Cypress Bend, located on the Mississippi River near McGehee and Arkansas City, met the necessary criteria, and in 1958 the company signed an option on 517 acres of open land. For a variety of reasons, construction did not move forward for nearly two decades, but in 1977, a 450-ton-a-day bleached pulp and paperboard mill went into operation at the site. Supplied with chips brought by rail from Potlatch lumber mills as well as others, the Cypress Bend plant began manufacturing paperboard for conversion into folding cartons, plates, cups, and other food-safe products.

In the years since, Potlatch has invested in the Cypress Bend complex to ensure that it remains one of the lowest-cost manufacturers of high-quality pulp and paperboard in the industry. Periodic improvements have increased capacity to 850 tons per day from the initial 450 tons. In late 2000, upgrades to the paperboard machine improved the surface quality and printability of the mill's paperboard, which has added to its appeal for packaging of some 5,000 products worldwide. Concurrently, the recovery boiler was retrofitted to meet the mill's future pulp production capacity needs and enhance environmental performance. Today Cypress Bend's paperboard is competitive with

the finest paperboard available and is in demand for high-end packaging of pharmaceuticals and luxury items such as cosmetics and perfumes.

Cypress Bend's long-standing reputation for excellence extends to manufacturing quality standards. In 1993, it became one of the first mills in the paperboard industry to receive International Standards Organization (ISO) 9002 certification, and in 2004 the facility was awarded the Governor's Award for Performance Excellence.

Over the past few decades, Potlatch has been able to modernize and expand its lumber and pulp and paperboard operations in the state knowing that it could count on a sustainable supply of timber. Along with intensifying forest management of company forestland, Potlatch established a seed orchard in 1976 at Warren to produce superior loblolly pine seeds. Today the tree improvement program has progressed to the point where seeds from the newest orchard produce trees capable of yielding 35 percent more wood at harvest than the average native pines. What's more, the trees exhibit straighter stems, which are ideal for higher-value sawlogs.

Since 1976, Potlatch has planted more than 142 million softwood seedlings on Arkansas land. The state's long, mild growing season and nutrient-rich soil enable these pine trees to reach harvest age in 30 to 35 years.

The company's dedication to sustainable management of its forests has now taken on a new dimension, one that has far-reaching implications for both the marketplace and the environment. Potlatch has implemented an environmental management system (EMS) in each of its forested regions, including Arkansas, that enables the company forestlands to meet the goals of the ISO 14000 environmental standards as well as the American Forest and Paper Association's Sustainable Forestry Initiative (SFI) and the Forest Stewardship Council (FSC) standards. The company also undertakes third-party certification processes, which the three respected organizations recognize as validating their program objectives. Third-party certification signals to global markets that Potlatch is committed to internationally accepted standards. It also complements the company's long-held philosophy that sustainability and responsible forest management are critical to future success. Potlatch was awarded the Arkansas Environmental Federation's Diamond Award in Environmental Leadership in 2005.

On January 1, 2006, Potlatch converted to a real estate investment trust (REIT) in an effort to be better positioned for forestland acquisitions and to offer overall greater value to shareholders.

TROTTER FORD
Family Values

Pine Bluff's Trotter Ford, founded in 1936, has entered its seventh decade of business, and the reasons for its successes are simple, according to third-generation owner Henry F. "Ford" Trotter III.

"We're part of the community and we enjoy being involved with this community," said Trotter. "We've supported and worked with the United Way of Southeast Arkansas, Susan G. Komen Race for the Cure and other endeavors. Plus, we're involved with the (Economic Development) Alliance (of Jefferson County), so that we can help contribute to our area's future."

Trotter compares the dealerships practices to "family values."

"Our business partnership with Ford Motor Company has been good and we work hard to make sure our customers are happy," he explained. "We have a 45 percent loyalty (repeat business) rate, and that's among the highest with Ford Motor Company."

Trotter also boasted of his 92 employees and the teamwork illustrated in the firm's average annual sales of 2,000 new and used vehicles.

The dealership has been located at 3131 South Olive St. since 1970, when it moved from its original site at East Fifth Avenue and State Street. The company has expanded to also sell and service Lincoln-Mercury and purchased Pine Bluff Toyota in 1998.

"Our Toyota business is steadily growing," said Trotter, "and Lincoln-Mercury is revitalizing by coming out with a new array.

Trotter's father, Henry F. Trotter Jr., remains active with the business, but isn't in his office each day.

Meanwhile, the younger Trotter recently marked his 20th anniversary in the business.

"I very much enjoy my job," he said. "I get to meet a lot of people, and selling cars is fun."

Right, Henry Ford Trotter I, second from right.

UNIVERSITY OF ARKANSAS AT MONTICELLO
Meeting the Challenges

As one of the few remaining open admissions universities in the region, the University of Arkansas at Monticello is proud of its heritage of offering educational opportunity to the people of Arkansas.

Founded in 1909 as the Fourth District Agricultural School, UAM enters its 97th year with a renewed commitment to meeting the challenges of higher education in the 21st century.

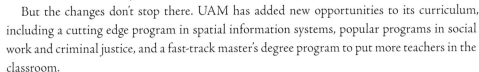

Take a walk across campus and you'll notice the dramatic changes taking place – from the renovation and landscaping of Weevil Pond to the implementation of an ambitious Campus Master Plan to change the face of the campus as we prepare for our second century.

In recent years, UAM has added a $7.5 million library and technology center, a new apartment-style residence complex and a new athletic facility in the north end zone of Convoy Leslie Cotton Boll Stadium.

But the changes don't stop there. UAM has added new opportunities to its curriculum, including a cutting edge program in spatial information systems, popular programs in social work and criminal justice, and a fast-track master's degree program to put more teachers in the classroom.

The University has made dramatic improvements in student retention and recruitment, and has expanded its extracurricular offerings to include an intercollegiate rodeo team.

In addition, UAM has created a comprehensive system of postsecondary education in southeast Arkansas with the acquisition of technical campuses in McGehee and Crossett.

UAM currently offers the bachelor of science degree in 13 fields, the bachelor of arts degree in eight major areas, the associate (two-year) degree in arts and applied sciences, and master's degrees in forestry and education.

Known in its early years as Arkansas A&M College, the University merged with the University of Arkansas System on July 1, 1971. UAM is governed by the UA Board of Trustees, which also oversees the operation of campuses in Fayetteville, Little Rock, Pine Bluff, Helena, Hope, Batesville, Fort Smith, and Morrilton.

UAM is fully accredited and holds mature institution status from the North Central Association of Colleges and Schools. The University holds specialized accreditation for its programs in forestry, nursing, teacher education and music.

Through the years, UAM has established a reputation for academic excellence in areas such as forestry, nursing, teacher education, pre-medicine and health-related sciences. The University is home to the Arkansas Forest Resources Center and one of the South's top exercise physiology laboratories.

UAM students have gained state, regional, national and international recognition in a variety of areas. Members of the University's award-winning debate team have traveled to Great

Britain, competing against top debaters from prestigious institutions such as Cambridge and the University of Glasgow. UAM students also travel to Costa Rica to Canada to study foreign language and culture.

The University counts among its former students such luminaries as Frank Hickingbotham, chairman and founder of TCBY Enterprises, Inc., Paul Carter, vice president and chief financial officer for Wal Mart, and Bobby Brown, president of Remington Arms, Inc., and Consolidated Coal, Inc.

Through education, research and public service, the University of Arkansas Monticello is continuing its commitment to providing educational opportunities to the people of the state, region and nation.

Quick Facts — University of Arkansas at Monticello

Year Founded: 1909 (First classes Sept. 14, 1910)

Merged: Joined the University of Arkansas System July 1, 1971 (was known originally as the Fourth District Agricultural School before becoming Arkansas A&M College in 1928)

School Mascot: Boll Weevils (men); Cotton Blossoms (women)

How UAM Became the Boll Weevils: The UAM Boll Weevil is one of the most unusual mascots in college athletics and the subject of much confusion (mostly among Yankees!). The Boll Weevil is a small gray insect that can wipe out a cotton crop in the blink of an eye. When UAM was founded in 1909, cotton was still king in Arkansas and the Boll Weevil was the more feared pest in the South. UAM's early students, most the sons and daughters of delta cotton planters, selected the Boll Weevil as their mascot in admiration of its toughness, its persistence, and the fear it caused whenever its name was mentioned. It's been said that the Boll Weevil is the only thing tough enough to ever truly lick the South.

Only At UAM: UAM has the only School of Forest Resources in Arkansas and is also home to one of the nation's leading programs in spatial information systems.

Famous Graduates:

Frank Hickingbotham, Founder, TCBY Enterprises, Inc.

Larry Lacewell, Retired Coach and Director of Scouting, Dallas Cowboys

Paul Carter, Executive Vice President, Wal-Mart

The 1956 Boll Weevils (13-9, AIC Champions)

University of Arkansas at Pine Bluff
From Humble Beginnings

The University of Arkansas at Pine Bluff is a university with a history of academic and personal success for our graduates — The kind of success that builds vital careers, raises the entrepreneurial spirit, and positively impacts our way of life. UAPB sets the path for the intellectual and social growth of our students—growth that can only be nurtured in a comprehensive university environment.

The University of Arkansas at Pine Bluff provides a setting for ambitious minds to flourish — an evolving campus that embraces new technology and nurtures a healthy social environment — under the guidance of an accomplished faculty. By responding to marketplace demand, our undergraduate and graduate degree programs provide an opportunity for our students and graduates to make a difference.

Branch Normal College was founded in 1873 by Act 97 of the 1873 General Assembly, and as a branch of the Normal Department of the Arkansas Industrial University. Branch Normal College opened its doors on September 27, 1875, in a rented frame house on the corner of Lindsey and Sevier streets (now Second and Oak). The college was designated as a Land Grant Institution under the Morrill Act of 1890. The college has undergone many changes. However, the growth and development of the college was slow until 1927. During the span of its existence, the school has had three name changes, from Branch Normal College to the Arkansas Agricultural and Normal School in 1921, to the Arkansas Agricultural, Mechanical, and Normal College in 1927, and now the University of Arkansas at Pine Bluff since 1972.

It is remarkable that the institution has survived against great odds, from within as well as those from outside its walls, to stand today shoulder to shoulder with other universities across this nation as a fully accredited institution of higher education by Arkansas and the Higher Learning Commission (North Central Association) since 1950, the National Council for the Accreditation of Teacher Education since the 1950's along with several accreditations for dis-

ciplines. The institution has survived, in part, because of strong men and women of vision and determination such as Joseph C. Corbin, Jefferson Ish, Robert Malone, John Brown Watson, Lawrence A. Davis, Sr., Johnny B. Johnson, Herman B. Smith, Lloyd V. Hackley, Charles Walker, Carolyn Blakely, Lawrence A. Davis, Jr., and others who have respected and supported their educational strategies and solutions.

From its humble beginnings in a rented frame building on the corner of Sevier and Lindsey streets (now Second and Oak) to its present day location on University Drive (formerly Highway 79), the institution has grown from a faculty of one to a faculty and staff of over 500. At the Fall 2005 term sixty-four percent of the faculty held doctoral degrees. The 20:1 student/faculty ratio made it possible to maintain a learning environment in which there is a close relationship between students and faculty, from one building to the current physical plant includes 56 buildings situated on 318 acres on the Pine Bluff campus and a research farm of 871 acres at Lonoke.

The school conferred its first degree in 1882. In the years that followed (until 1928), the school operated as a junior college with a grammar school and a preparatory department (high school). The Licentiate of Instruction (teaching certificate) was the only degree awarded until 1930 when two students were awarded the Bachelor of Arts. Now, UAPB has more than 16,000 alumni who represent the essence of a UAPB education in a variety of professions.

The William E. O'Bryant Bell Tower constructed in 1947, is known as the rallying point for alumni. It is listed on the National Register of Historic Structures. The Bell Tower is also a central focus for the historic quadrangle that is bordered on the east by Caldwell Hall, a 1929 structure that is also on the National Historic Register; on the north by Childress Hall, another National Register property, formerly Watson Memorial Library and currently home to the UAPB Museum and Cultural Center. On the west, the Bell Tower is bordered by the

Henderson-Young Hall and on the south by Dawson-Hicks and Caine-Gilleland Halls.

In the 1940's an extensive building program was launched including Larrison Hall, Woodard Hall, L.A. Davis, Sr. student union, Pumphrey stadium, Hazzard gymnasium, and Browne Infirmary. During the 1940's also the university saw the inaugurals of the Vesper Choir, Founders' Day and Homecoming, continuing traditions at UAPB.

Each chief officer of the institution served with distinction. Herman B. Smith, Jr. began his duties as chancellor on July 1, 1974. He continued the renovation of the campus and oversaw the construction of a new home economics building and later a new administration building in 1977.

Lloyd V. Hackley assumed the duties of chancellor on September 1, 1981, and inaugurated the first multipurpose endowment campaign, secured unprecedented state funding for the construction of the new (Johnny B. Johnson) dormitory complex and gave strong leadership to academic excellence. During this period also the University of Arkansas Board of Trustees designated Aquaculture/Fisheries as the UAPB Center of Excellence and identified Teacher Education, Science, Student Leadership, and Minority Business as UAPB areas of emphasis.

Charles A. Walker accepted the position of chancellor in 1986. During his tenure the University was successful in generating phenomenal research funds - ranking the school third among all Arkansas institutions of higher learning in terms of research funds received. Federal funds were secured for the expansion of the dormitory complex initiated by Hackley, and the establish-

ment of the Center for Multi-purpose Research and Sponsored Programs. The laboratory facilities for the television and radio facilities were developed during this time; facilities which continue to be critical to the academic and information services of the university. The organizational structure was modified to include four schools. In 1991, the State Board of Higher Education also approved Master of Education programs in Elementary Education and in the secondary education fields of English, General Science, Mathematics, Physical Education, and Social Studies, marking a milestone in the educational offering of UAPB.

Dr. Carolyn Blakely served as interim chancellor, becoming the first female to hold the position. Lawrence A. Davis, Jr. was appointed chancellor in November 1991 and embarked on moving UAPB aggressively to address

the challenge of finding new ways to better serve the University clientele and to serve a more heterogeneous student body.

The Lawrence A. Davis, Jr. administration has labored assiduously to address as many of the historical concerns as possible while giving impetus to enhancing and advancing the teaching, research, and service functions that the university had performed well for more than 100 years. The accomplishments during the Davis, Jr. administration include a range of projects from financial equilibrium and a $30 million appropriation from the state to upgrade campus facilities to fulfilling the aspiration of contributing to the economic development of

the University also impacts international workforces and promotes global understanding.

As a land-grant institution, the ultimate goal is to assist America in building a new social organism that will accommodate racial, ethnic, and cultural pluralism in a manner that will enhance the quality of lives, of patterns of living, and weld the nation into one people, a mission which seems essential to the future security and health of the nation.

Pine Bluff through the establishment of the downtown Business Incubator and Office Complex.

Today, this land-grant institution and the Flagship of the Delta builds on its past and continues to serve Arkansas and the nation with particular emphasis on the Delta. UAPB has a strong undergraduate program consisting of in-class and out-of-class learning activities; broad-based educational support services for students (e.g., counseling, advising, mentoring, and residence halls); and specialized research, education and public service. UAPB offers bachelor's programs, certificate and associate programs, and master's degrees, and prepares a cadre of professionals who contribute to the diversity of the state, region and national workforce. Significantly, UAPB offers the world's only undergraduate regulatory science degree program, which prepares its students for entry-level employment in four of the U.S. Department of Agriculture's regulatory agencies—Agriculture Marketing Services, Animal and Plant Health Inspection, Food Safety and Inspection Services, and Federal Grain Inspection Service. Through the International Program,

SMART MOTOR COMPANY
100 Years of Smart Selection, Smart Savings and Smart Service

In 1906, the San Francisco Earthquake shook the city by the bay into the bay. Closer to home, sons of Sooners looked forward to Oklahoma becoming the 46th state in the nation.

And in Pine Bluff, Arkansas, Felix G. Smart II, a former real estate man, opened the F.G. Smart Motor Company in a 14' x 60' building at 213 West Barraque, west of the courthouse. Among his shining array of newfangled horseless carriages were brass-bound Maxwells and sturdy steel Franklins in roadster reds, racing green, and soon-to-be-standard black.

That was a century ago. The Maxwell and Franklin automobile companies are now history. Felix G. Smart's company, though, is still serving the automotive needs of people in this region with the family legacy of Smart selection, Smart savings and Smart service.

The First Hundred Years

By 1912, Felix Smart had become a Ford franchisee and soon had growing dealerships in Star City, Rison, Sheridan, and Malvern, as well as in hometown Pine Bluff. In 1915, Mr. Smart passed away at age 39. His son, Felix Smart III, immediately left high school to carry on the family business — though he was only 17 at the time.

During the 1920s, the thriving F.G. Smart Motor Company moved from Barraque to much larger facilities at 306 West 2nd Avenue.

In 1933, Felix Smart III gave up his Ford franchise to become a Chevrolet Dealership.

Following the death of Felix Smart III in 1957, his son, Richard L. Smart, took charge of the dealership.

Felix G. Smart, the founder of Smart Motor Co. — circa 1906.

Richard L. Smart retired in 1990 at which time his sons, Roger Smart and Lee Smart, stepped in to guide the company.

Today Smart Motor Company sells and services Chevrolet, Cadillac, and Mitsubishi cars, trucks, vans, and sport utility vehicles. Smart also handles Chevrolet medium duty trucks for commercial customers.

The Road from 1906 to Now

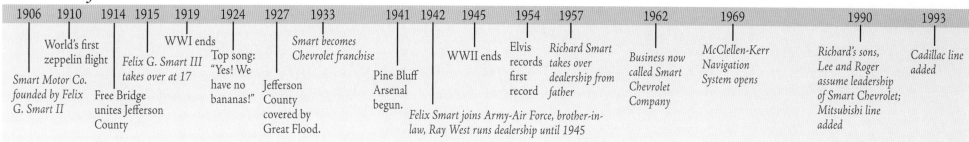

1906	1910	1914	1915	1919	1924	1927	1933	1941	1942	1945	1954	1957	1962	1969	1990	1993

World's first zeppelin flight

WWI ends

Top song: "Yes! We have no bananas!"

Smart becomes Chevrolet franchise

WWII ends

Elvis records first record

Richard Smart takes over dealership from father

Business now called Smart Chevrolet Company

McClellen-Kerr Navigation System opens

Richard's sons, Lee and Roger assume leadership of Smart Chevrolet; Mitsubishi line added

Cadillac line added

Smart Motor Co. founded by Felix G. Smart II

Free Bridge unites Jefferson County

Felix G. Smart III takes over at 17

Jefferson County covered by Great Flood.

Pine Bluff Arsenal begun.

Felix Smart joins Army-Air Force, brother-in-law, Ray West runs dealership until 1945

SMART MOTOR COMPANY
100 Years of Smart Selection, Smart Savings and Smart Service

In 1906, the San Francisco Earthquake shook the city by the bay into the bay. Closer to home, sons of Sooners looked forward to Oklahoma becoming the 46th state in the nation.

And in Pine Bluff, Arkansas, Felix G. Smart II, a former real estate man, opened the F.G. Smart Motor Company in a 14' x 60' building at 213 West Barraque, west of the courthouse. Among his shining array of newfangled horseless carriages were brass-bound Maxwells and sturdy steel Franklins in roadster reds, racing green, and soon-to-be-standard black.

That was a century ago. The Maxwell and Franklin automobile companies are now history. Felix G. Smart's company, though, is still serving the automotive needs of people in this region with the family legacy of Smart selection, Smart savings and Smart service.

The First Hundred Years

By 1912, Felix Smart had become a Ford franchisee and soon had growing dealerships in Star City, Rison, Sheridan, and Malvern, as well as in hometown Pine Bluff. In 1915, Mr. Smart passed away at age 39. His son, Felix Smart III, immediately left high school to carry on the family business — though he was only 17 at the time.

During the 1920s, the thriving F.G. Smart Motor Company moved from Barraque to much larger facilities at 306 West 2nd Avenue.

In 1933, Felix Smart III gave up his Ford franchise to become a Chevrolet Dealership.

Following the death of Felix Smart III in 1957, his son, Richard L. Smart, took charge of the dealership.

Felix G. Smart, the founder of Smart Motor Co. — circa 1906.

Richard L. Smart retired in 1990 at which time his sons, Roger Smart and Lee Smart, stepped in to guide the company.

Today Smart Motor Company sells and services Chevrolet, Cadillac, and Mitsubishi cars, trucks, vans, and sport utility vehicles. Smart also handles Chevrolet medium duty trucks for commercial customers.

The Road from 1906 to Now

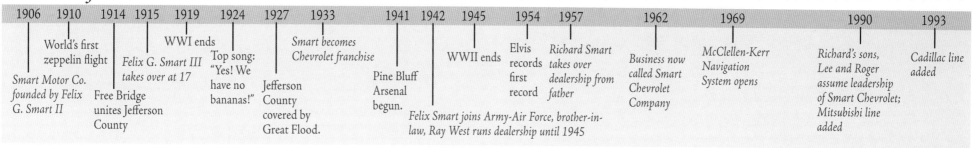

1906	1910	1914	1915	1919	1924	1927	1933	1941	1942	1945	1954	1957	1962	1969	1990	1993
	World's first zeppelin flight		WWI ends		Top song: "Yes! We have no bananas!"		Smart becomes Chevrolet franchise		WWII ends		Elvis records first record	Richard Smart takes over dealership from father	Business now called Smart Chevrolet Company	McClellen-Kerr Navigation System opens	Richard's sons, Lee and Roger assume leadership of Smart Chevrolet; Mitsubishi line added	Cadillac line added
Smart Motor Co. founded by Felix G. Smart II		Felix G. Smart III takes over at 17				Jefferson County covered by Great Flood.		Pine Bluff Arsenal begun.								
		Free Bridge unites Jefferson County							Felix Smart joins Army-Air Force, brother-in-law, Ray West runs dealership until 1945							

PHOTO CREDITS FOR *BAYOU COUNTRY*

Page 74 – Pine Bluff/Jefferson County Museum; Ralph Fitzgerald, *Pine Bluff Commercial*; Pine Bluff/Jefferson County Historical Museum

Page 76 – Courtesy of the author

Page 77 – White Hall Museum; Ralph Fitzgerald, *Pine Bluff Commercial*

Page 78 – Pine Bluff/Jefferson County Historical Museum; Ralph Fitzgerald, *Pine Bluff Commercial*

Page 79 – Ralph Fitzgerald, *Pine Bluff Commercial*

Page 80 – Courtesy of the Moore family; courtesy of Willie Van Winkle

Page 82 – Courtesy of the editor; Ralph Fitzgerald, *Pine Bluff Commercial*

Page 83 – Upper left, clockwise, courtesy of Scott Melton; Ralph Fitzgerald, *Pine Bluff Commercial*; Ralph Fitzgerald, *Pine Bluff Commercial*

Page 84 – From upper left, clockwise, Pine Bluff/Jefferson County Historical Museum; courtesy of Bob Curry; courtesy of the author

Page 85 – At left, courtesy of Scott Melton; Scott Melton; Ralph Fitzgerald, *Pine Bluff Commercial*

Pages 86 and 87 – Courtesy of Scott Melton

Pages 88 and 89 – Courtesy of Diane Hellums Mazanti

Pages 90 and 91– Left clockwise, Pine Bluff/Jefferson County Historical Museum; courtesy of the author; courtesy of Scott Melton; Unknown; courtesy of the editor; background, Ralph Fitzgerald, *Pine Bluff Commercial*

Page 92 – Courtesy of the editor, courtesy of the author

Page 94 – Courtesy of the editor; Pine Bluff/Jefferson County Historical Museum

Page 95 – Courtesy of the editor

Page 96 – Ralph Fitzgerald, *Pine Bluff Commercial*

Page 97 – Left, clockwise, courtesy of Wayne McGriff; courtesy of Wayne McGriff, courtesy of the author; Pine Bluff/Jefferson County Historical Museum

Page 98 – Ralph Fitzgerald, *Pine Bluff Commercial*; Pine Bluff/Jefferson County Historical Museum

Page 99 – Ralph Fitzgerald, *Pine Bluff Commercial*

Page 100 – Library of Congress

Page 101 – Courtesy of Deborah Moon Taylor

Page 102 – Ralph Fitzgerald, *Pine Bluff Commercial*

Page 103 – Pine Bluff/Jefferson County Historical Museum

Pages 104 and 105 – Courtesy of the author; Ralph Fitzgerald, *Pine Bluff Commercial*

Page 106 – From left, Ralph Fitzgerald, *Pine Bluff Commercial*; courtesy of the author

Page 107 – *Pine Bluff Commercial*

Page 108 – Ralph Fitzgerald, *Pine Bluff Commercial*

Page 110 and 111 – Pine Bluff/Jefferson County Historical Museum

Page 112 – Pine Bluff/Jefferson County Historical Museum

Page 114 – Ralph Fitzgerald, *Pine Bluff Commercial*

Page 116 – Courtesy of the Arkansas Department of Correction

Page 117 – Library of Congress

Page 118 – Courtesy of the author

Page 119 – Courtesy of the Arkansas Department of Correction

Page 120 – U.S. Army Corps of Engineers; Pine Bluff/Jefferson County Historical Museum; Pine Bluff/Jefferson County Historical Museum

Page 122 – Pine Bluff/Jefferson County Historical Museum

Page 123 – Courtesy of Wayne McGriff; Courtesy of Glenn Crain

Page 125 – Pine Bluff/Jefferson County Historical Museum

Page 127 – Pine Bluff/Jefferson County Historical Museum

Page 128 – Courtesy of Joseph Torres

Page 129 – Courtesy of Wayne McGriff; courtesy of the author

Page 130 – Pine Bluff/Jefferson County Historical Museum

Page 131 – *Pine Bluff Commercial* file photos

Page 132 – Courtesy of Wayne McGriff

Page 134 – Ralph Fitzgerald, *Pine Bluff Commercial*

Page 135 – Ralph Fitzgerald, *Pine Bluff Commercial*

Page 136 – Ralph Fitzgerald, *Pine Bluff Commercial*

Page 138 – Courtesy of the author

Page 139 – Courtesy of Pat Brown

Pages 140, 141, 142, 143, 144 and 147 – Courtesy of the author

Page 148 – Ralph Fitzgerald, *Pine Bluff Commercial*

Page 149 – Pine Bluff/Jefferson County Historical Museum

Page 150 – Ralph Fitzgerald, *Pine Bluff Commercial*

Page 151 – Pine Bluff/Jefferson County Historical Museum

Page 152 – Courtesy of Pine Bluff Fire Department

Page 153 – Courtesy of the author

Page 154 – Courtesy of the Pine Bluff Fire Department; courtesy of the Museum of the Arkansas Grand Prairie

Page 155 – Courtesy of the Museum of the Arkansas Grand Prairie; courtesy of Joseph Torres

Page 156 – Courtesy of Myrt Bobo; courtesy of the author

Page 157 – Ralph Fitzgerald, *Pine Bluff Commercial*

Page 158 – Courtesy of the author

Page 160 –Courtesy of the author

Page 162 – Courtesy of Pat Brown

Page 163 – *Pine Bluff Commercial* file

Page 164 – Pine Bluff/Jefferson County Historical Museum

Page 165 – Courtesy of the author

Page 166 – *Pine Bluff Commercial* file

Page 169 – Courtesy of the author

Pages 170 – 175 – Ralph Fitzgerald, *Pine Bluff Commercial*; *Pine Bluff Commercial* files;

Page 176 – Ralph Fitzgerald, *Pine Bluff Commercial*

Page 202 – *Pine Bluff Commercial* archives

Bayou Country **sources:**

Newspapers: *Pine Bluff Commercial*, *Pine Bluff News*, *White Hall Journal*

Arkansas Press Association

Arkansas Old State House Museum

The Department of Arkansas Heritage

The Encyclopedia of Arkansas History and Culture

The writings of: Kenneth Hensley, Dallas T. Herndon, Ken Parsons Jr., James W. Leslie, Dave Wallis and James Carter Watts.